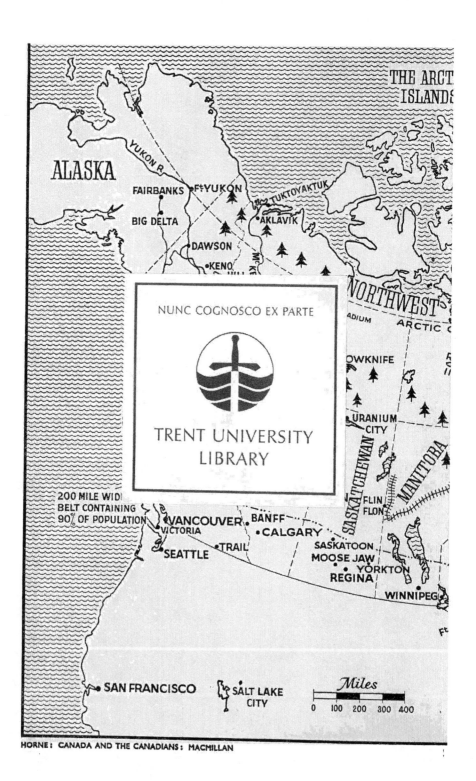

THE ARCT
ISLAND

ALASKA

FAIRBANKS

BIG DELTA

YUKON R.

Ft YUKON

DAWSON

KENO

TUKTOYAKTUK

AKLAVIK

NORTHWEST

ADIUM

ARCTIC

OWKNIFE

URANIUM
CITY

200 MILE WID
BELT CONTAINING
90% OF POPULATION

VANCOUVER
VICTORIA

SEATTLE

BANFF

CALGARY

TRAIL

SASKATCHEWAN

FLIN
FLON

MANITOBA

SASKATOON
MOOSE JAW
YORKTON
REGINA

WINNIPEG

Ft

SAN FRANCISCO

SALT LAKE
CITY

Miles

0   100   200   300   400

HORNE: CANADA AND THE CANADIANS: MACMILLAN

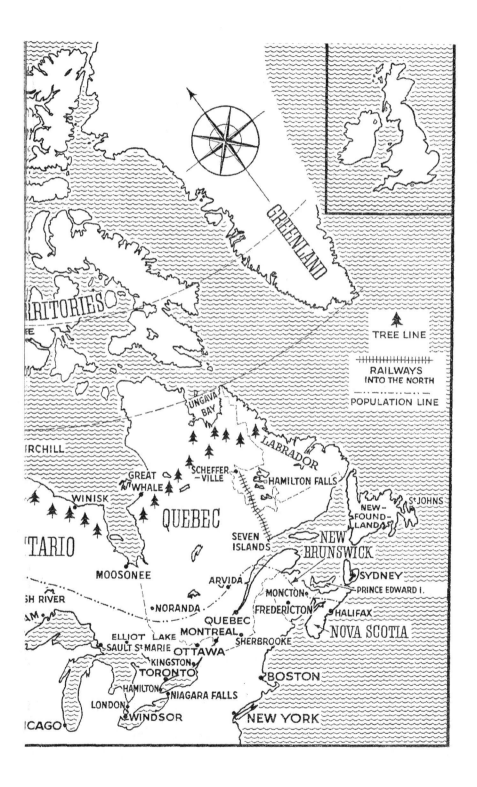

CANADA AND THE CANADIANS

CANADA AND THE CANADIANS

BY

ALISTAIR HORNE

TORONTO

THE MACMILLAN COMPANY OF CANADA LIMITED

1961

To
WILLA AND DAVID
Old and New Canadians

FOREWORD

How can a Canadian talk to England of Canada when he knows that the average Englishman . . . understands little or nothing about Canada and sees no particular reason why he should learn?—HUGH MACLENNAN, in *The Times Supplement on Canada*, 1956.

THERE have been many books on Canada since the war, some good, some bad. The only excuse for yet another is the ignorance about the most important nation within the Commonwealth that still persists in Britain. Just before I left for Canada to collect material for this book, a Londoner asked me 'will it be their summer or winter?' Barely had I returned when I overheard the following exchange between a well-dressed woman, sending off a parcel to Montreal in a Knightsbridge Post Office, and the P.O. clerk:

CLERK: 'Which part of Canada is Montreal?'
LADY: 'It's near Toronto.'
CLERK: 'Yes, but is that East or West Canada?'
LADY: 'Oh, I've no idea!'
2ND P.O. CLERK *(coming to rescue)*: 'It's on the Hudson River, so it must be East.'

After meeting hundreds of British immigrants in Canada, I came to the conclusion that a great many — perhaps the majority — of them had crossed the ocean little better informed than the trio in the London Post Office. It is for the British 'New Canadians', recent and future, that this book is particularly intended.

In the course of research, it also struck me that a number of the post-war books about Canada were too starry-eyed to be of much help either to Canada or to the immigrants planning to make their homes there. If in places this book seems critical of certain facets of Canadian life, it may be an error on the right side, and is certainly not intended in an unkindly spirit.

This is no easy country to write about. Even the last
Governor-General, the Rt. Hon. Vincent Massey, warned
me of the difficulties I might encounter; because, as he said,
'Canada is changing and moving on every minute of the day'.
Like a horse fancier, one could study the form for a lifetime
and still be wrong on the day of the big race. The best one
can do here is to show a slow-motion film of the horse in
action over a few furlongs, study its pedigree and past showing a little, and from all this attempt a daring deduction on
its future career.

The ingredients of this book are two years of research,
involving the consumption of some fifty books on Canada,
and the sifting of two trunkloads of official handouts, company reports, etc., and a two-foot mound of press cuttings.
Above all it involved a four-month tour (my third visit to
Canada since 1943), during which I travelled nearly 20,000
miles inside the country; eight thousand of them by car,
and the remainder by cargo-ship, ferry, canoe, 'boom-
scooter',[1] aeroplane, helicopter, bus, train, gas-truck, snow-
mobile and horse. In fact, almost every form of conveyance
one can think of — except a dog-sled (which I regret) and a
Hovercraft (which had not yet been invented). I visited all
ten Provinces, Labrador and the Yukon, returning with six
full notebooks that totalled some five hundred illegible pages
(my wife contributed another invaluable and rather more
legible two hundred pages during the two months she was
with me), a head spinning with the grandeur of Canada and
a heart full of admiration for, and gratitude to, the Canadian
people. Everywhere public figures, from the Governor-
General and the Prime Minister down, gave up crowded
hours for me to consult them; busy factory managers
turned over their offices to me so that I could interview
British immigrants in private. Without the almost unbelievable help and kindness I received I would never have seen
as much as I did during these all-too-short four months.

It would be impossible to mention here all to whom I owe
my thanks, but I feel I must record my gratitude to the
following in particular: The Departments of External
Affairs, National Defence, and Citizenship and Immigration,

---

[1] For a definition, see Chapter Six.

Ottawa; The Royal Canadian Air Force; Trans-Canada
Airlines; Canadian National Railways; The White Pass
and Yukon Railway; The Royal Bank of Canada; The
Canadian Federation of Agriculture; The Industrial De-
velopment Department, Government of British Columbia;
The Saskatchewan Wheat Pool; The Iron Ore Company of
Canada; The International Nickel Company; The Alu-
minium Company of Canada Ltd.; Grosvenor-Laing (BC)
Ltd.; The Consolidated Mining and Smelting Co.; Rio
Tinto of Canada Ltd.; AVRO Aircraft Ltd. and the
Dominion Steel and Coal Co.; Macmillan and Bloedel
Ltd.; United Keno Hill Ltd.; The Canadian Broadcasting
Corporation; Mr. Campbell Moodie of Canada House,
London; Dr. George Lindsey of the Defence Research
Board; Mr. Floyd Chalmers, President of the Maclean-
Hunter Publishing Co.; Colonel L. H. Nicholson, former
Commissioner of the Royal Canadian Mounted Police;
Mr. D. W. McLean of McLean, Budden; Mr. Michael
Langham and Miss Mary Jolliffe of the Stratford Festival
Foundation; Air Vice-Marshal Sir Cecil Bouchier of the
Migration Council; Colonel Allan Magee; Brigadier
C. H. Dewhurst; Mr. Austin Taylor Senior; Mr. Allister
Grosart; Mr. and Mrs. Jim Cartwright; Mrs. Graham
Spry; Mr. Donaldson of Ontario House, London; Mr.
Murray Armstrong, Agent-General for Manitoba, Lon-
don; Mr. John Gray of The Macmillan Company of
Canada, and Mr. Lovat Dickson of Macmillan and Co. Ltd.
for making this project possible in the first place; Miss P.
Brennan-Thorpe for her secretarial services; and, finally,
my wife — for her assistance and stamina in standing up so
cheerfully to a fairly killing pace.

ALISTAIR HORNE

CONTENTS

ILLUSTRATIONS

The marked photographs are reproduced by courtesy of
* The National Film Board of Canada; † Port of Toronto
Public Relations Department; ‡ Provincial Archives, Victoria,
BC; § Agent General for the Province of Ontario; and ‖ Pro-
vincial Publicity Bureau, Quebec: photo Driscoll. Those
unmarked were taken by the Author.

CHAPTER ONE

WHAT IS A CANADIAN?

I saw a great and wonderful country; a land containing in its soil everything that a man desires; a proper land, fit for proper men to live in and to prosper exceedingly. (FIELD-MARSHAL LORD MONTGOMERY, September 1946)

You should see them on the seventeenth of March, for example, when everybody wears a green ribbon. . . . On St. Andrew's Day every man in town wears a thistle. . . . And on St. George's Day! . . . why shouldn't a man feel glad that he's an Englishman? Then on the Fourth of July there are Stars and Stripes flying over half the stores in town. . . . (STEPHEN LEACOCK, *Sunshine Sketches of a Little Town*)

Two hundred years ago when summer was at an end but the maples had not yet turned to the gloriously fiery colours that characterise the Canadian autumn, a powerful British force lay ringed about the dejected remnants of a French army on the isle of Montreal. With no natural defences and provisions for less than a fortnight, the position of the two and a half thousand French troops was hopeless. In fact, it had been hopeless for almost exactly a year, ever since General Wolfe had led his men up on to the Plains of Abraham at Quebec the previous September; though at one time after the winter, when the St. Lawrence was still closed to the supporting Royal Navy, it had looked as if the 3000 sick and hungry British soldiers in the fortress of Quebec might have to surrender it once again.

By September 8th, 1760, the French Governor, Pierre de Rigaud, Marquis de Vaudreuil-Cavagnal, was forced to capitulate to Wolfe's successor, General Murray. Under the Articles of Capitulation, the French leaders and most of their soldiers were returned to France aboard British men-of-war. Their departure marked the extinction of the colony of New France, after a courageous existence of a century and a half. It was the end, once and for all, of French ambitions in

1

North America.   Yet another huge segment of the earth's
surface had come under British rule, and nobody then could
tell what would emerge from it.

Both the triumphs of Quebec and Montreal were in fact
but the final battles in a war that had gone on in spasms
virtually since New France was founded; the New World's
extension of Britain's struggle with France for supremacy in
Europe.   In the latter stages of this war, the French in
Canada — together with their Indian allies — had shown
remarkable skill in guerrilla forays into the British colonies
of New England and New York.   As with most guerrilla
wars, the attackers with greatly inferior forces (at the time
of the Capitulation the 60,000 French *habitants* of Canada
were outnumbered twenty to one by the British in the
American colonies) were able to inflict deadly wounds on
greatly stronger forces.   Many were the British generals who
lost their names, and sometimes their lives, fighting in the
fearful jungle of the so-called 'American Wilderness'.

Disaster followed on disaster, one incompetent followed
another, until at last Pitt arrived on the scene to provide the
first unified plan of action Britain had ever had in the New
World.   From then on, as Sir Winston Churchill remarked,
'it seemed as if Fortune, recognising her masters, was changing sides.' [1]

In the history of warfare, the fruits of victory seldom
resemble the aims for which the war was actually fought.
This was certainly the case with the Seven Years War.   If
Pitt could have seen what, indirectly, the Conquest of
Canada was to lead to, would he ever have launched his
masterly plan?   When Wolfe stormed Quebec, neither he
nor his superiors had any more intention of founding a great
new realm than had Montgomery at Alamein.   Canada just
happened to be the place where New England's vulnerable
back door could be closed and a deadly blow struck at
France.   But with the closing of the back door came the need
to administer the conquered territories, and with administration came the Quebec Act.   In the eyes of the New Englanders who had played a vital part in the war against the
French in Canada, the Quebec Act, with its concessions to

[1] *A History of the English Speaking Peoples*, vol. iii.

the French Catholic clergy and its restoration of the coveted Mississippi-Ohio territories to Canada, became one of the 'Intolerable Acts' that was to touch off the American Revolution. So the Plains of Abraham, in part, led to Concord, Yorktown and the Declaration of Independence.

And so it could be said that Canada as we know it happened by mistake. Had it not been for George Washington — who served a useful apprenticeship as a major in the French-Indian wars — and had Louis XV devoted his vast energies more to diplomacy than to the boudoir, Canada with its almost entirely French population might well have been handed back to France in return for a wider settlement. As it was, the British Government at the time of the Peace of Paris in 1763 (Pitt was no longer there) was strongly urged to trade what Voltaire scornfully wrote off as a 'few acres of snow' for the commercially more attractive sugar isle of Guadeloupe. But after the American War of Independence, thousands of refugee British-Americans, whose only crime had been loyalty to their King and backing the wrong horse, flooded into Canada. The die was cast; Britain had lost one Empire to gain another. Canada was henceforth destined to grow into a great and vital entity that would be neither all-French, all-British, nor all-American.

A hundred years passes. Almost to the day, the first centenary of the Capitulation was marked by the visit to British North America (as Canada was then called) of the 19-year-old Prince of Wales, the future Edward VII. The fact that this was the first state tour to the colonies ever to be made by a member of the Royal Family indicates the importance which Canada had already assumed. But most of the two thousand miles between Lake Huron and the Pacific were still empty, inhabited only by a handful of scattered settlements totalling no more than just a few thousand. Out on the Pacific, British Columbia, which had just become a Crown Colony, could number her permanent settlers by hundreds only; and all the Canadian colonies were economically dependent on Great Britain.

As one of the highlights of his tour, the Prince of Wales 'shot' the perilous Lachine Rapids on the St. Lawrence, close to the scene where Vaudreuil had capitulated a century

B

earlier.   In those days the Rapids formed part of the sole link between Upper and Lower Canada,[1] and only a small shallow-draughted craft could negotiate them.   Ninety-nine years later, the Prince of Wales' great-granddaughter, Queen Elizabeth II, passed through this waterway to open the greatest single enterprise in Canadian history, the St. Lawrence Seaway.   Henceforth, great ships of twenty thousand tons would be able to travel unimpeded for 2400 miles from the Atlantic to the far end of Lake Superior, deep into the heart of North America.   The transformation of the St. Lawrence symbolised what had happened to the country as a whole.   A population of somewhere over three million in 1860 had grown to more than seventeen million.   In the year following the Queen's tour, the bi-centennial year of Vaudreuil's capitulation, the two-millionth immigrant since the war arrived in Canada.   No longer a dependant of Great Britain in any way, Canada had become a great sovereign nation, in area the world's second largest.   Her counsels were now heeded by nations with several times her population; her armed forces were playing an important and independent part in the defence of the Western World.   She had, of her own right, attained the position of the world's fourth trading and sixth manufacturing nation;   she had become the greatest source of raw materials in the Free World, and her forests provided it with half of all its newsprint.   Her manufacturing industries employed more than twice as many as in 1939;   her dollar was worth more than her mighty neighbour's;   and the standard of life of her people was second only to that of the United States.   The average Canadian was earning more than double the wages his father or grandfather had earned at the beginning of the century, for 16 fewer hours' work per week.

And what of the 'average Canadian' himself?   What has he become in the two centuries since the British burst so rudely in upon the bucolic serenity of New France?   What manner of man is he now?

Like so much in modern Canada, he has become complicated.   There are times when he does not even quite know what he is himself.   No longer is it possible to point to

[1] Now Ontario and Quebec.

any Canadian and reckon, with certainty of being right —
as one might have done in 1860 — that his ancestors came
from either France or Britain. The English, the Scots and
the Irish together still account for the biggest racial block in
Canada (with the Scots giving the impression that they are
far more numerous than in fact is the case), but this block
now amounts to less than half the total population. Miraculously, the descendants of New France have managed to
maintain a proportion of nearly one in three Canadians. In
between the two main blocks, however, is an ever-widening
gap containing representatives of a hundred different races
and nations. At the present rate, these will soon constitute
one quarter of Canada's total population. In this alone the
country resembles the United States a little more closely
each year.

Some of Canada's various racial groups are spread evenly
across the country; others concentrated in small pockets,
often still virtually unassimilated, speaking their own tongues
and wearing strange garbs that did not originate in North
America. The British Canadians, of course, are everywhere;
and so are the three-quarters of a million of German extraction, the third biggest ethnological group in Canada. The
French-Canadians, however, still cling proudly to their
ancient home of Quebec, though spilling over increasingly
into neighbouring New Brunswick, and with a large outpost
on the Prairies adjoining Winnipeg. The two hundred
thousand of Jewish descent in Canada are largely concentrated in Montreal, Winnipeg and Toronto; the Italians,
now numbering about the same, also seem to follow in much
the same orbit as the Jews, with Toronto perhaps in second
place. Wherever there is successful farming you will find
enclaves of the quarter of a million energetic Dutchmen,
many of whom have immigrated since the war. The various
Slav nationalities, now jointly totalling over three-quarters
of a million, with the Ukrainians well to the fore, are to be
found largely on the Prairies; perhaps because the flatness
reminds them of home. Also on the Prairies, chiefly by Lake
Winnipeg, are solid little communities of Icelanders with
their beautiful women, representing the more than three
hundred thousand of Scandinavian stock who live in Canada.

The Scandinavians have concentrated on the Prairies and around the Lakehead in N.W. Ontario, but they are also to be found anywhere there are trees to be chopped down. Except for the countless Chinese who have found their way into restaurants across the continent and except for a substantial Chinese community in polyglot Toronto, Canada's fifty or sixty thousand Chinese do not stray far from Vancouver. Finally, the latest racial group to arrive in Canada *en masse*, the Hungarians,[1] have not yet really had time to decide where to distribute themselves.

Just to make matters still more complicated, there are the special little groups within the country that have made their own peculiar contribution or not, as the case may be, to shaping the character of the Canadians. These are the various pacifist sects who were forced to seek refuge from militarism in Germany or Russia towards the end of the 19th century. First to arrive were the German Mennonites, who settled near Winnipeg in 1875, and became some of Canada's most industrious and valuable pioneers. Today, in the small town of Steinbach, they still produce their newspapers in German, using the old Gothic script now largely obsolete in modern Germany; men in their forties still speak with a strong accent, but their children are almost completely integrated into Canadian life. More exclusive are the Hutterites, fine patriarchal figures with their strong faces, large black hats, beards and green blouses; also Germans and also living on the Prairies. The Hutterites lead a strongly communal life in settlements where all property belongs to the community. The most exclusive, unassimilated and extreme in their pacifist views are the Russian Doukhobors, in their settlements largely concentrated around Nelson, in the interior of British Columbia. The Doukhobors, helped out of Russia by Tolstoy some eighty years ago, have been at odds with the Canadian authorities for a long time. The principal issue has been the refusal by one Doukhobor faction, the 'Sons of Freedom', to pay taxes or send their children to Provincial schools; on the grounds that taxes are partly spent on weapons of war, and that the schools teach non-

---

[1] Of the post-1956 refugees from Hungary, Canada took the largest number of any nation: some 42,000.

pacifist doctrines. From time to time over the years, the centre of BC has erupted in strangely un-pacific acts of violence by 'Freedomites', such as the blowing up of railway tracks.

Adding to the diversity of the Canadian people are the two-hundred-thousand-odd descendants of two races that originally inhabited Canada, the Indians and the Eskimos. At a place called Caughnawagga,[1] near Montreal, lives a tribe, a branch of the once ferocious Iroquois, whose members — it was discovered — are immune to vertigo. Today they are to be found perched on skyscraper girders all over New York, and they probably have the highest *per capita* income of any Canadian Indian today. The industrialised Caughnawagga Indian has little in common with the proud and magnificent Blackfoot and Stony Indians of the Prairies, contented to live disdainfully on their reserves, appearing once a year in all their finery at the Calgary Stampede. These Plains Indians, too, bear slight resemblance to the depressed and indigent Dogrib and Loucheux Indians of the Northwest Territories. Still more different are the Indians of the Pacific Coast, with their round faces, highly developed totem-pole art and prosperous salmon fisheries. Among the Eskimos, the igloo-dweller from the borders of Alaska, who passes his winter making delicate carvings from fossilised walrus teeth or mammoth ivory, will very likely not understand a word spoken by the soapstone-carving tent-dweller from Hudson Bay.

Thus there is no such thing — if there ever was — as a 'typical Canadian'; a fact that deters the generaliser. Yet it is difficult to discover what kind of people the Canadians really are, in a mass, without casting forth a few broadly true, but vulnerable, generalisations; and perhaps it is safest to begin by generalising on what Canadians are *not*. Few things irritate any Canadian more, when he visits England, than to be asked if he is 'an American'. This barbaric ignorance of the natives can positively ruin his pilgrimage to 'The Old Country'. And it happens again and again; because, of course, to the untuned English ear all North American dialects sound the same, and, if you

[1] Pronounced 'Kog-na-wogga'.

plump for American (meaning US American), the odds are after all ten to one in your favour. But the Canadian is *not* an American — at least, not entirely, not yet.

To identify a Canadian by speech alone is, at first, certainly no easy task. With the rising generation, heavily influenced as it is by voices heard on US radio and TV, it promises to become even harder. As it is, 99 times out of 100 when there is a discrepancy between English and American usage, the Canadian chooses the American. He speaks of 'drug store' instead of 'chemist', 'coal oil' for 'kerosene' and 'gasoline' for 'petrol'. He goes 'hunting' when we would go shooting; pays the 'check' at a restaurant, and shops at a 'store' on the 'Instalment Plan' instead of hire-purchase. He sometimes keeps his 'pants' (trousers) up with 'braces', but more usually with 'suspenders' (though perhaps most often with a belt). He has a 'roast' on Sunday instead of a joint; on the other hand, in the more temperance-conscious parts of Canada, an American may still sometimes have difficulty in getting directed to what he understands by a 'joint'.

On top of all this, the Canadian uses the American flat *A*, and talks about 'Aloominum' instead of 'Aluminium'. (As one tiny compromise to Britain, he still terminates his alphabet with 'zed', not 'zee'). Yet there are certain phonetic Shibboleths that give him away after a while. The sounds *-all* and *-out* always seem to me the two most revealing; 'Montreal' pronounced by (British) Canadians usually sounds something like 'Montre-oll', 'all right' like 'oll right'; and 'about' comes out somewhere between 'aboot' and 'abote'. The Canadian tends to clip his words more than most Americans; he gives his *R*'s a pleasing burr, and many Canadians betray most markedly their Scottish origins in their speech. Generally, it is a pleasant accent. Nowhere in Canada will you find the rasping twang of the American Midwest, or the lilting whine of the Deep South that, enchanting at first, can drive you to distraction after too prolonged a dose.

These may sound hopelessly misleading generalisations; as soon as you have identified one Canadian accent, you may well meet somebody from another part of the country with a totally different manner of speaking. It is probably true to say, however, that there is far less regional diversity of speech than in the United States. But perhaps the most universally valid quality about Canadian speech is its *quietness*. And this quietness points to a general dislike of noise, to a distrust of ostentation, and to a tendency towards conservatism that is distinctly more British than American. One evening early on in our tour, my wife and I were eating in a café in Cornwall, Ontario — a small town on the St. Lawrence where it forms the frontier with the United States. There were a number of teenagers in the café, casting longing eyes at a huge juke-box in the corner. Strangely enough, it was silent. A waitress explained, 'We don't allow them to play it before 9 o'clock, so as not to disturb the diners.' We wondered how many restaurants you would find like this on the other side of the St. Lawrence.

The Canadian has, in fact, been described as a 'Quiet American' long before Graham Greene gave the expression a rather different meaning. He wears quieter suits, less spectacular ties than his southern cousins; builds his cities of sober grey stone instead of coloured glass and bronze. He may be a little slower to take a newcomer to his bosom than an American, but when he does his friendship may be less fickle. Canadian 'quietness' extends also to the worlds of both business and politics — though perhaps to less obvious degrees. To a new arrival, the rush and scurry of Toronto's business tempo may seem every bit as alarming as New York, when compared with London, but there is, in fact, an underlying leisureliness in Canadian affairs seldom to be found in the northern United States. Canadians at work always seem to have time, or be happy to make time, to have a chat about this and that. It is one of the pleasanter features of Canada. The rat-race exists, of course; the North American urge to get ahead, to keep up with the Jones's, is all there, but in Canada it seems to be kept to a healthier mean. The frenzy is absent (it may be significant that more Canadians die from flu each year than from ulcers), and one gets the impression that the man from Montreal or even Toronto is more contented and more in harmony with the world than the New Yorker.

One of Canada's leading actuaries, an intelligent and thoughtful man, claimed to me that there was probably more integrity in Canadian business practices than in the United States. He went on to qualify this by saying: 'It's not that we're fundamentally more honest — just that in such a small population if you get a reputation for being a bit "hot", everybody gets to hear about it, and that's the end of you.' On the other hand, the Canadian 'way-of-business' is totally shackled to the North American chariot of advertising and public relations; the importance of which is still lost on all too many British firms trying to sell things to the Canadians. Though he has a habit of shifting jobs more rapidly, when at work the Canadian seems to be generally a steadier worker than today's Briton. He is more self-reliant and better able to stand on his own feet; in the not-too-distant pioneer past he had to do so to survive. Canada is no welfare state and the Canadian has less security than a Briton, but at the same time he is less ridden by the prejudices and fears that the European has inherited from generations of insecurity.

When one Canadian wishes to be really derogatory about another, he will quite frequently stigmatise him as 'one of those tiresome Canadians who thinks he combines the best of both the British and the Americans'. But the truth, of course, is that he does have much of both worlds — good and bad. Nowhere is this more true than in his political being. Though, like an American, a Canadian politician speaks of 'running' rather than 'standing' for office, the difference is more one of semantics than tempo. The charivari and hurly-burly of the US 'convention' is unknown to Canada, and though there is more beating of drums and disbursement of invective in a Canadian election than in Britain, when it comes to the polls there is no soberer or more reflective electorate in the whole world. History has shown that the Canadian prefers his governments to die of senility rather than by the electoral knife. Regardless of party, he tends by inclination to be more of a Gladstone Liberal than either a true-blue Conservative or a left-wing radical.

As 'democratic' as the Americans, he cannot tolerate

arrogance; he does not believe in aristocracy or inherited privilege or nepotism. He supports the Commonwealth, though he does not believe in colonies or colonialism or racial discrimination (none of these being problems that press upon him anyway). He is loyal to the Crown, though sometimes he privately wonders how the Monarchy fits into the facts of life in modern North America.

Few Americans, I think, would deny that Canadian society is as a whole more disciplined, more law-and-order conscious than their own; even if they may think it is also duller. Despite the fact that in all Provinces, except only Newfoundland, the police carry sidearms and look every bit as forbidding as their American counterparts, and despite the fact that crime (particularly juvenile delinquency) has shown an alarming increase in the cities in the last two or three years, statistics indicate that Canadians are also more law-abiding. As the bootlegger chieftain of *Juan in America* warned Juan when they crossed into Canada: '"It's different from the States. You've got to look for pedestrians here. . . ."'

A Canadian generally marries younger than a Briton — about as young as an American; but, again according to statistics, he stays married longest of the three. At the census of 1951 there were a total of 31,998 divorced persons in all Canada; the average *yearly* divorce rate in the United States is about 380,000, in Britain 25,000, and in Canada only 6000 (although the respective populations of the three countries are roughly in the ratio of 10 : 3 : 1). A visitor to Canada as long ago as 1795 [1] remarked that '. . . a Canadian never makes a bargain, or takes any step of importance without consulting his wife . . .' Nevertheless the hand that rocks the cradle does not also rule the roost to the same extent that it does in the United States. Canadian women do not control such a large percentage of the cash, and their sphere of interest does not trespass upon the male prerogatives at so many points. At social gatherings in Canada one frequently notices that curiously British phenomenon of

[1] Isaac Weld, jr., 'Travels Through the States of North America, and the Provinces of Upper and Lower Canada, During the Years 1795, 1796 and 1797', from *Early Travellers in the Canadas*, edited by Gerald Craig.

men filtering off to one side to discuss 'hunting' and fishing and other exclusively male topics, leaving the women (apparently happily) engrossed in feminine chit-chat.   Never would such churlishness be permitted in the Great Matriarchy.   On the other hand, Canadian children are raised — increasingly — on the American pattern.   The harassed Canadian father living in a small frame house knows that his children will make themselves both seen and heard and there is nothing he can do about it.

Like an American, the average Canadian is deeply concerned about the educational and cultural shortcomings of his society.   He probably shows more interest in what is being taught in the local school than a Briton, but his interest is not always effectual or constructive — doubtless due in part to confusion currently prevailing over all North America as to what are the real aims of education.   He will talk to you till four in the morning of the cultural needs of Canada, but he will not always himself do anything about it as drastic, for instance, as buying tickets for the biennial production of the local theatre group.   My impression was, however, that in general he is more interested and usually better informed on international affairs than the average American.   The reasons are not hard to find ; for the greater part of Canadian history, the political last word rested with men an ocean's width away ; in each World War, Canada was in it from the start ; today she is still economically dependent on foreign markets.   These factors alone have never allowed Canadians the luxury of absolute intellectual isolation, of not caring what happens in the rest of the world.

'Mobility' is one of the cardinal virtues preached to every would-be 'New Canadian' by the Immigration Services ; be prepared to follow where the work is.   It is sound advice, and the Canadian worker is distinctly more mobile-minded than his British opposite number ; yet, compared with the United States where, like the bombers of the Strategic Air Command, a third of the nation seems to be in the air all the time, Canadians tend to be relatively static. (It was in Canada that, for the first time in my life, I met somebody of my own age who had never seen the sea ; a pretty girl, born in Winnipeg and married in Edmonton, presumably quite well off, yet she had never had the urge or the curiosity to travel the few hundred remaining miles across the Rockies.) Canadian industrial structure and communications are such that a Canadian working for a firm in Toronto is less likely to be shipped off suddenly to Vancouver or Edmonton than a New Yorker to San Francisco or Los Angeles. In several out-of-the-way mining settlements across Canada, I met many men who had been in the one place for ten or fifteen years. The very nature of his society permits a Canadian to put down deeper roots than an American, and this may also partly explain the reluctance of young Canadians today to seek their fortunes in the great unrolling canvas of the North; a reluctance which causes older generations to shake their heads and say that the pioneer spirit is dead.

Finally, in two really fundamental relationships does the Canadian differ from the American: in his attitude to his environment, and his attitude to his nation. A Canadian's attitude to his environment — so often a harsh and relentless one — might be summed up in one word: GARDENS. A few years ago, when travelling around the more untamed parts of the United States (notably the deserts of the Southwest), one of the attributes of the Americans that most impressed me was their ability to settle down, almost casually, in the most inhospitable wilderness one could imagine. With them they bring all the gimcracks of modern technics — deep-freeze, air-conditioning, TV and Hi-Fi — to make life on the frontier as tolerable as anywhere else in the United States. But they would do little to improve or beautify their austere surroundings; perhaps life was too short, any day the word might come to pack up and move back to Cincinnati. Even in the temperate and well-to-do parts of the Eastern Seaboard, what an Englishman understands by a garden is a rarity. On the other hand, in Canada, from the beautiful Annapolis Valley of Nova Scotia to Vancouver Island, you seldom see a house without its patch of carefully tended flowers, or a construction worker's trailer without its window boxes crammed with gleaming nasturtiums. There are gardens even across the arid Prairies and up in the frozen Yukon; they should be one of Canada's great prides, for man has few better ways of displaying his triumph over his environment.

Americans have a reputation for being sensitive to what the rest of the world thinks about the Americans as human beings. Yet no people are as critical of the nation itself, of the American 'Way', the American Philosophy or American *Realpolitik*; an American will occasionally even admit criticism from an outsider, provided it is not aimed at his personal Gods, or the Holy Constitution. (Britons, of course, to the eternal aggravation of foreigners, are too old and too cynical to care what anybody says about them or their country.) The Canadian, however, is rather the reverse. He can be remarkably rude about the shortcomings of his fellow nationals, and he will never ask you for your opinion of the Canadians. Or if he does, often the question will be loaded for a negative response — 'Don't you think we're the world's *dullest* people?' But Canada itself is sacred; criticise any aspect of it if you dare. The British immigrant would do well to remember this, and that even implied criticism can lead to trouble.

One of the first questions his first Canadian will ask him, even when he has barely stepped off the immigrant ship, will be: 'What do you think of Canada?' This question will pursue him till his accent no longer betrays him. Those who believe discretion to be the better part of valour might well favour fore-arming themselves with a stock response — even a glib one. Canada's great humorist, Stephen Leacock, derived one when travelling through the Canadian West; on being demanded: 'How do you like our city?' he would reply, non-committally, 'It seems alright; I don't see anything the *matter* with it.' [1] (Ernest Bevin, on his first trip to the United States, produced an even more devastating parry when American newsmen asked him for his views on America: 'Your newspapers are too big, and your lavatory paper's too small,' and nobody loved him any the less for it.) But a 'new boy' to Canada should not expect the indulgence accorded the venerated Leacock. To a Canadian — like all North Americans — no praise, or restrained praise, equals dispraise. So when faced with this deadly question, a Briton

[1] Stephen Leacock, *My Discovery of the West.*

had better just fling his traditional understatement to the winds and be ready with a suitably enthusiastic stock reply. This may sound dishonest, but he will soon find things about which he can express genuine and unstinted admiration; if he doesn't, there must be something wrong with him, and he should return home at once.

Canada, as she is today, is a much 'newer' country than even the United States, and she has all the sensitivity and national feeling of a new country. No people in the Western World are more fiercely proud of their country than the Canadians; nor is there any that is more entitled to this pride. From the one in nine of her population that Canada has taken in from abroad since the war, the Canadians have absorbed a great deal of punishment in the way of criticism. Before a British immigrant opens his mouth to criticise, he should reflect on just what Canada has achieved since 1760, 1860 — or even since 1945 — and on the fact that these things have been achieved against a background of far greater odds than any that ever faced her mighty southern neighbour after the Declaration of Independence. The following chapter should make some of these odds apparent.

CHAPTER TWO

SPACE IN THE BLOODSTREAM

Space enters the bloodstream . . . this is an immense country.
(Royal Commission on Canada's Economic Prospects, 1957)

Every man of sense, whether in the Cabinet or out of it, knows
that Canada must, at no distant period, be merged in the
American Republic. (*The Edinburgh Review*, 1825)

What is the matter then . . . ? they ask.
The matter is the sections and the railways,
and the shouting lost by the way and the train's whistle like
wild-life in the night. (PATRICK ANDERSON, 'Poem on Canada')

DURING the Montreal Commonwealth Trade and Economic Conference, I met a British immigrant in Toronto who was positively seething with rage. For the short time that he had been in Canada he had done quite remarkably well for himself, was earning what I thought was an astronomic salary with a public relations firm, and had obviously made a more than average attempt to get to grips with Canada. He was not very flattering about his fellow countrymen in Canada, but the particular cause of his indignation was an encounter he had just had with one of the correspondents of a leading British newspaper covering the conference. The journalist had asked him whether it would be possible to make a week-end trip to Vancouver and back by '*overnight*' train. 'And yet he claimed to be an expert on Commonwealth affairs. If an Englishman can't understand how big this country is, how can he possibly understand what makes it tick? It's one of the main faults of our immigrants, too; they're totally unprepared for the sheer size of Canada — and, my goodness, how their ignorance infuriates the Canadians!'

Canadians like to ensure that visitors appreciate the bigness of their country. And they are quite right to do so, because, next to her people, her size is the prime conditioning factor of Canada. It affects every aspect of life; as the

16

Gordon Commission Report [1] put it in one of its more eloquent passages — 'Space enters the bloodstream.' For an inhabitant of our tiny islands it is not always easy to come to terms with this Canadian spaciousness. Though I had travelled all the way across the United States, and most of the way down Africa, I was constantly receiving nasty shocks at the distances I had to cover in Canada. After I had travelled some 15,000 miles inside Canada, I thought I was beginning to grasp its true size — until I paid a visit to a RCAF Group HQ. The Commanding Officer (at 38, one of Canada's most brilliant young commanders — born in England, he had won the DSO, DFC and AFC with the RAF) had just finished pointing out the area covered by his group of interceptors — an amorphous-looking piece of land somewhere in the back areas of Quebec — and then asked me how large I thought it was. I guessed about 250 by 100 miles. He laid a celluloid outline of the British Isles over the map; it fitted comfortably within the boundaries of his sector.

Even looking at a map, it is not easy to realise that Canada is appreciably bigger than the United States, with Alaska. Second in size only to Russia, it occupies one-thirteenth of all the world's land surface, and contains about one-third of the planet's fresh-water area. It is *forty times* as big as Great Britain, which could fit six times into the Province of Quebec alone, and still leave something over. In fact, of the ten Canadian Provinces, only three are smaller than Great Britain. In the uninhabited vastness of the Northwest Territories, the British Isles would be lost in one small corner.

The British journalist who thought he could reach Vancouver by overnight train from Montreal would in fact have found himself spending three nights *en route*, even on Canadian Pacific's fastest transcontinental express. By pre-jet Super-Constellation it was still the best part of a day or night's flying. And Montreal is another thousand miles away from St. John's, Newfoundland, at Canada's eastern

[1] The Report of the Royal Commission on Canada's Economic Prospects, headed by Mr. W. L. Gordon, which will be referred to frequently on ensuing pages under its more popular and less ponderous title, the Gordon Report.

extremity. Even distances that on the map look like infini-
testimal fractions of the 4000 miles from coast to coast, can
spin out to alarming lengths. Toronto to Ottawa, for
instance, which appears to be hardly farther than from
London to Reading is alone an overnight train journey.

Because of the way her population has concentrated in
the South, one also tends to think of Canada in terms of all
width and little depth. But in fact, from Cape Columbia on
Ellesmere Island, Canada stretches from less than 7° short of
the North Pole to the same latitude as Naples and Madrid at
the southernmost tip of Ontario. Once at Edmonton, the
farthest north of the major Canadian cities, you still have 900
miles of flying to get to Port Radium, the uranium centre on
Great Bear Lake; and over 1200 miles to reach Aklavik,
the most important communications centre on the Arctic
coast, at the mouth of the Mackenzie River — or nearly as
far as London to Leningrad. And from this coast the Arctic
Islands — at present still largely uninhabited except for the
American DEW-Line camps and Hudson's Bay trading-
posts, but one day likely to have permanent settlements
extracting their oil and other as yet unestimated mineral
wealth — stretch for another thousand miles farther north.

In all this vastness, there is no country in the world —
not even Russia — with so much uninhabited land, that,
under modern technology, could be inhabited. Yet, if you
travel by land through Canada, its emptiness is even harder
to grasp than its overpowering size. Many times as I drove
along the immense length of the semi-completed Trans-
Canada Highway I found myself refusing to believe that the
country's entire population could be supplied from a circle
with its centre on Hyde Park Corner and a radius of rather
less than 100 miles. Every few miles one came across evidence of some form of intensive activity that seemed to
reflect the energy of a far more populous nation; there were
battalions of bulldozers at work, ripping a path for the new
transcontinental highway through the bush, scraping away
whole sides of mountains in the Rockies; new bridges and
causeways being built, and everywhere new factories and
new housing estates. For the best part of a day we drove
alongside the mammoth excavations of the St. Lawrence

Seaway project; a few days later, several hundred miles to the west, we met up with the head of the new natural gas pipeline, striking rapidly for Montreal, like a monster snake slithering across the Prairies and the forests. Yet even the 200-mile-wide belt along the US border that contains some 90 per cent of Canada's people still accounts for ten times the area of Great Britain but has less than a third of its population.

It is partly psychological, too; the statistics of Canadian achievements can become hypnotic. And Canada thinks and acts bigger than she is. In international affairs she has developed, particularly since the war, such a degree of sensibleness, of maturity beyond her years and influence beyond her numbers, that when she speaks one thinks one hears the voice not, in size, of a Turkey, an Egypt, or a Jugoslavia, but of a great nation of forty or fifty millions.

But this is a deception, and a dangerous deception because it conceals the intrinsic nature of Canada, and glosses over the causes of its most serious problems. To understand what Canada really is, you have to explore it by air, as well as by land. When you fly for hour upon hour over the awful desert nothingness of the 'Barrens' around Hudson Bay, the grim furrowed rock of Labrador, the endless empty Prairies, or the unbroken dark green of Northern Ontario's fir wilderness, if you are not gripped by a sense of fear and awe, then you are less than human. These are the right feelings with which to approach Canada. For it is not a small, comfortable and warm England, with a village, a telephone kiosk and a teashop over each hillock. The Jesuit missionary-explorers risking the fearful tortures of the Iroquois to discover the Great Lakes, Mackenzie groping his way overland towards the Pacific, Fraser shooting the terrifying rapids of the river later named after him, and Franklin lost in the ice of the illusory Northwest Passage, did not find it so. Despite all Canada's material advances, the 'frontier' is still not all that far away; challenge is always at hand.

Sometimes challenge is accompanied by danger, and disaster. People still get eaten by wolves, killed by bears, get frozen to death or lost in the wilderness. This is not being melodramatic. While I was visiting the 'Mid Canada'

C

radar line with the RCAF in October, the worst flying month in the North, I found myself momentarily stranded in Labrador. The reason for this was that every available plane in the area — 35 in all — had been called out on an air-rescue search. No less than three separate aircraft had been reported missing simultaneously somewhere in the vast emptiness of Labrador and Newfoundland. After more than a week of search, one of the planes was spotted on a lake, one or two hundred miles north of the St. Lawrence. An amphibian flew down to the plane and discovered a note left by the pilot, an American, saying that he had grown desperate of waiting for rescue, had found an Indian canoe on the lake, and was going to 'paddle his way' out to the St. Lawrence. He was never seen again, and, when I left Canada, still no trace had been found of the other missing planes.

You do not, though, have to go to Labrador to experience the untamed forces of Canada; even in the big cities, they are never very far away. A Canadian girl told me how she still remembered her emotions as a child when there was a long power cut in Montreal one winter: 'It just seemed as if all our civilisation had come to an end. It was a bitterly cold winter, and I could feel the house getting colder every minute. I began to feel really quite frightened, and then, for the first time in my life, I realised what a tough country Canada was.' In the winter of 1960, four men in a car became stuck in a snowdrift not very far from New Brunswick's largest city. When they were found, they had died — not from the cold — but from suffocation. The snow had piled up so quickly that they had been literally buried alive while huddling around the car's heater.

These are not intended to be bogy tales, designed to scare any sensible-minded immigrant away from Canada. But you have to be at least tough in mind to measure up to life in Canada. It is not a quality especially demanded by the physical facts of life in modern England, but most Canadians possess this toughness of mind — perhaps their inheritance from pioneer days — and they are not prepared to be sympathetic to an Englishman who fails in Canada through lack of it.

Of the natural forces that have moulded Canada, none has played a more vital role than a geological phenomenon called the 'Laurentian Shield'. Until a relatively short time ago the 'Shield' was a distinct minus sign in Canadian affairs. It was looked upon as a stumbling-block to settlement and communications and was held responsible for much of the harshness of the Canadian climate. Today, it is recognised as one of the principal sources of Canada's current prosperity.

Geographically, Canada is composed of three principal features that recur like the layers of an onion. At the opposite sides of Canada are chains of mountains or hills running north and south; in the Atlantic Provinces, the low continuation of the American Appalachians; in the West the massive ranges of the Rockies, which, under one name or another, extend almost unbroken from the Arctic to Cape Horn. Then come the interior lowlands; in the East, these are restricted to the St. Lawrence Valley, running down into the great rich peninsula of Southern Ontario; in the West, they comprise the vast sweep of the Prairies, continuing up to the Arctic as the Mackenzie River basin, themselves a continuation of the Great Plains of the United States. Around the core of the onion, shaped like a great heart and sprawling across more than half the land mass of Canada, lies the Shield. Look at a geological map, and you will see how intimate it is to the lives of the huge majority of Canadians. For the Shield reaches to the back doorstep of Quebec and Montreal, where it forms the Laurentian Mountains' playground for Canadian skiers. It comes down to less than a hundred miles of Toronto, cleaves Canada in two by submerging into the very waters of Lakes Huron and Superior; its edge lies only 50 miles from Winnipeg, just over 200 from Saskatoon and not much more than 250 from Edmonton. Composed largely of granite and other volcanic rocks, geologists believe the Shield to be one of the oldest, perhaps the oldest, feature in the world. The receding glaciers of several Ice Ages were not kind to the Shield, and scraped it clean of soil. As a result, except for a few scattered semi-fertile pockets, nothing will grow on it.

Nothing, that is, but trees — fir and jackpine; jackpine

and fir, fir, fir. Stephen Leacock once described the Shield
as 'a billion Christmas trees without a Christmas'. In fact,
Christmas lasts rather longer in the Shield than in most other
parts of Canada. For at the very core of the onion, in the
centre of the Shield, lies the dismal grey expanse of Hudson
Bay, a gigantic natural refrigerator. The Bay must surely
be the most useless — almost worse than useless — of the
world's major salt-water bodies. In the 17th century it
provided a back door for the British fur traders, to get a
foothold in Canada at the rear of New France; today, for
three brief months in the year, it provides a shorter route
for the Prairie grain ships, via Churchill. Apart from this it
serves as a breeding ground for millions of Canada Geese.
That is about all. There are no fish of value in it, and just
enough seal and beluga to maintain a few handfuls of
Eskimos at barest subsistence level. For the rest, its principal
role is to freeze out a large part of Canada. 'I never see such
a miserable place in my life,' complained Captain James
Knight in 1717. Another early explorer's account of winter
in the Bay inspired Coleridge to write some of the unpleasanter
parts of 'The Ancient Mariner'. Arctic water and ice flow
constantly into it from the North, and so Canada's cold iso-
therms follow closely along its contours, thrusting deep down
into the heart of the country. Its presence accounts for the
severe winters of the big cities on the fringe of the Shield;
for the fact that Montreal has a harsher, longer winter than
Boston or New York. Recently, as Canada has begun to
think bigger and the enticing promises of the Atomic Age
have begun to manifest themselves, there has been talk about
building a series of dams across the narrow neck of the Bay,
to keep out the Arctic waters, and even to raise further the
temperature of its shallow waters by studding them with
atomic piles! This would entirely alter the climate of
Canada, and it is not altogether idle talk. The dams alone
would probably present rather less of a construction problem
than Russia's ambitions (with similar objects in mind) of
putting a dam across the Bering Straits.

The Shield country lying around Hudson Bay is some of
the grimmest in Canada. Flying over it just before freeze-up,
much of its treeless Barrens reminded me of a vast magnifica-

tion of the surface of an English country lane after a heavy
rainfall; everywhere great puddles of water, unable ever to
drain away because of the underlying *Permafrost*. No trees,
no life; the only thing I have ever seen from the air to resemble its swampy desolation is the Sudd of the Upper Nile.
But not all the Shield is grim; in the South, the rolling
pleasant Laurentians contain some of Canada's loveliest
countryside, and in Northern Ontario, just above the Great
Lakes, where the wild, pitted surface of the Shield actually
consists of more water than land, are a myriad still blue
lakes, each one more idyllic, and with better fishing, than
the last.

In 1883 railwaymen blasting a way through the Shield's
granite came across a huge pocket of almost pure metal at
what is now Sudbury, Northern Ontario. Between then and
now, that pocket has produced 80 to 90 per cent of all the
nickel used by the Free World, as well as vast quantities of
copper. In 1903 construction of another railway just to the
north of Sudbury led to the discovery of silver deposits at
Cobalt. Then came discoveries of gold, lead and zinc, iron
ore and almost every known metal, in profusion; and finally
uranium. With the end of the Second World War, many of
the United States mineral deposits were approaching exhaus-
tion and world demand for metals was reaching higher and
higher peaks. No other single factor contributed so much
to Canada's sudden increase in prosperity. Within the
memory of many Canadians still living, in fact almost overnight, the Shield had been transformed from Principal
Villain to Fairy Godmother. And nobody yet knows the full
extent of her bounteousness.

Of the three main geographical features described earlier
in this chapter, only the Shield belongs truly and exclusively
to Canada. The others are, broadly speaking, simply northern extensions of physical features of the United States. For
on the North American continent, geography runs strictly
vertically, not horizontally, and even the Shield cleaves
Canada on a North-South axis. Ideally, it would perhaps
have been a fairer deal if the continent had been divided
down the line of the Mississippi–Missouri, into an East and a
West nation, instead of along the 49th parallel. By the laws

of both geography and economics, British Columbia is more at one with the US Pacific Coast States than with its neighbour beyond the Rockies, Alberta; to say nothing of its more distant relatives, Toronto and Montreal. The cattle and wheat Prairie Provinces of Alberta, Saskatchewan and Manitoba form a natural unit with Montana .and the Dakotas. The Great Lakes and St. Lawrence closely link the industrial southern portions of Ontario and Quebec with the US Midwest; divided by a narrow strip of water the twin automobile cities of Detroit and Windsor seem like one unit. Temperament, hardship, history and the Atlantic give the Canadian Maritimes and most of New England a common denominator often little appreciated in the 'interior'. Add to this the effect of climate which has concentrated Canada's population in a thin belt of shreds and patches stretched out along the highly artificial frontier with the United States — 50 per cent of her numbers within 100 to 125 miles, and 90 per cent within 200 to 225 miles from the border — and one can begin to appreciate against what unnatural odds Canada has created and maintained her identity.

The economic problems posed by her small population scattered over so vast an area are brought out very clearly in one example cited by the Gordon Report. In the United States, the president of a big electrical manufacturing company told the Commission, a plant of minimum efficient size to manufacture refrigerators would have to have an output of 250,000 to 350,000 units per year. In comparison, the Gordon Report noted, the total Canadian output of refrigerators in 1955 was 267,000 units — produced by nineteen different manufacturers. As it remarked soberly elsewhere: 'It is doubtful whether Canada would be a separate nation today if economic forces alone had been allowed to determine our destiny.'

Throughout her history, Canada has had to pay a huge price for running counter to the laws of nature and resisting assimilation by the southern giant. She still continues to pay a heavy price. Compared with the sorry experience of most European nations, no country has had a better neighbour, for the best part of a century and a half, than has

Canada — except possibly the United States. But even so, the powerful centripetal forces unconsciously emitted by the United States have frequently had a thoroughly disruptive effect in Canada, as will be seen in a subsequent chapter. And relations have not always been so cordial.

A quick glance at the story of Canada gives one the impression that whenever the Canadians felt themselves threatened by engulfment, they started building communications. It started after the War of 1812, with the construction of the Rideau Canal to bypass the most vulnerable section of the St. Lawrence. In the 1860s two unrelated but significant events occurred. An enterprising Lancastrian called Walter Cheadle decided to trek through Canada, all the way to Victoria BC without dipping down into the United States. Travelling by rail, steamer, canoe and horseback, swimming unbridged rivers and finally walking, it took him a whole year and a half. At the same time, Britain, through backing the losing side in the American Civil War, incurred the wrath of the Unionists. When the war was over, the restored Union, heady with victory and military might, turned its wrath on Canada and for a time it seemed as if there might actually be a repetition of 1812. While temperatures were still high, in 1868, a US Senate Committee declared: 'The opening by the United States of a Northern Pacific Railway seals the destiny of the British possessions west of the ninety-first meridian' (*i.e.* west of Ontario). The Canadians took the hint and set to work feverishly to build their own first transcontinental railway, the Canadian Pacific. (It was the price exacted by British Columbia for joining the Federation.) As if setting a seal on Cheadle's discovery that, like geography, communications in North America also tended to run north and south, British Columbian delegates to the first conference on the new railway in Ottawa had to travel by ship to San Francisco, and thence by rail across the United States.

The construction of the Canadian Pacific across nearly a thousand miles of granite Shield, another thousand of empty prairie, and another eight hundred of almost uninterrupted mountains, was one of modern civilisation's epic feats. Even in the sophisticated mid-twentieth century, accustomed to all manner of engineering marvels, it is impossible not to feel a thrill as from the 'Scenic Domes' you watch the great stainless steel train winding ahead of you through the famous 'Spiral Tunnels' that hoist the railway over Kicking Horse Pass in the Rockies. With its three mighty diesels flexing their muscles to the accompaniment of deep rolling rumbles, its double-decker coaches twice the size of any British rolling stock, departure on the Canadian Pacific from Vancouver is still an exciting event — more like the sailing of an ocean liner than a mere train leaving a terminus.

Though it took six years longer to build than it should have done, and brought down a government through corruption in its financing, the CPR provided the backbone Canada so badly needed. Immigrants flooded out along it to fill up the empty Prairies. Its success also provided the impetus for the building of more and more Canadian railways. Railways, as somebody once remarked, became the national genius. There are some Canadians, no doubt, who would call it the national folly. By 1915 there were no less than three transcontinental lines completed, for a population of seven and a half millions. Over long stretches, some of the lines merely duplicated each other along the opposite banks of rivers. By 1920 two of the railways were bankrupt. One of those built during the railway spree earned itself the name of the line that 'went from nowhere to nowhere'. But it was part of the price of developing the nation and exorcising the spooks of American annexation. This rail-building 'folly' also helped save Britain from starvation in two World Wars. If it had not been for the railways, immigrants would never have come to grow wheat on the Prairies; if it had not been for the great complex of unprofitable, semi-bankrupt grain-gathering lines in the Prairies, their wheat would never have got to Britain.

When the First World War was over, Canada tried to piece together again the crazy jumble of her railways by bundling all the bankrupt lines (virtually all but the original Canadian Pacific) into a vast, nationalised railway — Canadian National. The CNR inherited some 25,000 miles of railway — which make it still the world's biggest system under one management, with the largest working force in

Canada and the highest turnover of any Canadian corporation. It also inherited crippling debts. The problems that faced it at its birth, and almost non-stop ever since, were at least as great as, if not greater than, those facing British Railways upon nationalisation (and nobody would dispute which system has made the better job of it). Today CNR runs a highly modernised and efficient network that could compare with most of the world's major railways. Its Phoenix-like ascent from the ashes of 1920 was largely due to the unique genius of its first chief, a Briton called Sir Henry Thornton. Only its inherited debts defeated Sir Henry, as indeed CNR's finances have defeated every other President since. Year after year, the Annual Report opens on the same note: 'last year was not financially rewarding for Canadian National Railways'. But the reasons for these repeated deficits lie beyond the control of any railwayman, however inspired. They stem from the deep natural defects of Canada that I have mentioned earlier in this chapter; they are the price Canada continues to pay for independence.

Look at some of the facts. Canada has twice as much railway mileage *per capita* as the United States. Despite her far lower national income, she pays a considerably larger proportion of it in transportation. For example, for all Canada's superabundance of cheap hydro-electric power, according to the Gordon Report the average cost of energy in Canada is 50 per cent higher than in the United States due to the distances that oil and coal fuels have to travel. Whereas population in the United States is large enough to allow a large amount of industrial decentralisation, in Canada raw materials have to travel fantastic, costly distances before reaching processing plants or their final markets. An extreme example of this is Keno Hill, in the far north of the Yukon. Silver, lead and zinc ores mined at Keno have to be shipped out first over 350 miles of unpaved road to Whitehorse, another 110 miles by narrow gauge railway to Skagway on the coast of Alaska, a thousand miles by sea to Vancouver and a final 400 miles to the smelter in the interior of British Columbia; total, over 1800 miles, and the raw metals are still hundreds, perhaps thousands, of miles away from the processing industries. Again, raw steel produced at Sault

Ste. Marie, on the juncture of Lakes Huron and Superior, has to travel nearly 700 miles east to Hamilton on Lake Ontario before it can be turned into oil- and gas-piping for shipment west again to the Alberta oilfields.

Most of the freight traffic in Canada is in bulk goods — such as metal ores, grain and lumber — on which producers simply cannot afford to pay high freight rates. As it is, the Gordon Report estimates that, as a proportion of final selling prices, freight charges on an average haul of 1000 miles amount to 'as much as 50 per cent on lumber and coal and 25 to 35 per cent on pulpwood and steel bars'. Of the total freight tonnage carried by Canadian railways today, some 30 per cent is grain; but, in order to protect the Prairie farmers, statutory agreements forbid the railways from charging any higher rates than those which prevailed in *1899*. At the same time, freight services in the Maritimes have to be heavily subsidised to safeguard the delicate economy of these Provinces. It is therefore hardly surprising that CNR can claim that 25 per cent of their ton-mileage contributes nothing to overheads and that another 30 per cent is marginal. Ideally, both railway companies would like to close down many of their unprofitable lines, but this could not be done without striking a deadly blow at Canada's economic growth. In fact, if her growth is to continue, she is faced with the inescapable necessity of building still more financially risky railways to extract the unexploited mineral wealth of the north.

Meanwhile, since the war, the troubles of the Canadian railways have been accentuated by a decrease in revenue caused by the huge expansion of road transport, and by a sharp increase in wages. The pattern has been the same as in Britain; between 1945 and 1958, railway wages rose 112 per cent. The worst blow yet came in 1958, when the railways had to pay out $60 million in increased wages. Speaking as one, both railways claimed that to meet these rises, they would have to pass them on to the public in the form of a *35 per cent increase* in freight rates. It was an alarming figure, and eventually the Board of Transport Commissioners compromised on a 17 per cent increase. In itself, this was the biggest single increase since the war, and a severe shock to the Canadian economy still suffering from the effects of the 1957 recession.

At the time of the 1958 rail crisis, one of Vancouver's leading businessmen remarked to me that the increased freight charges would have the effect of placing a 'tariff' on goods travelling between east and west Canada, as if they were passing into another country. 'In the short term, it may help British Columbia by protecting and stimulating the growth of her new secondary industries, but it can't help but be bad for the country as a whole. What in effect it will do will be to subdivide the country into separate zones — and probably make each zone more economically dependent on its neighbouring section of the United States.'

Here indeed is a vicious circle. Canada pays a high price for economic sovereignty in terms of exorbitant freight charges or heavy rail subsidies. Yet, when the price becomes too high, the very dangers she pays to avoid grow with it. The 'subdivision' of Canada is quite a real danger; even that development which will greatly advance progress in parts of Canada, the St. Lawrence Seaway, may add to this subdivision by improving as well the natural north-south communications with the United States. In the long run, Canada's only answer to the problem is — more people. More people to provide more local markets and counterbalance the effects of distance.

CHAPTER THREE

'DOWN WHERE THE EAST BEGINS'

Down where the sun is about like water,
Ma sold a drop till the Mounties caught her,
And you spent the rest when you hadn't oughter,
Down where the East begins.
(Old Maritime ballad)

This is their culture, this — their master passion
Of giving shelter and of sharing bread,
Of answering rocket signals in the fashion
Of losing life to save it . . .
(E. J. PRATT on Newfoundland)

WHEN you ask a Canadian what is the most important date in his history, he will be almost certain to reply — regardless of whether his ancestors came from France, Britain or elsewhere — that it was 1867. This was the year of the signature of the British North America Act. The Act created the Dominion of Canada out of four weak and divided British colonies and laid the foundations of the powerful sovereign nation that Canada is today. From 1867 the road led, logically and inevitably, to the Statute of Westminster in 1931, which gave all the Dominions complete control over their own affairs. Today the Act still forms the framework of the Canadian Constitution (a fairly rigid harness of formal documents which provides Canada with one similarity to the United States, and a contrast to Great Britain).

Unlike the Declaration of Independence, the British North America Act was not wrested by force of arms from the mother country. In fact, opposition to it was far more savage in Canada than in Westminster. The father of Canadian union, Sir John A. Macdonald, remarked caustically that disinterested and bored British officialdom had treated the BNA Act as if it 'were a private bill uniting two or three English parishes'. Though it was largely compounded from the elusive, unwritten British Constitution,

from British law and British colonial experience, in both its
contents and in the acceleration of its actual signature, the
Act was heavily influenced by recent events in the United
States, which had just emerged from its Civil War. The new
menacing tone of the triumphant Unionists changed the
minds of Canadians who for years past had hesitated to
take the plunge into Confederation; now, out of the same
motives that led to the construction of Canadian Pacific,
they jumped. But still more important, historically, was the
effect that the grim lessons of the recently ended American
Civil War had upon the framers of the BNA Act. They
were determined not to commit the same error as the
American Founding Fathers, who had bestowed upon the
individual components of Confederation 'States' Rights' so
powerful that these one day nearly blew the whole Union
sky-high. On the contrary, Canada was to have — from
the first — a strong centralised Government. In direct contrast to the United States, Canada's Federal Government
was granted a 'Right of Disallowance' over any legislation
passed by a Provincial Government; the country was to be
governed on the British Cabinet system, rather than the
American principle of an elected Executive; members of
the Upper House, or Senate, instead of being elected by
voters of the Provinces, were to be appointed for life by the
Federal Cabinet; the Lieutenant-Governors of each Province
were to be appointed by the Governor-General in Ottawa.

Thus (in theory) the BNA Act took the first step to
counter the potent natural forces — of geography, population, climate, economics and communications — that have
traditionally threatened to tear Canada in fragments and
draw the fragments towards the United States. But, in
practice, over the course of time, things have worked out
rather differently. Largely due to the insistence of French
Canada that '*nos institutions, notre langue et nos lois*' be safe-
guarded under the BNA Act, the Provinces were given full
powers over property, civil rights and education. They were
also made responsible for direct taxation, a power that they
obviously did not take too seriously at a time when income
tax in Britain was only 4d. in the pound. Yet, in two World
Wars alone, this has presented the Federal Government with

dreadful headaches in finding ways to finance national expenditure without depriving the Provinces of their rights under the BNA Act. Even today, Ottawa collects the national revenue only through an elaborate series of 'Tax-Rental Agreements', whereby the Provinces (Quebec excepted) surrender most of their taxation rights in return for various grants from the Federal Government. In the present age, the potential power that authority over property and civil rights accords each Provincial Government is also enormous. In British Columbia, for example, the socialist Co-operative Commonwealth Federation has a platform far to the left of any other regional faction of the party, and has openly declared that it stands to nationalise (perhaps 'provincialise' is more appropriate) many of BC's principal industries. In the event of the CCF coming to power, a right-wing Conservative Government in Ottawa might find itself standing by more or less impotently while another government was carrying out strongly un-Conservative legislation in one of Canada's most important Provinces.

As things have turned out, the Canadian Provinces have in fact, paradoxically, come to gain more power, and a greater degree of autonomy, than the States in post-Civil War America. Long terms under different forms of Provincial Government have left indelible stamps on many of them; fifteen years of CCF Socialism in Saskatchewan and nearly twenty-five years of the Social Credit Party's curious brand of messianic Conservo-Socialism in Alberta have left these two western Provinces with little in common with the traditionally free-enterprise, essentially conservative 'Empire Province' of Ontario. Problems are different; the wheat grower on the Prairies views freight subsidies from a standpoint diametrically opposed to that of the high-tax-paying industrialist from Toronto — and different problems make people different. Distance and isolation, the factors mentioned in the previous chapter, have all contributed to the separateness of each part of Canada, towards an individuality and a particularism that seems almost certain to grow, rather than decrease, over the years — at least until Canada has a population so great as to give the country a homogeneity and unity comparable to that of the United States.

This separateness, this subdivision into zones, makes it all the more difficult to describe Canada as a unit. Tempting generalisations about the country and people as a whole collapse on the idiosyncrasies of each Province, or block of Provinces. They need examining piecemeal.

Geographically, the farthest eastern portion of Canada is a convenient place to start; historically, it also has some claim to priority in that it was the site of the first attempted permanent white settlement in Canada (in fact, the first in the New World north of Florida), and the site also of the preliminary skirmishes between Britain and France in the battle for North America. Until just over a decade ago, this part of Canada consisted of the three 'Maritime Provinces', the three tiniest in Canada; Nova Scotia, New Brunswick and Prince Edward Island. Of the three, the largest, New Brunswick, is a little smaller than Scotland. Then in 1949, the Maritimes were joined by a fourth, Britain's oldest colony of Newfoundland, bigger than all three put together. Today the four 'Atlantic Provinces', as they are now called, form an increasingly integrated bloc. The background and problems of Newfoundland, however, are so different to those of the original three that it may be wiser to leave it till later, and deal first with the three Maritime Provinces.

When one thinks of earliest Canada, it is usually in terms of Quebec, then Upper Canada, rather than the Maritimes, though here there were both French and British outposts well before the existence of 'New France'. In 1604 that enterprising Frenchman — geographer, explorer, writer and soldier — Samuel de Champlain, landed a 'colony' of 125 men at St. Croix Island, near the mouth of the river of the same name that now marks the easternmost part of the frontier between Canada and the United States. For a man who had once been Geographer Royal to the King of France, it was a remarkably inept choice. By the following spring, 35 of the company had died of scurvy, thirst and starvation; a grimly fitting introduction to the hardness of life that has been the lot of the Maritimes ever since. Champlain then transplanted the colony across the Bay of Fundy to what is now known as the Annapolis Basin, on the sheltered side of

Nova Scotia. For nearly three years the colony, christened Port Royal, flourished — enjoying fleshly comforts that only Frenchmen know how to provide under awkward conditions. They established the first wining-and-dining society, the 'Order of Good Cheer', and wrote and produced the first drama on North American soil. Then suddenly their royal charter was revoked, and the colony was re-embarked for France. In 1608 Champlain switched his attention from the Atlantic coast to the natural fortress up the St. Lawrence which Jacques Cartier had discovered seventy-three years earlier, and Quebec was founded.

Though Quebec was henceforth to be the centre of gravity of French colonisation, two years after its inception de Poutrincourt, a member of Champlain's first colonising attempt, sailed to re-found Port Royal. It is a sad commentary on the affairs of man, particularly European man, that no sooner were the first toeholds secured in the New World than the colonists set forth to expunge the settlements of rival powers. In 1614 Samuel Argall, a young English sea captain from the recently founded colony of Virginia, descended on Port Royal and sacked the French settlement. Thus was struck the first blow in the Franco-British struggle for supremacy in the New World, which was to continue intermittently until 1760; and thus did Britain get her foothold in the Canadian Maritimes. James I hastened to change the French name of the area, Acadia, to Nova Scotia, and his son, Charles I, reinforced this by creating his dubious 'Nova Scotia baronetcies'. But Stuart colonisation attempts were a failure and it was not until the Treaty of Utrecht in 1713 that Nova Scotia (and Newfoundland) were finally ceded to Britain. In 1749 the English built Halifax — as a counterpoise to the mighty French fortress at Louisburg on the northernmost tip of Nova Scotia's Cape Breton Island, the key to the St. Lawrence and Quebec. In the last years of the final campaign, the British sealed their claim to Nova Scotia with the expulsion of 6000 of the unhappy Acadians, heirs of the 'Order of Good Cheer', who were dispersed far and wide over the New England colonies.

Barely a generation later the boot was to be placed on the other foot, when thousands of Loyalist Britons either were expelled or fled from the successfully rebellious American colonies into the British possessions north of New England. Many came to swell the established settlements in Nova Scotia, but 28,000 crossed into the more or less empty territory beyond Champlain's first abortive settlement on the St. Croix River, to create the new colony of New Brunswick. Some went to Prince Edward Island, the fertile sliver of land cupped by the northern coasts of the other two Maritimes. Many of the refugee Loyalists were well-educated people who had occupied the highest strata of society in the American colonies, and pioneer life in the inhospitable brush of New Brunswick came as a dreadful shock. 'It is, I think, the roughest land I ever saw,' was how one woman described the St. John Valley in 1783.

Hardship, suffering, and often tragedy, have been the almost constant companions of the Maritimers, from earliest to most recent times; it is perhaps what gives them as people a very special attractiveness. For a brief halcyon period in the mid-19th century, however, the shipbuilders of New Brunswick and the 'Bluenose' fishermen of Nova Scotia enjoyed remarkable prosperity. At one time, in terms of registered tonnage, Saint John NB[1] actually laid claim to be the world's fourth port (it still boasts the second biggest dry dock). No New England state could rival the Nova Scotia merchant marine. Then came the ship of iron and steam, and (despite the fact that the compound engine had actually been invented in New Brunswick) it struck a mortal blow at the Maritimes, whose prosperity had been based on the wooden ships constructed from their inexhaustible forests. Typical of the tragedy was Shelburne on Nova Scotia's Atlantic coast, one of Canada's prettiest towns. Founded by 10,000 Loyalists, Shelburne was once the largest town in British North America and launched some of the most famous sailing ships in Atlantic history. It now has a population of barely two thousand.

As the internal canal system of New York State and the Great Lakes grew, so trade also began to pass the Maritimes by, and Saint John and Halifax were eclipsed by Montreal

[1] Always called Saint John, in contrast to the St. John River that flows through it, and St. John's, the capital of Newfoundland.

D

and New York. In 1867, with considerable reluctance, Nova Scotia and New Brunswick joined with Quebec and Ontario to become the original four Provinces of the Canadian Confederation. Prince Edward Island did not come in till six years later — although the initial meeting to discuss Confederation was held in its capital, Charlottetown. But, despite the links that were forged to give Confederation a meaning, as Central Canada has galloped ahead Fate seems to have continued to push the Maritimes to one side.

To this day, many Maritimers feel that the world — and Canada herself — has not been fair to them. Some even have misgivings about 1867. The very first person I spoke to as I stepped on to Canadian soil in 1958 — an amiable Customs Officer on the quay of Yarmouth NS — was particularly bitter. 'I detest the Federal Government,' he said. 'Not just because of its politics, but because we in Nova Scotia are always ruled by two Provinces — Ontario and Quebec. Why should eight Provinces always be ruled by two? Because of this, we have never got our fair share of the country's revenue.'

Some of the Maritimes' grievance against the Confederation stems from the resentment of an object of charity towards its benefactor. No people could resent being dependent upon charity more than the proud Maritimers, but they know that, as things are, the society they have so painfully constructed would cease to exist without it. And they do not consider that the charity they receive is anywhere near adequate for them to create for themselves a standard of life comparable to that of the rest of Canada. No other part of Canada suffers quite as much from the effects of distance has the Maritimes. Their tiny combined population of one and a quarter millions provides far too inadequate a market for their produce; their nearest markets in Central Canada lie hundreds of miles through the great empty forests of northern Maine and the interior of New Brunswick. Without generous rail subsidies, the whole Maritime economy would collapse. As it is, they receive freight reductions of 30 per cent and still their goods are barely competitive with those of Central Canada. Their coal receives a Federal Transportation subsidy amounting to perhaps a quarter to a third of its cost per ton; but still Ontario finds it cheaper to buy coal from West Virginia — another example of Canada's north-south orientations. Their cod and lobster fishermen can obtain subsidies from the Government to build new boats; yet still, although they account for more than half the value of all Canadian fisheries, the value of their average catch per head amounts to perhaps only a fifth, or even a sixth, as much as the harvest reaped by the salmon fishermen of British Columbia.

Whereas the once poverty-stricken Prairies have farmers who own (though by no means all of them) planes and spend their winters in Florida, the great majority in the Maritimes are 'subsistence farmers', living in tar-papered shacks and scratching a precarious existence out of a few acres of acid soil, without any thought of taking their produce to market — even if there were one. And so it goes on.

In addition to transportation subsidies, under Tax Rental agreements each of the provinces receive substantial special grants from the Federal Government. But when the Maritimers chastise Ottawa for being miserly in the 'charity' without which they know their economy must wither away, they can produce one incontrovertible fact; according to the Gordon Commission Report, in 1955 the average income *per capita* of the three Provinces was 33 per cent below the rest of Canada.[1] Since the war, while the rest of Canada has boomed, the gap has widened still further; in 1946 the income discrepancy was only 24 per cent.

One of the tragedies of the Maritimes is that, more than any other part of Canada, they badly need people; people to create new markets that could raise personal income and standard of life for all. In the long run, only a great increase in population can mitigate the traditional hardships of the Maritimes, yet while these hardships exist they are constantly driving people away. A truly vicious circle. Over the past thirty years, nearly a quarter of a million people have left the four Atlantic Provinces. Each year they lose approximately 8000 people in 'driftage' to other parts of Canada, or the

[1] With the inclusion of Newfoundland, average income *per capita* figures for the four Atlantic Provinces sinks as low as 37 per cent below the rest of Canada.

United States. (Boston is reputed to have more Newfoundlanders in it than St. John's.) At the same time, the
four receive only 2 per cent of the country's immigration
intake. Yet, surprisingly enough, despite driftage and the
by-passing of the immigrant influx, between the censuses of
1951 and 1956 a high birth-rate has in fact increased Nova
Scotia's population by 8 per cent, New Brunswick by 7 per
cent (compared with only 2 per cent for England and Wales)
— a hopeful omen for the future.

The damage that 'driftage' has done to the Maritimes,
however, lies not in numbers. It is so often the most adventurous and daring that have left. Those that remain tend
to be too conservative, over-cautious and prone to accept
things as they have always been. The author of a recent
book on Canada [1] has aptly likened Nova Scotia and New
Brunswick to Scotland — 'a reservoir of talent on which the
rest of the country has drawn'. Many are the heads, past
and present, of Canada's great banks that have originated
from the humble Maritimes. The list of Maritimers who
have found fame or fortune in the outside world is a long one.
It includes Samuel Cunard, the founder of the shipping line,
born Halifax 1787; Sir James Dunne, the steel magnate,
probably Canada's richest man when he died; R. B.
Bennett, the last pre-Diefenbaker Conservative Premier of
Canada; Andrew Bonar Law, the first British Prime Minister to be born outside Great Britain; and, of course, William
Maxwell Aitken, the first Lord Beaverbrook [2] — all New
Brunswick men. What was the secret behind all the great
men that this tiny, rather backward corner of Canada had
produced? In Fredericton, the capital of New Brunswick,
I asked this of a dynamic, one-eyed British ex-Brigadier
called Mike Wardell, a former lieutenant of Lord Beaverbrook, who had migrated, fairly late in life, in the reverse
direction to the 'Beaver'.

'I can tell you exactly what makes them,' he replied.
'It's the challenge of having to creep out to the outhouse
every winter's day at 30° below zero!'

Not all the Maritimers who left their land migrated for

[1] Ernest Watkins, *Prospect of Canada*, Secker and Warburg, 1954.
[2] Though only by adoption; Lord Beaverbrook was in fact born in Ontario.

good; as soon as they could, after the American War of Independence, many of the banished French Acadians returned. In the southern parts of Nova Scotia you will find their villages, often sprung up from one family. At Comeauville and Belliveau's Cove everybody still seems to be called Comeau or Belliveau. Although the Acadians have been isolated from the parent body for centuries, their villages are as unmistakably part of French Canada as any village in Quebec Province. Everywhere the church spires, on which, during the war, lost RAF trainees used to set their compasses, dominate town and plain. Typical of them is St. Bernard's great stone church, thirty-two years abuilding by local labour and designed for the kind of population growth that typifies French Canada, with a seating capacity of a thousand in a village of only 290. From the handful of Acadians, Nova Scotia's French-speaking population has now multiplied to some 75,000; more than one in three New Brunswickers are now French Canadians, their long lines of washing attesting to the land pressure that has forced them to spill over from neighbouring Quebec. Now, for the first time in her history, New Brunswick actually has a French Canadian Premier, Louis Robichaud.

Among the other minorities in the Maritimes, are some 30,000 of German descent who settled in the peaceful fishing villages near Halifax in the 18th century, and have since become completely assimilated. More recent emigrants are about the same number of Dutchmen (again, mostly in Nova Scotia) who have proved themselves to be highly successful farmers, and, as a group, probably the Maritimes' most hard-working and satisfactory immigrants. Finally, the Maritimes have — strangely enough — by far the largest portion of Canada's estimated 25,000 negroes, of whom no less than 15,000, many of them descendants of runaway slaves from the Southern States, live in a dispirited slum on the outskirts of Halifax, called 'Africville'.

But the Maritimers are more solidly of undiluted British stock than any other section of Canada. In many parts of the three Provinces, the flavour is predominantly of the Highlands. Despite the failure of early Stuart attempts at settlement, Nova Scotia particularly has come to live up to its name. The fact that much of Nova Scotia's scenery, as well as its damp, temperate climate, is remarkably like parts of Scotland, was more responsible than the name for luring out some 50,000 Highlanders in the early 19th century. As you approach Cape Breton, sign-posts proudly proclaim 'The Road to the Isles'. It is virtually a Scottish colony. The ancestors of many of the coal-miners at Sydney worked in Scottish pits. At Ingonish, one of Canada's greatest beauty spots, and really reminiscent of the Highlands, there are so many Macdonalds (a Mackenzie in Halifax told me) that they are simply known by their nicknames. Highland culture still proudly flourishes after more than a century and a half of separation from the glens; at St. Ann's is the only Gaelic college in North America, and each July Antigonish celebrates its Highland Games.

Hard as the economic facts of life may be in the Maritimes, there are compensations. A Briton who could survive away from the hubbub of a metropolis would, I think, find them a good place to live in, compared with the unnerving relentlessness of Toronto or Montreal. This is an essentially rural society; unlike most of Canada where the tendency is to concentrate more and more around the big cities, in the Maritimes the majority of the population still live in the country or in small settlements. Its towns are quiet, unhurried places, hidden under ancient avenues of shady elms and maples, with lawns that run right down to the street, closely resembling the smaller towns of old New England. With the exception of the interior uplands of New Brunswick, their climate is considerably less harsh than the rest of Canada, with the exception of the Pacific coast. Virtually everything that grows in the British Isles will also grow in Nova Scotia. And it is beautiful country, some of the loveliest in North America. All of it is on a smaller, neater, almost more English scale than you will find in the other gargantuan Provinces of Canada. New Brunswick is a peaceful land of gently rolling hills, heavily forested, with pleasant pastures and small farms that cling mainly to the broad, winding valley of the St. John River, sometimes called (with only just a touch of exaggeration) 'The Rhine of North America'. Nova Scotia, deservedly enough, is one of

Canada's principal tourist attractions[1] for visiting Americans;
by and large, everything is just a little prettier, a little softer
and a little more prosperous than its western neighbour. It
has a great range of varied scenery; from the picturesquely
pretty fishing villages that nestle in the rocky coves of the
Atlantic coast, to the more subdued, sheltered land on the
Bay of Fundy with its remarkable, 60-foot tides. Between
coasts lie the glorious, fertile Annapolis Valley, the Garden
of Eden of the ancient Acadians and now one of Canada's
chief apple orchards, and the wild spruce and pine forests of
the interior with their wonderfully sweet smells, where the
moose, bear and wildcat roam. And finally, up north, the
rugged, Highland beauty of Cape Breton Island, split down
the centre by a great salt water inlet, which, as the sinking
summer sun shines across it, lives up to its Acadian name:
'Bras d'Or'.

Chief of the Maritime cities is Halifax, Canada's great
eastern port and rail terminus, now with a population of
some 95,000. Halifax is the most British of all Canadian
cities, far more so than Victoria BC which for so long has
held that reputation. A little Victorian in atmosphere, it is
very conscious of its Loyalist past; recalling with perhaps
more pride than they deserve the not very creditable sojourns
of the future William IV and his brother, the Duke of Kent.
Halifax is immensely, and justifiably, proud of the vital role
played in two World Wars, and of the fact that geography
brought it closer to Britain and the actual conflict than any
other city of Canada. During the last war, I can remember
no more moving sight than the hundreds of grey, battered
merchantmen assembling in the huge Halifax Basin for the
desperate sortie into the Atlantic. Fifteen years later, a
moustachioed old soldier, guardian at Halifax's mighty star-
shaped Citadel, delighted to find someone from 'the Old
Country', reminisced to me of the war before: 'I was a
Sergeant here, and that fellow (taking down the flag) was my
trumpeter. In 1918 we had sixty-eight ships leave here and
two were sunk right before our eyes — but we got two U-
boats and we put the crews in cells under the ramparts here.

---

[1] Nova Scotia's official travel bureau, incidentally, puts out one of the most
informative and well-written guide-books I have come across anywhere.

There were rats this big in 'em. . . .' Halifax paid a heavy
price for its participation; in 1917 a French munitions ship
collided with a freighter in the harbour, and the resulting
explosion flattened half of the city, killing two thousand
people. History nearly repeated itself at least twice in the
Second World War, and in 1941 many Haligonians were
convinced that the *Bismarck* was heading their way when
apprehended by the *Hood*.

Halifax at night is one of the quietest towns I know. In
this at least it resembles its English namesake; after nine
o'clock, nothing stirs. But this is deceptive. In fact, since
the war much has stirred in Halifax. Many new industries
have opened up — some, like Fairey Aviation and Cossor,
built with British capital; an imposing, new $11 million
suspension bridge — second longest in the Commonwealth
— now links two parts of the city previously divided by the
harbour. On the scrub-covered hill whence, fifteen years
ago, I had watched the convoys forming, a whole new
suburb has sprung up; between the censuses of 1951 and
1956 alone, Halifax has added nearly another tenth to its
population.

The same is true of Moncton, at present New Brunswick's
second city but rapidly becoming its first, the fastest growing
of all the Maritime cities. I wandered for an hour or more
searching for the air base where I had spent several months
during the war. I remembered it as being on the far outskirts of town. Eventually I found it; a new settlement had
engulfed it and moved on beyond, only the hangars (now
used as warehouses) showed where some 10,000 Canadian
and British airmen had once trained. In those days, Moncton had been a sleepy, rather dreary town of 10–15,000, with
seemingly little more excuse for its existence than its railway
junction. Now it is a thriving, bustling city of 40,000, full
of confidence in its future and the assurance that if ever the
four Atlantic Provinces become consolidated into one 'super-
Province', Moncton with its central position and good communications will be the logical choice for a capital.

Saint John (52,491), New Brunswick's biggest and oldest
city, famous for the unique 'Reversing Falls' that the extra-
ordinary Fundy tides cause at the mouth of its river, has, as

I mentioned earlier, never quite recovered from its 19th-century decline. All the maladies of old age — narrow streets, antique buildings and conservative ideas — afflict it. Its nose is constantly being put out of joint by ebullient Moncton, and its population has barely moved over the last decade. But the promises are there. It is still a great port, one of the few in Eastern Canada to be ice-free all year round, and if a project to cut a canal across the Chignecto Isthmus ever comes to pass, Saint John would experience a great revitalisation. It already boasts one of Canada's largest sugar refineries, and a number of new industrial developments include a $50-million oil refinery shortly to be completed by Mr. Kenneth Irving, who has also been responsible for the erection recently of a steel processing plant, an important expansion of the St. John paper industry, and the conversion of the famous dry dock into an up-to-date shipyard.

Farther up the St. John River lies Fredericton, the Provincial capital, the birthplace of Bliss Carman and home of Charles G. D. Roberts, two of Canada's best-known poets. In the eyes of perhaps its most enterprising contemporary citizen, Mike Wardell, it has potentialities that could make it 'the Leipzig of Canada'. Today, however, Fredericton is a charmingly drowsy city of about 20,000 inhabitants, missed out by both the mainline railways and remote from the rest of the world, apparently more concerned about the preservation of its handsome elms than Wardell's grandiose ambitions for its future. It boasts a few sawmills, a few small industries, a small but distinguished university — one of the oldest in Canada — and the favours of Lord Beaverbrook. The mantle of the 'Beaver' lies closely about Fredericton. On the banks of the St. John stands the million-and-a-half-dollar Lord Beaverbrook Art Gallery, interposed between the Government buildings and their view of the river; to the New Brunswick legislators, *si monumentum requiris* . . . but there is a monument as well. Next to the Lord Beaverbrook Art Gallery, stands the Lord Beaverbrook Hotel, and a few paces farther on, the Lord Beaverbrook Statue. If some New Brunswick parents disapprove of the dimes collected from their children at school for the erection of the great man's statue during his own lifetime, nobody in the Province will deny the good that he has done for it as a whole, and Fredericton in particular. Above all, the University of New Brunswick has benefited from his generosity, in the form of scholarships, new buildings and notably the Bonar Law–Bennett wing added to the university library — to the tune of over $2,000,000.

So far I have said very little about the third member of the Maritimes, Prince Edward Island — Canada's smallest Province with (until his defeat in 1959) the largest Premier. Though history and geography make the island, which lies at one point only eight miles off the mainland, an integral part of the Maritimes, where hardships and economic problems are concerned it is something of an exception. And it likes to be the exception, to be different from the rest of Canada. The leading newspaper, the *Charlottetown Guardian* (which makes the endearing boast that it 'covers Prince Edward Island like the dew') has been known to call it the 'island continent'. The Indians christened it *Abegweit*, or 'cradled-on-the-waves'; other Canadians call it 'the Garden of the Gulf', or just 'The Island' — all of which should suggest that it is both different and lovely, and so it is. Jacques Cartier, probably the first European to see it, wrote ecstatically: 'All this land is low and most beautiful it is possible to see.' If Nova Scotia is the Scotland of Canada, 'the Island' is its Devonshire. It is one long landscape of lush green meadows set off by the bright, Indian red soil that peeps through in places, of white well-cared-for farms with high gables and vermilion doors and window sashes, and barns of traditional New England salthouse red. Even Charlottetown's diminutive Parliament, where a painting depicts the Fathers of Confederation notionally clad in togas, is both the most artistically pleasing of all Canadian Legislative buildings, and the most different; it is the only one where the Opposition sits to the right of the Speaker. An idyll of bucolic contentment, 'The Island' hardly seems to belong to the bustling New World at all — somebody once aptly described it as 'the last outpost of leisure and of dreams'. It even runs on its own special time, an hour behind the mainland. Although it is the most densely inhabited of any

Canadian Province (population remaining fairly constant at just below 100,000 in an area about half the size of Jamaica), Prince Edward Island unquestionably has the highest overall prosperity of the Maritimes. The reason for its prosperity is its rich red soil. Farming is its principal, indeed, almost its only industry; out of a total area of some 1·4 million acres, 1·1 million are farmland. Potatoes are the largest crop, and for many years the Province has had an important export market in selling seed potatoes to the States and even South America. Cattle do extremely well in its mild moist climate, and currently number about 25 per cent more than 'The Island's' human population. Silver fox farming has also been fairly successful.

Outside 'The Island', farming in the Maritime plays an unsatisfactory role. In the past, too much has been carried out in small, infertile patches. In New Brunswick alone there are 25,000 smallholders of whom perhaps four-fifths farm on a subsistence basis, supplementing meagre earnings by cutting pulpwood, fishing and sometimes doing part-time roadwork. The problem of 'driftage' is nowhere more acute than on the Maritime farms today. Legion are the number of eldest sons, disgruntled by the sad story of farming in the past, who sell up as soon as their fathers die, and then move to the big city. Without a ready buyer, many do not even bother to sell; they simply 'realise' what machinery there may be, board up the farmhouse, and get out. All over New Brunswick and Nova Scotia, one comes across the depressing sight of these boarded up farms, with fir seedlings already thrusting through land once so laboriously cleared by the Loyalist pioneers. In Halifax, an agricultural official waved a thick bundle of 'Farms For Sale' notices at me — it was, he said, just a week's crop. Even in fertile Prince Edward Island, the percentage of the population on the farms sank from 63 to 48 per cent between 1931 and 1951, and many excellent farms are unoccupied today.

That farming *can*, however, be made to pay in the Maritimes has been proved by three hundred Dutch families who have settled on the land since the war, and who — almost without exception — have done extremely well. British immigrants as a whole have not been so successful ('they won't learn,' an immigration official complained to me in Halifax, the first of many hundred times I was to hear this remark across Canada). It requires courage to move in where Canadians themselves have been failing; nevertheless, farms are notably cheaper in the Maritimes than elsewhere in Canada and, although there may be a surplus of such crops as apples and potatoes, meat, poultry and vegetables are predominantly in short supply for home consumption, and markets are constantly growing over the border in Quebec and Ontario. All Canadian Provinces have schemes to assist immigrants in the purchase of farms and machinery; Nova Scotia, for instance, has a system of farm loans whereby the applicant has to put up only one-third of the price of the farm himself, with remainder repayable at $4\frac{1}{2}$ per cent interest over a period of from ten to twenty-five years.

In the four Atlantic Provinces taken as a whole, agriculture constitutes the third or fourth most important industry, in terms of value — though it barely exists in Newfoundland. Forestry products (including pulp and paper) still take the lead — particularly in New Brunswick — with fisheries and the coal and steel industries closely behind them. Mining and manufacturing are growing gradually in importance in various parts of the area, but are still in their infancy compared with the scale of things in Quebec or Ontario.

Of all the black spots that still plague the Maritime economy, coal is perhaps the blackest (it sounds like a poor pun) and the most persistent. Yet Nova Scotia's depressed coal and steel industry plays a vital role in the prosperity of all four Provinces. Furthermore, its tribulations point to some of the fundamental weaknesses of the Canadian economy, so that it is essential to give it some space here. As long ago as 1720, the French were digging coal out of the Cape Breton cliffs to heat their garrison at Louisburg. Today the coal of Cumberland County and Cape Breton comprises between a third and a half of Canada's total production. At Sydney, built on top of the Cape Breton coal deposits, has sprung up one of Canada's three major steel industries (the other two are in Ontario, at Hamilton and Sault Ste. Marie), with a capacity of some 900,000 tons a year. It has direct access to the sea and its iron ore comes, also entirely by cheap sea transportation, a relatively short distance across the Cabot Strait from Bell Island, Newfoundland. In theory, then, the Sydney coal and steel industry should be one of the most prosperous in North America. In fact, for almost as long as anybody can remember, it has been Canada's South Wales. Why?

The reasons, in a nutshell, are those twin bogies of distance and lack of population. Largely because of increased freight rates, the cost of a steel product delivered from Sydney to Toronto increased 97 per cent between 1948 and 1955; the same product from Hamilton increased only 8 per cent. One of the leading men of Dominion Steel and Coal Co. at Sydney, a former Doncaster coal-miner who had emigrated in 1949 and was now largely responsible for DOSCO's new mechanisation programme, put it to me this way: 'Sydney to Yarmouth [at the opposite ends of Nova Scotia] equals the distance of Newcastle to London, but whereas over this distance in England there are some 40 million potential coal consumers, here there are less than 700,000.'

The Nova Scotia coal deposits are difficult — and sometimes dangerous — to work. At Sydney, the ancient seams are now being mined up to six miles out under the sea. Consequently costs are more than double those of US mines; though, since British-owned A. V. Roe Canada Ltd. took over control of DOSCO, mechanisation has boosted productivity over 50 per cent in five years. In Cumberland County, as if the Maritimes' burden were not already great enough, coal seams are faulty and have repeatedly caused terrible accidents; culminating in the Springhill disaster of October 1958, which entombed seventy-four miners, and finally led to the closing down of the colliery.[1] But these are no more than contributory factors — in Britain, less-productive seams are still being worked by the National Coal Board.

Throughout Canada, the coal industry (none of which, incidentally, is nationalised) presents one of the principal minus signs of the Canadian economy. Its problems are in many ways akin to those of the railways. It is also about the only sector of the economy actually to show a decline since

[1] In previous disasters at Springhill, 122 were killed in 1891, and 39 in 1956.

the war. In 1938 Canada produced 13·3 million tons of coal;
in 1949 production had risen to a peak of 19·1 million but by
1957 it had sunk again to 13·1 million, below even the 1938
totals. Yet the great industries of Ontario currently consume
as much coal as the whole of Canada produces; and almost
all of it imported from the United States.

Apart from the constant of distance, two special reasons
are advanced for the sharp decline in coal production; rapid
dieselisation of the railways (in 1946, in the Maritimes alone,
the railways used 1·2 million tons of coal — ten years later
the figure had sunk to less than half, and conversion to diesel
is expected to be virtually complete during the early '60s);
and the discovery of oil and natural gas in western Canada,
which has led to a great increase in the consumption of these
fuels. In western Canada, which contains perhaps as much
as 97 per cent of all Canada's estimated coal reserves, the
picture of declining production is repeated. Between 1950
and 1957 it was nearly halved, and Alberta, home of most of
the oil and gas, has been particularly hard hit. The most
depressed towns I saw in all Canada, close facsimiles of the
Rhondda Valley, were those of Alberta's Crowsnest Pass.[1]
Once again the melancholic phenomenon of ghost towns has
made its appearance in Canada's West; this time, not as the
aftermath of a goldrush, but of a coal slump. Only three or
four years ago, one such town in the Albertan Rockies had
two and a half thousand inhabitants and a nine-hole golf
course; now its population consists of one caretaker. It is a
fantastic situation. Alberta alone has an estimated 48 billion
tons of coal at least — representing probably a greater energy
reserve even than her fabulous oil and gas resources — and
much of it in rich, thick seams close to the surface. Yet, all the
time, for want of accessible markets, she is closing down coal-
fields that Britain's Coal Board would sell its soul to possess.

For all Canada's coal producers, the situation is likely
to get worse, rather than better, over the immediate future.

---

[1] Superstitious Albertans claim that a curse was placed on the area by an
Indian Princess, who was seduced by a rascally white, wanting to penetrate the
secret of her tribe's gold mines. In 1903 a whole mountain literally collapsed
on top of the mining town of Frank, killing sixty-six; the 'Frank Slide' and
recurrent economic disasters that have struck the Crowsnest Pass have been
blamed on the 'Indian Curse'.

By 1965, it is estimated that conversion to oil and natural gas will have reduced coal used for central heating and transportation to less than a third of 1955 consumption. Nearly half of Nova Scotia's coal goes to Quebec, and DOSCO hopefully expects that the St. Lawrence Seaway will help increase this export — but on the other hand it is even more likely to facilitate transportation downstream of cheaper American coal. At the same time, pipelines bearing oil and gas are reaching towards Montreal and those valuable Quebec markets.

To prosperous Alberta, the depressed coal industry is but one small slice of the cake; but to Nova Scotia it is nearly everything. At least, it is the Province's principal source of both wealth and employment, as well as being the basis for the only major industrial combine in all the Atlantic Provinces. Thus economists (generally from other parts of Canada) who from time to time recommend that the Maritime coal industry be gradually 'folded up' are completely out of touch with reality. The authors of the Gordon Report were nearer to the mark when they suggested that what was needed was not for Ottawa to raise transportation subsidies on Nova Scotia coal exports, but to encourage construction of thermal power stations that would utilise the coal locally. In fact, for the salvation of the Maritimes, what is really needed is a much more daring plan that would found a whole new industry on Sydney's coal and steel. A petrochemical industry is one possibility, and — with plentiful supplies of cheap, high-grade iron now assured from recent discoveries in near-by Labrador — a motor-car and machinery industry that could revolutionise gloomy Sydney into a minor Detroit is not all that fantastic. Cars are certainly far cheaper to transport to distant markets than coal or raw steel ingots. One thing is certain — some day Canada's vast coal reserves, whether in the East or the West, must come into their own, but, if the industry is meanwhile permitted to atrophy as at present, it may well do irreparable harm to the Canadian economy as a whole.

Despite more than a decade as citizens of the youngest Canadian Province, many of the 430,000 Newfoundlanders still speak of 'going to Canada' when they cross the Cabot Strait. Isolated by the cold waters of the Gulf of St. Lawrence and the fogs that traditionally swirl around her coast, still (despite a decade of remarkable progress) bedevilled by centuries-old problems of poverty of a degree that no other part of Canada has ever shared, Newfoundland remains a little apart from the rest of the country. Ever since John Cabot reported in 1497 that 'the sea there is swarming with fish', the Newfoundlanders have traditionally been a race of cod-fishermen, living totally isolated existences in the twelve hundred 'outports' that are scattered among the bays and islands of their heavily indented coastline. In the outports, settlements as remote from civilisation and each other as any in the Western World, even the houses lean perilously on rickety piles out over an inhospitable sea. Before radio and the helicopter, the sea was the only means of communication for most of them, as well as a sole source of livelihood that was often tragically hard and unrewarding.

Behind the outports lies a rocky, infertile country, much of it of great beauty, but it is a hard, unyielding beauty that reminds one of the outer islands of the west coast of Scotland. The vast hinterland of Newfoundland (the island itself is a quarter again as large as Ireland) is a wilderness of fir and muskeg, rock and lake, one of the most unexplored areas of any Canadian Province; a paradise for fishermen and big-game hunters. Great new lumber plants, like Bowater's at Cornerbrook on the western end of the island, are gradually cutting their way into the interior, but it is a mere nibble. There is still no road across Newfoundland; the only surface link being a narrow-gauge railway ironically nicknamed the 'Newfoundland Bullet', which for slowness and squalour might embarrass even a Balkan state.

On only a few small acres can farmers scratch a living out of the poor soil, and almost all of Newfoundland's food has to be imported from the mainland. Contrary to expectations, the Newfoundlanders eat remarkably little fresh fish (perhaps they have had too much of it over the centuries), as attested by the monstrous piles of empty tins that mar the beauty of many an outport. Dried cod and 'Brewis', a kind of hardtack, is still a great favourite with the outporters,

The Cabot Trail, Cape Breton Island, Nova Scotia

THE CANADIAN SCENE, EAST AND WEST

Mount Rundle and Vermilion Lake, Banff National Park, Alberta

Mixed farm on prosperous Prince Edward Island

Fishing 'outport' near St. John's, Newfoundland

usually washed down with a good tot of 'Screech' — a suitably named liquor apparently distilled from the dregs of
rum barrels. But, despite the fierceness of 'Screech', alcohol-
ism is a problem that barely exists in Newfoundland. The
island maintains a reputation of being one of North America's
most law-abiding communities; the only Province in
Canada where the police still feel they can get along without
side-arms. Divorce is almost unheard of; in 1958 there were
only ninety-three divorced persons listed on the whole island.
Life is closely centred around the various Churches, which
are still responsible for education. Predominantly of English
and Irish descent, the Newfoundlanders remain strongly
loyal to Britain — even though, in their long years as a
Crown Colony, they were not always treated magnanimously
by the Mother Country — and probably no other section of
Canadians is more devoted to the Royal Family. They are
by tradition among the most hospitable people in the world;
but if courage and hospitality are their principal virtues,
laziness is almost certainly their greatest vice. It could
explain why the streets of St. John's strike one as being the
dirtiest in all Canada; people apparently just throw their
rubbish into them, and nobody bothers to collect it. More
than just laziness, the island suffers from a sort of fatalistic
indolence bred of centuries of insecurity and hardship. St.
John's today claims the highest rate of construction of any
Canadian city, yet one cannot help feeling that any progress
there requires more effort than elsewhere in Canada.

The past has not been kind to Newfoundland. Few
people have suffered more from a conspiracy of history and
geography. For a century after the first serious attempt at
colonisation in 1610, the Newfoundland settlements lay
under constant threat of fire and sword during the intermittent French-English wars for control of the New World.
Even once the French threat was removed by the Treaty of
Utrecht, the unhappy Newfoundlanders continued to be
plagued almost as much by their own countrymen. For
many years British governments, under pressure from West
of England fishing interests, toyed with notions of winding
up the settlements that could never feed themselves, and of
utilising the island purely as a transient fishing camp. It was

E

not until 1811 that the right to hold property on Newfoundland was actually confirmed by Westminster.

As if the unkindness of man, the rigours of nature and the occasional devastating failure of the dried cod market were not enough, with alarming regularity fire wiped out its wood-built capital. It happened in 1816, twice in 1817, and again in 1846 and 1892. Then in 1894 the banks collapsed. In the First World War, The Royal Newfoundland Regiment fought with immense courage (it won one VC, 38 MCs, 32 DCMs and 105 MMs) and suffered appalling casualties. By the late 1920s, the island was beginning to recover from her losses and, through the growth of new industries, seemed at last in sight of a viable economy. Then came the Great Depression. Nobody wanted Newfoundland cod, and by 1932 one-third of the whole population was on winter relief at a rate of 6 cents a day. By a combination of bad luck, bad management — and worse — the Government had run out of cash and was even unable to make the relief payments. Unwillingly, Britain had to step in, suspending the colony's constitution and appointing a Commission Government.

Things had already begun to improve noticeably by 1940, when the Americans arrived to establish a base 'leased' in exchange for fifty obsolete destroyers. With them they brought about $15 million a year into the islanders' pockets. In 1946 Britain — anxious for any solution that might bring lasting solvency to Newfoundland — called a convention to discuss its political future. Two years later a plebiscite was held, but results were so close that a second was required. This time Newfoundland voted for confederation with Canada, by a margin of only 10 per cent. Newfoundlanders had not always felt kindly disposed towards their new foster-parent; an ancient ballad taunted 'Come at your peril, Canadian wolf!' Twice in the 19th century they had turned down proposals of confederation. But for the persistence of one man — Premier 'Joey' Smallwood — history might easily have repeated itself a third time. The very closeness of the two plebiscites is testimony to the ardour with which Smallwood had to hammer home his cause.

Former journalist, radio commentator and pig-farmer —

for a time the only Liberal in power in Canada — Smallwood is one of the more remarkable figures on the Canadian
political scene. A small owlish man in his sixties, with a
puckish sense of humour, he possesses a dynamic energy rare
in Newfoundlanders. As well as being Premier, he is his own
Minister of Economic Development, and likes to confound
the experts with his mastery of facts and figures. Working in
his shirt-sleeves from a small office in St. John's, for the last
eleven years he has run Newfoundland with his own special
brand of Liberalism mixed with patriarchal Socialism.
Politically, 'Joey' looks upon himself as the guardian angel
of the outports, and the arch-enemy of the merchants of
St. John's (whom he unflatteringly refers to as 'uncreative
waffle-iron salesmen'). It is at their expense that his suggestively socialistic programme of 'redistributing' the very uneven purchasing power of Newfoundland has been aimed.
Whatever may be thought of his methods of government
there has never been any doubt as to the strength of his
following in Newfoundland.

When I visited St. John's, Mr. Smallwood explained to
me why he had so ardently sought to transfer Newfoundland
from British to Canadian patronage. 'We were lying between two continents. All our interests and emotions were
British, but we were resting snugly against the American continent. Two wars had made it increasingly impossible for
Newfoundland to paddle her own canoe, and Confederation
relieved her of her futile efforts to be a single nation and
linked her with a great coming nation.'

There is no doubting the benefits that this most backward
corner of North America has received since Confederation.
(On the other hand, Canada has also gained in acquiring a
territory with great potential wealth.) When the British-
appointed Commission Government took over less than a
generation ago, unemployment insurance and family allowances were unknown; in 1959 allowances received by Newfoundland parents actually exceeded the total value of the
cod landed by her fishing fleet.

Prior to Confederation, health was — next to bankruptcy
— Newfoundland's gravest problem. Medical facilities
were generally limited to the primitively equipped 'cottage

hospitals' scattered among the outports. The island had one of the highest TB rates in the world. But in the past ten years, funds from the Fairy Godmother in Ottawa have enabled her to spend as much on health as in the previous seventy-five years. A fleet of ambulance helicopters has been bought to service the outports; in 1956 Newfoundland became the first community in North America to introduce free hospitalisation for all children; and a year ago the TB rate had dropped so drastically that St. John's was able to close down one-half of its sanatorium. Newfoundland now boasts the lowest death-rate in Canada. She also has the highest birth-rate, eclipsing French-Canadian Quebec for the first time, and it is hardly surprising that nearly half of the island's population is under 15. Since Confederation Ottawa's financial support has enabled the Smallwood Government to meet this acute 'bulge'; last year it claimed to have spent $15 million on education, compared with $3·5 million in 1948, and Mr. Smallwood was able to assure me: 'I can remember when 25 per cent of the island was illiterate — now we don't even bother to keep figures on it.'

On the economic scene, great advances have also been made during the last decade. Some sixteen major industrial plants have been built; several with Government money, then sold or leased to private enterprise. Foreign capital has greatly expanded the island's pulp and paper industry, and several important new mines have been started. The yardsticks of prosperity are that personal earnings have risen from $120 million in 1949 to a current level well above $300 million, and nearly twice as many new jobs have been created as those in existence ten years ago.

Newfoundland is, as *The Times* once remarked, 'under-developed rather than basically poor.' Potentially, it is immensely wealthy, with great unexploited riches lying in the bleak and forbidding mainland 'colony' of Labrador that belongs to it. Within the last six years, the US-backed Iron Ore Co. of Canada has invested some $400 million at Schefferville, astride the Quebec–Labrador boundary, from which Newfoundland is already drawing substantial royalties. One of the biggest hydro-electric projects ever undertaken in Canada is also being actively surveyed on Labrador's

Hamilton Falls, cheap power from which could revolutionise Newfoundland's economy.

The last decade has made big changes in Newfoundland's traditional way of life. Though she still provides one-third of Canada's commercial fish catch, her once staple product has ceded first place to the pulp and paper industry. Many fishermen have abandoned the rigours of the outports for the comparative luxury of the towns. Immigrants still pass by her rugged outline on their way to more prosperous parts of Canada (out of the 280,000 admitted in 1957's bumper year, Newfoundland received only 408), but the hopeless, despairing driftage away from the island has nearly ceased. She still has a long way to go, however; there are still less than 200 miles of paved road on the whole island, and you have only to walk to the outskirts of St. John's to the dilapidated fishing community of North Battery to find evidence still of really grim poverty.

Future progress for Newfoundland, as well as maintenance of the relative prosperity she has come to enjoy over the past decade, depends greatly on the subsidies she receives from Ottawa, amounting in 1958 to nearly $18 million. At the time of writing, these stand to be sharply cut as a sequence to the explosive row which broke out in 1959 between Mr. Smallwood and Mr. Diefenbaker, provoked by the former's banning of an American-controlled logger's union. Instead of the jubilation which would otherwise have greeted the tenth anniversary of Confederation in St. John's, Mr. Diefenbaker was hanged in effigy in front of black-draped public buildings. To some extent, the Smallwood regime, hugely optimistic, has fallen into that Newfoundland fault of spending on credit — on the assumption that Federal subsidies would top up the coffers. Thus if the Diefenbaker threats are fulfilled, the island could even be brought back to the brink of bankruptcy whence it was rescued by the Commission Government of the '30s. Whatever the outcome, however, the Newfoundlanders, toughened to adversity in the hard school of history, are unlikely to let it dishearten them, or cause them to turn their backs on Canada.

On the way out to an outport with the entrancing name of Blow-Me-Down, where fishermen were bringing in cod from a bleak November sea as their ancestors had done for centuries past, I came across an old adage on the wall of a country pub :

'I COMPLAINED BECAUSE I HAD NO SHOES,
UNTIL I SAW A MAN WHO HAD NO FEET.'

It seemed to epitomise the Newfoundland spirit.

Expert opinion in Canada is divided as to the future of the Atlantic Provinces. The Gordon Report, which singled out the area for special attention, proposed that the Federal Government might actually have to assist the further emigration of its people to other parts of Canada, if economic prospects did not improve — a suggestion condemned to me by an eminent Maritimer as 'a wretched, dispirited outlook'. In its section on the Atlantic Provinces, the Report is certainly at its least good; if Canada is to grow into a really great nation, it seems hopelessly unrealistic to allow four of its Provinces to lapse into a kind of monster rotten borough.

Meanwhile, men of the Atlantic Provinces with more faith in their future than Ottawa have decided that the time has come to make a common approach to their problems — to help themselves if, as they claim, Ottawa will not. One of the fruits of their endeavours in recent years has been the formation of APEC — the Atlantic Provinces Economic Council; another was to set up a joint office in London, to encourage immigration and attract British industrial enterprise. There is no doubt that, partly due to the activities of APEC, industrial interest in the area has been greatly stimulated. In the depressed years of 1959 and 1960, capital investment in the Atlantic Provinces actually showed a healthy increase over 1958, while in the rest of Canada there was a decline. Tourism, mostly from the United States, now brings in about $100 million a year. New development schemes (to the extent of some $250 million) already under way, or projected, make impressive reading. There are the Irving refinery and the new pulp mills at Saint John, and in Newfoundland. Vast, newly discovered base metal deposits in New Brunswick may well turn the Province into one of the more important Canadian mining centres over the next decade (though, true to Maritime luck, development of these was just under way when the slump in metal prices struck in 1957). There is the Hamilton Falls project in Labrador, capable of supplying all four Provinces with vast quantities of power. Whereas Ontario has nearly run out of accessible hydro-electric potential, the Atlantic Provinces have barely begun to tap theirs. Serious oil exploration is under way in all four Provinces; chemical industries, based on timber by-products, are being set up in New Brunswick; and many small secondary manufacturing units are springing up in most centres. Age-old schemes such as the damming of the 40-foot tides in New Brunswick's Passamaquoddy Bay to produce electricity are once again being revived. In the further distance are more ambitious projects to link Prince Edward Island to the mainland by an eight-mile-long causeway, and to establish an international 'free-port' at Newfoundland's Mortier Bay that would serve the whole St. Lawrence Seaway.

If the Maritimes (I exclude Newfoundland) are backward today, it is only in relation to the rest of Canada — boasting as it does the world's second highest standard of living. In fact, on arriving in Nova Scotia direct from England, as the first part of Canada we saw, my wife and I found ourselves constantly being surprised at the signs of prosperity and the high tempo of activity and growth almost everywhere. It was only on reaching Central Canada and having our eyes opened still wider that we began to realise that things might have been a bit slow on the Atlantic Coast.

The fact that Britons with drive can triumph in the Maritimes today is nowhere better illustrated than by the story of Mike Wardell. When Wardell emigrated to Fredericton eight or nine years ago, he admittedly had considerable capital behind him — but against this his background of hunting, society and the Establishment was everything that Canadians tend to find most suspicious in a Briton. His first act was to buy up the local newspaper, *The Gleaner*, with a not very spectacular circulation of 7000. Since he took over, it has doubled. In 1956 he bought up a local magazine, changed its name to the *Atlantic Advocate*, and increased its circulation from a paltry 1000 to approaching 20,000. Apart from this, the enterprising ex-Brigadier has in his brief time in Fredericton become regarded as one of the leading generals in the battle to unite the four Atlantic Provinces into an integrated, prosperous economic unit, and get them a 'fair deal' from Ottawa.

Backward they may be in material ways, but the Maritimes have some distinct advantages over the rest of Canada. In most parts of them, winter is less severe than elsewhere; coupled with the fact that their industries are not so subject to the grim spectre of seasonal unemployment that haunts much of Canadian life. It is also worth noting that the area as a whole has suffered rather less from the recession than British Columbia, Alberta or Ontario. Then the Maritimes have long held a tradition of high educational standards. Nova Scotia alone has no less than seven recognised universities, including the first to be founded on Canadian soil (Kings), and even Prince Edward Island has two junior colleges for its 100,000 inhabitants. Finally, there is the leisurely pleasantness of their environment, and, perhaps of special value to any Briton considering settling in the Maritimes, the prospect of finding in their British Loyalist background a possibly more sympathetic welcome than he might encounter in some other parts of Canada; particularly those that have had more than their fair share of immigrants in recent years, and where any pro-British zeal has worn somewhat thin.

CHAPTER FOUR

THE EMPIRE PROVINCE

The Earthly paradise of Canada. (FATHER GALINÉE, on Southern Ontario, *c.* 1670)

Loyal She Began, Loyal She Remains. (Motto of Ontario)

Returning to Toronto was like finding a Jaguar parked in front of the vicarage and the padre inside with a pitcher of vodka martinis, reading Lolita. (Article in *Maclean's,* January 3rd, 1959)

NEXT to the Maritimes, looming over them with its huge bulk, lies the Province of Quebec, the largest in Canada — *the* original Canada. Together with its giant rival to the west and south, Ontario, the two Provinces form a great chunk of land, one million square miles, equalling in area a third of the continental United States or half of Europe. They contain eleven million people of Canada's seventeen million, and jointly draw 70 per cent of all the immigrants.

Of these eleven million, all but a fraction are still concentrated around the areas of the St. Lawrence Valley and the Great Lakes that were first colonised by the French and the British Loyalists. Consisting broadly of the southern section of Quebec and the southern and eastern parts of Ontario, this is the industrial heartland of Canada. If one disregards the frontier (culturally so important) that divides this area along the Ottawa River, it is geographically and economically one powerful unit accounting for about 80 per cent of all Canada's manufacturing output.

Connected by the great artery of the St. Lawrence, the fates of the two provinces — industrially and commercially speaking — have become so interwoven that it is difficult to think of one without the other. Factors that affect the one affect the other too. But the character of French Canada, and its problems, are so different from those of the rest of the country that I shall by-pass Quebec for the time being and hasten on to Ontario; in itself a difficult enough task to describe.

Americans have long emblazoned New York, the mammoth that confronts Ontario along a vital section of its 2400-mile fresh-water shoreline, with the title of 'The Empire State'. Ontario deserves just as richly to be known as 'The Empire Province'. In size, potential wealth and diversity it is far more of an Empire even than opulent New York State; just in terms of people and actual wealth does the latter still excel.

Second only to Quebec in size, and equalling the sum area of fourteen American States (of which New York is one), 'The Empire Province' measures 1000 miles across and another 1050 from north to south. Its climate varies from the semi-Mediterranean, producing tobacco and wine, to the sub-Arctic along Hudson Bay that will grow nothing at all. It is Canada's leading mineral producer and fur producer, and easily beats all the Prairie Provinces for the place of No. 1 in Canadian agriculture. It has a third of Canada's population, with five of her twelve biggest cities, and has attracted more than half of all the immigrants to come to Canada over the past ten years. Its people own half the cars on Canada's roads (and most of them seem to be in Toronto), and produce something like 99 per cent of all the vehicles that leave Canada's factories. Needless to say it is far and away the biggest manufacturing Province, with an output exceeding all the rest of Canada put together. It accounts for over three-quarters of Canada's rubber products, half its aircraft, industrial machinery and chemicals; and more than half its publishing and printing. Though only third in the Canadian forestry industry (British Columbia top, Quebec second), its woods produce about one-sixth of all the world's newsprint. Its great concentration of wealth continues to give Canada a slightly lopsided appearance.

Ontario has grown to this position of overwhelming predominance with remarkable speed. It had a slow start. In 1615 the indomitable Champlain reached Georgian Bay on Lake Huron, which he first believed to be the 'South Sea'. In a corner of a factory ground at Sault Ste. Marie at the entrance to Lake Superior there sits a cracked and forgotten cairn commemorating the discovery of the lake by Étienne Brulé — later to suffer martyrdom at the hands of cannibalistic Huron Indians. By the mid-17th century much of Ontario around the Great Lakes had been explored either by the French Jesuit missionary-explorers, converting as they went — and often being hideously martyred — or by the intrepid '*coureurs de bois*'. Yet, until after the American War of Independence, the vast, fertile areas remained a wilderness; a no-man's-land inhabited only by the grim Iroquois, a few handfuls of the nomadic '*coureurs*' in search of furs, and a scattering of French forts. The fateful year of 1783 saw the first real colonisation attempt, with the advent of some 10,000 of the United Empire Loyalists. In the years that followed they were heavily outnumbered by a powerful flow of the ordinary breed of Americans, following, quite unpolitically, the westward course of empire into the empty land beyond the lakes. In the War of 1812, these Americans could have provided the most devastating of Fifth Columns — but for the gross tactlessness of the invading American generals. As it was, the 'Americans' of Upper Canada[1] for the most part resisted the invaders as vigorously as the rest.

The only participant to win out of that most pointless of all pointless conflicts was Canada. Of the few engagements won by the British side, most were those fought on land in Canada, with the indispensable assistance of Canadian militiamen. Some notable victories were gained; including one where, through a Gideon-like strategy of buglers deployed in the woods, some three hundred militiamen put to flight 4000 Americans. York (later Toronto) was burnt, but the British went one better and razed the White House in Washington. Out of the war (barely mentioned in British school history books, but given great and deserved emphasis in Canadian schools) Canada emerged for the first time with a national identity and a new-found confidence in itself. By 1812 Upper Canada's population had reached 80,000; following the Napoleonic Wars, a great wave of immigrants came in from the British Isles — including a

[1] In 1791 the land taken from France thirty-odd years previously was divided into two Provinces, Upper and Lower Canada, which—when Confederation took place in 1867—were to become Ontario and Quebec respectively.

large number of 'Orangemen' from Northern Ireland, who
have left their stamp on modern Ontario in the same way
as Highlanders on Nova Scotia. During this period much of
its virgin wilderness was cleared — strangely enough not
primarily for the rich farmland beneath it, but because of
the demand for pit-props in Britain's Industrial Revolution.
As late as the mid-1870s, even the heart of Ontario was still
empty land, with Lady Dufferin, the wife of the Governor-
General, describing Orillia (not more than 70 miles north of
Toronto) as being 'on the edge of the settled country'.[1] It
is really only in this century — and particularly since the
Second World War that Ontario has become the Empire
Province that she is today. Statistics make dull reading, but
a few here may be relevant to show just how remarkable
Ontario's expansion has been; in fifteen years since 1938,
the net value of manufacturing output rose from $758 million
to $4130 m.; of construction, from $73 m. to $853 m.;
forestry from $19 m. to $103 m.; and consumption of electricity from $50 m. to $164 m.[2] Between 1946 and 1956,
gross values in manufacturing increased by just under 180
per cent; over the same period, the rate of capital investment
in the industry had multiplied two and a half times. In all
sectors of Ontario's economy, overall output had increased
175 per cent over the decade from 1948 onwards.

Broadly speaking, the reasons for Ontario's tremendous
surge forward since the war are the reasons for the boom
that echoed right the way across Canada, with varying
intensity. First it was the urgency of war that rushed the
building of great new industries in Ontario; then the accumulated spending power of war-time wages that kept the
industries going, and helped convert them to peacetime
production. When things began to slacken up again, along
came the Korean War with its vast demands for raw
materials. But perhaps most of all, it was the huge post-war
demand, especially from the United States with her seriously
depleted resources, for metals and mineral products of all
sorts that boosted Ontario's economy; for nobody had more
to offer than the Empire Province. Add to this the rapidly

[1] The Marchioness of Dufferin, *My Canadian Journal* (1891).
[2] Source — The Toronto Dominion Bank.

expanding domestic market provided by the deluges of immigrants, the presence of a further market of some sixty-five million in the adjacent American States (something denied the poor Maritimes), and you have the picture in a nutshell.

Because of the size, wealth and importance of Ontario, and the great bulk of British immigrants it has attracted over the years, in Britain more is known about the Province than any other. Probably more Britons have gained their knowledge of Canada from the novels of Mazo de la Roche with their gentle tales of life in southern Ontario than from the works of any other Canadian writer; every other Briton seems to have some kind of picture of Toronto from a brother or cousin who emigrated there. For these reasons, and the fact that there is also more material available about Ontario, the description in this chapter may seem less detailed than others. No slight is intended to the Empire Province.

Bruce Hutchison, one of Canada's most distinguished journalists (though a British Columbian, and thus perhaps apt to see Ontario in a less kindly light than a native), describes it as having 'no recognisable image, accurate or inaccurate. In the National Gallery its portrait is a blur.' [1] There is, however, something in this remark — if only because Ontario is composed of so many contrasting fragments. The Empire Province falls roughly into six basic parts, several of which could well be Provinces in their own right. Four of them, with nearly 90 per cent of the population, but perhaps less than a quarter of the total area, lie pressed together between the line of the St. Lawrence, Lakes Ontario and Erie, and a line drawn from Lake Huron's Georgian Bay to just west of Ottawa — in fact, the southern limit of the Laurentian Shield.

Nearest to Montreal, a triangle formed by the St. Lawrence and the Ottawa River contains Eastern Ontario. On its section of the St. Lawrence, the International Rapids, the main bulk of the Seaway project has been carried out. When we were there it was a scene of tremendous activity. Stretching two-thirds of a mile across to the United States, the huge dam with its thirty-two generators, each as big as a four-storey house, was nearing completion. Within a matter of weeks, it would be producing over a million horsepower of

[1] Bruce Hutchison, *Canada — Tomorrow's Giant.*

electricity for both New York State and Ontario. Behind it
the waters were already rising, flooding some 38,000 acres of
Eastern Ontario — and several towns and villages. Inhabitants had been given three alternatives: demolition with
compensation; bodily removal to a new community, with
neighbours 'A' and 'B' to right and left, as before; or
re-location with an entirely new set of neighbours! The
operation took place so smoothly that families breakfasted on
their old site and dined at home on the new site, perhaps
eight miles away, with all services reconnected. It was an
unnerving — though not uncommon sight — to see a whole
church tottering towards you on gigantic rollers along the
highway. In one place, we spotted someone who, with a
truly North American sense of enterprise, had already
erected a 'Boatel', complete with jetty and sand beach; but
standing in the middle of a field waiting for the waters to
reach it. We hoped he had not miscalculated. The Seaway
will have a big impact on this part of Ontario; though not
every community will benefit. Badly left out is Cornwall, a
pleasant, typical Ontario small town of 48,000. Right on the
site of the dam, Cornwall boomed while construction engineers lived and spent their large pay packets there. Now
the engineers have departed and the main channel of the
St. Lawrence by-passes Cornwall on the other side of the
river. To her chagrin, a mere village called Massena on
the New York side has attracted two major aluminium
industries and a new General Motors plant, on the basis of
the power available from the dam, while Cornwall has heard
itself described in Parliament as one of the most depressed
corners of Canada.

The other old-established small and medium towns along
Ontario's stretch of the Seaway — like Brockville, Gana-
noque, Prescott and Kingston — seem unchanged and un-
changing. Nearly a hundred and twenty years ago, Charles
Dickens wrote of Kingston, in his critical fashion, that 'one
half of it appears to be burnt down, and the other half not
to be built up', but noted it had an 'admirable jail'.[1] Today
Kingston is a bustling city of nearly 60,000, with rapidly
expanding industries — including two aluminium plants and

[1] Charles Dickens, *American Notes*, 1842.

a branch of the Dupont chemical empire — as well as being the home of Canada's Sandhurst, the Royal Military College. Its narrow, rather meandering streets remind one that Kingston is no upstart, that for a brief time in Dickens's day it was actually the capital of Canada before Ottawa was thought of. The heart of Loyalist Ontario, Kingston and its neighbours have to this day a more strongly English flavour than other parts of the Province, and many of them boast battle honours from 1812 of which they are immensely proud. It is beautiful country; the 1000 islands near Kingston, reminding one in parts of the Italian Lakes, is one of eastern Canada's gems; and it is on the Ottawa River that the fiery fall colours of the maples, 'the blood of the Mohawks and Tuscaroras', produce their most spectacular effects. Much of this gentle, undulating land, with its hedgerows so like Britain's, is good farm country; not generally as productive as in the southwesterly parts of the Province, though it is claimed that a big new drainage scheme on the Ottawa River may produce one of the richest market gardens in North America.

And then Eastern Ontario contains the nation's Capital. Some of those few Canadians not in the Government service tend to be scathing about Ottawa, but a foreigner had better not try. It was generally believed by Canadians (so a 19th-century traveller reported) that the site of Ottawa had been chosen by Queen Victoria, just to 'spite' them.[1] No, said Stephen Leacock, it was chosen because 'no enemy from the States would find it'.[2] 'A sub-Arctic lumber village converted by royal mandate into a political cockpit', was how a controversial 19th-century Canadian called Goldwin Smith termed it. Bruce Hutchison has a notional American querying, '"We know what Washington means to us. What does this mean to you?"'[3] The answer is: a lot symbolically, but perhaps not much else — except to the Easterners, Westerners, Northerners and *Québecois*, to whom Ottawa is simply the cold monster that does them down. In a very brief meeting with Mr. Lester Pearson, the Liberal leader,

[1] *Early Travellers to the Canadas*, edited by Gerald Craig.
[2] Stephen Leacock, *Canada, the Foundations of its Future*.
[3] *Canada — Tomorrow's Giant, ibid.*

the remark I most clearly recall was, 'Ottawa's a bad place
to visit to find out about Canada.' Having spent several
years in Bonn, I think I knew what he meant; there is
something faintly sterilised about a town dedicated solely to
the art of governing, to politics and the tittle-tattle of diplomats and journalists.

Ottawa's 350,000 inhabitants are very much given over
to the business of government, and it is a business that is
expanding perhaps even more rapidly than any other branch
of industry in Canada. Even Professor Parkinson might be
surprised; according to the Gordon Report, between 1931
and 1951 the percentage of the labour force in the Government Service (including the armed forces) more than
doubled, while the labour force itself had increased by barely
a third. *Excluding* the armed forces, this percentage is
expected to double again between now and 1980, though
over the same period the total population will only rise by
an estimated 60 per cent. The Federal Government today
has no less than twenty-four Cabinet Ministers, most of them
backed by heavily staffed ministries — despite the very large
degree of duplication in the semi-autonomous Provinces —
which gives Ottawa a slightly top-heavy appearance. For
all the importance attached to government, however,
Canada's lower-grade civil servants are one of her worst
paid groups today. In Ottawa it is not uncommon for them
to take on part-time jobs, like the taxi-driver who drove me
out to the airport; which means that employment is generally hard to find there for newly arrived immigrants.

In the three visits I made to Ottawa in 1958, I sensed an
atmosphere of flurry and some disorganisation. After their
huge landslide victory that spring, Mr. Diefenbaker and his
colleagues still seemed to be left gasping at their own success.
Although they had already had a brief session in power, one
could almost hear the grinding of rusty wheels as a party that
had been in the wilderness for twenty-two years found its feet
and discovered how governments are run, before settling
down itself (in the comfortable Canadian way of things) to
perhaps a generation of governing. The Conservative leaders
radiated enthusiasm, which seemed to go some way to make
up for political immaturity. In the entourage of Mr. Pearson

TORONTO

*Looking down
University Avenue
towards
Lake Ontario*

Iroquois Lock and Dam

ST. LAWRENCE SEAWAY

Grain storage, Lakehead, Port Arthur, Ontario

was an atmosphere of tired wisdom and a great deal of intelligence. An immigrant should spend a long time in Canada before trying to understand the differences between the two major political parties; he may need a microscope to help him at moments. Divisions are far more subtle than between the British parties; or even between the Republicans and Democrats of the United States. Often the Liberals and Conservatives in Canada tend to be all things to all people; there are no sharp ideological gulfs. Elections are fought on issues, not principles. In the earliest days, the Liberals came to stand for Provincial Rights, while the Conservatives favoured the superior power of the central government. Something of this still exists today. In external affairs, the Liberals traditionally have stood for the development of Canadian nationalism, and the Conservatives for co-operation with Britain and the Empire. During the long Mackenzie King–St. Laurent era, Liberal policy brought Canada into strong support of the United Nations and close alignment with the United States. (There may even be something symbolic in the fact that on the walls of their offices in the Parliament Buildings, Mr. Diefenbaker displays a portrait of the Queen, Mr. Pearson a picture of the United Nations building.) By 1957 alarming revelations of the extent of American economic domination of Canada were largely instrumental in putting the Liberals out of power; though, in retrospect, it is difficult to see that things would have been much different if the Conservatives had been in power during the post-war years.

Ottawa is a city of contrasts. The Parliament Buildings dominated by the stately Peace Tower, where the Mounties stand guard magnificently and disdainfully — shrouded in buffalo skins in winter, red tunics during the tourist season — are a special brand of austere 19th-century Gothic that peculiarly suits Canada, that *is* Canada. They have majesty. Along the Ottawa River and the Rideau Canal are parks and gardens as handsome as in any capital, and it has about the most inspiring war memorial I have seen anywhere. Yet for all this, parts of Ottawa present a curiously *ad hoc* appearance — more so even than Bonn, which is after all only supposed to be a temporary capital. Down Rideau Street — a few

F

yards from Parliament Hill, and Ottawa's principal thorough-
fare — weathered and twisted telegraph poles lurch in a
disorderly fashion. It might be any small town on the
Prairies. From Parliament itself, looking out across the
river, MPs are confronted with the homely sight of great
pyramids of sawdust at the sawmills in Hull (the view from
the sawmills, however, is superb !). But it may be that this
mixture of the stately with reminders of the homely provides
just the right atmosphere for legislators in a great, but still
becoming country like Canada. Meanwhile, Ottawa's planners have grand schemes for the future ; $100 million is to be
spent over the next ten years on a face-lift for the waterfront,
on greenbelts and 40 miles of new parkway. If Ottawa then
resembles at all closely the planners' model I have seen, it
will undoubtedly have become one of the world's more
beautiful capitals.

Next to eastern Ontario comes the key, South-Central
part of the Province. It includes the famous 'Golden Horseshoe', the stretch of Lake Ontario's shoreline from Oshawa,
just east of Toronto, to beyond Hamilton and into the
Niagara Peninsula. Within the Horseshoe lies the centre of
gravity of all Canada's industry, banking and commerce. A
semicircle fifty miles in radius, with Toronto at its centre
(so the Secretary of the Toronto Stock Exchange told me)
would embrace about one-third of Canada's purchasing
power. Toronto itself, with only 8 per cent of the country's
population, pays about a quarter of its income tax. Its
Stock Exchange, the most highly automated in the world,
in 1958 had the largest volume of transactions of any in
North America — including Wall Street. A hundred years
ago, Hamilton, with a strongly Scottish population of some
30,000, was known as 'the ambitious little city'. Today its
ambitions have been more than realised. It is Canada's
sixth city, with nearly 350,000 inhabitants, many of them
still bearing strong Scots accents ; a great steel and manufacturing centre, and a major port that the Seaway will give
even more significance. Beyond it, quite suddenly, the
smoke-stacks of the Horseshoe blend into sunny fields and
orchards. A fertile Kent merges into a prosperous Burgundy
in one of Canada's major fruit-growing areas, where peaches,

strawberries, cherries and grapes grow in rich abundance. The only part of Canada to produce wine, its vineyards and orchards continue right up to the brink of Niagara Falls.

Between Niagara and the opposite end of Lake Erie is sandwiched Southwest Ontario, Canada's southernmost extremity, sharing the same latitude as New York City and Naples. Almost on the tip of this extremity lies Windsor, the inseparable twin of America's Detroit; though, its sky-line a little lower and its character a little more conservative, unmistakably a Canadian town. Like Detroit, Windsor is also the automobile empire of Canada. In this section of the Province, there are many big towns of ever-growing commercial and manufacturing importance. One is London, sitting athwart its River Thames, boasting a university, and founded by a fiercely despotic Irishman called Colonel Talbot, who 'settled' much of this part of Ontario, and who apparently hated Scotsmen, women and teetotallers with equal passion (though one would have thought that, in Ontario, this must have somewhat restricted his circle of acquaintances!). Another increasingly important centre is Sarnia, the eastern terminal of the Inter Provincial Pipeline from the Prairie oil-fields, and hub of Canada's petro-chemical industry. For its size, Southwest Ontario contains more diversity than any other part of the Province. There are the bustling factory towns like Kitchener (originally called Berlin, because of its large German population, until in World War I feelings demanded a change, bringing it more closely into line with its twin city — Waterloo). The density of population of its section of Canada can be judged from the fact that Kitchener–Waterloo number some 80,000 and London 100,000; each larger than any Maritime city except possibly Halifax. Near by there is the stone city of Guelph, where law says that every building on the main street must be faced with native grey limestone, a contrast to the other cities of brick and clap-board. There are the charming, peaceful county towns like Stratford (it couldn't have been better named) with its willows, swans and leisurely river — of course, the Avon. There are thriving ports, and mile upon mile of golden, sun-drenched sand beaches lapped by the Great Lakes.

A hundred years ago southwestern Ontario was also the granary of Canada. Today it is still the biggest, and probably the most prosperous, farming centre in Ontario; producing a third of the Province's wheat. Sometimes called the 'banana belt', its mild climate makes it the main tobacco-growing area in Canada; a crop that has grown to considerable importance in recent years, with an output worth about $75 million a year. There is good farming land (on the whole, the best in Canada) to be found in all three of these parts of Ontario. Ontario also has the lowest rate of 'driftage' from the farms of any Canadian Province; it is not therefore surprising that good land also tends to be the most expensive in the country, and prices are steadily rising.

As you leave Toronto and head north into Central Ontario, the gently rolling farmland with its broom-shaped maples gradually becomes more broken, with savage black rocks peeping through the surface. Soon it gives way to more and more rock, chain after chain of lakes dotted with small islands and week-end cabins, and fir and jackpine drive out the deep-rooting maples. This is the beginning of the Shield. There are few large industrial towns in this part of Ontario — it is first and foremost a holidaying area.

From here on, the two remaining monster parts of the Empire Province are unadulterated Shield. Northern Ontario, running from the southern fringe of the Shield east to the Quebec border and north to James Bay, contains the bulk of the vast mineral and timber treasury of the Province. First comes Sudbury, where the world's greatest nickel mine gapes amid a grim, granite desert, denuded of trees by the ruthless smelting operations of earlier years, and of almost all other growth by the sulphur fumes that pour out of the towering smoke-stacks. International Nickel's fabulous mine also produces a major part of Canada's copper, and most of the world's platinum; to say nothing of incidental gold, silver, cobalt, selenium, tellurium and less exotic iron ore. Northwards from Sudbury lies the important area of Timmins-Kirkland Lake, principally gold mining, with its unexpected 'clay-belt' patches in the middle of the Shield, now containing Ontario's northernmost farming communities; over the boundary in Quebec it runs into the Noranda-Rouyn

mines (gold, copper, lead and zinc). Westward from Sudbury, along the north shore of Lake Huron, are the uranium
mines of Blind River and Elliot Lake. What six years ago
was little more than an untamed wilderness of rock and tree
has now become probably the free world's greatest producing source of uranium. Closely linked to its production,
at the farthest east end of northern Ontario, on the upper
Ottawa River, is another new community called Chalk River,
the headquarters of Atomic Energy of Canada, and the site
of Canada's first commercial atomic power station.

There could hardly be two more different townships than
Sudbury and Elliot Lake. Sudbury with its slightly seedy
main street of well-used brick buildings, the derelict shanty
towns on its outskirts, the bottomless pits and the blasted bare
rock screaming of the uncontrolled spoliation of two greedy
generations, is the old-style of Canadian mining town.
Elliot Lake — though its own future now seems precarious —
is typical of the new Canadian towns, like Kitimat and
Schefferville, that will become the homes of increasing
numbers of Canadians over the next generation.

The first axe was wielded at Elliot Lake in 1955; three
years later it was a flourishing centre of 27,000 people.
When we visited it — though most of its streets were still
unpaved, and rows of automobiles were wallowing like
elephants at the edge of the lake, having dust washed off
by their owners — it was well on the way to becoming
a carefully planned, attractive community; certainly no
hastily thrown up shanty town. On a superb position
between two lakes, its inhabitants were living in sturdy,
pleasantly designed houses (many of them carrying mort-
gages of $10,000), surrounded by trees and already lawns of
turf trucked in from 30 miles away. All its shops were
gathered together, dominated by a marvellously well-stocked
Hudson's Bay supermarket, that offered everything from
peanuts to caviare. Its Algoden Hotel was one of the most
comfortable we stopped at in Canada. (It should have been,
it was also easily the most expensive.) Five banks, five fine
schools and several churches of imaginative modern architecture, were already functioning; there was an indoor curling
rink, a cinema, a newspaper, a radio-station, a spacious

municipal hall with a stage regularly occupied by an active amateur group, and a 100-bed hospital. I doubt if any British 'New Town' could offer much more than Elliot Lake.

Despite its laudable externals, there was something vicious and faintly sinister in the atmosphere at Elliot Lake. There did not seem to be much happiness in its pleasant setting. A sad-eyed Czech, who had lost his wife to a miner earning twice his salary, told me over a bottle of beer that he was the only one of his race in the community. 'Why? Because Czechs enjoy living too much. People only come here to work, work, work — get rich and get out. But they don't get rich, even though some of the fellows around here have been picking up as much as $1600 a month — because they spend it on beer and the high costs of living. Everybody is just fighting for himself; fighting over women like animals over a loaf of bread. The sex-hunger is terrible. Sometimes you just can't work because of it.' On the day the new hotel opened, a man was killed in a fight, and in 1958 there was still no mistaking the underlying toughness of Elliot Lake. The *Elliot Lake Standard* was full of items of arrests of 'impaired drivers', of brothels raided in the trailer camps. Several times we were warned on no account to pick up hitchhikers in the area. On Saturday night, the Algoden reverberated with angry noises from the all-male saloon in its basement, as the last of three thousand cases of beer brought in that day ran out. The signs on the pitheads of 'Don't go short on SLEEP — weariness spells accidents' showed that the mine managers also knew what went on in town at night.

Perhaps the most sinister thing about the place, however, was the shadow cast by the object which gave Elliot Lake its purpose. It confronted you at every turn; in the un-naturally blotched, satanical rocks flanking the road in; in the cheery station identification—'this is the Radio-active voice of Elliot Lake'; in the nuclear patterns on the carpets of the Algoden; and in the female Jehovah's Witness out-side, heralding, appropriately enough, the end of the world in fire and destruction.

The atom bomb, however, was not the only shadow hanging over Elliot Lake. The uranium companies opened up the area on the gamble that they could pay off their huge expenditure on a US Government purchasing contract valid till 1963, and in the expectation that the contract would be extended. Hopes crashed at the end of 1959 when the United States (no doubt influenced by the thawing of the Cold War) announced that she would not renew. As a result, Rio Tinto, the leading company in the Elliot Lake area, announced that it was to close four of its six mines, guaranteeing employment only until 1965 for the remaining miners still employed. Elliot Lake itself, five years after its inception, may be reduced to less than a third of its former population; an imaginative new town possibly doomed to become a luxury version of Canada's ghost mining towns of yester year. Such are the trials and risks still facing a country that is the West's greatest supplier of raw materials; and, apart from anything else, the plight of Elliot Lake demonstrates all too clearly how sensitive Canada's economy still remains to the whims of her giant neighbour.

Beyond Elliot Lake, where the waters of thundery Lake Superior tumble into Lake Huron, is the world's busiest waterway, the 'Soo', otherwise known as Sault Ste. Marie, with cities of the same name on both the US and Canadian side of the rapids. The Canadian city numbers some 40,000 and is the home of Algoma, the third of Canada's big iron and steel industries. From the 'Soo' to the borders of Manitoba lies the immensity of Northwest Ontario; 212,000 square miles (= England plus Wales times 4) with the same number of inhabitants. All rocky, forested Shield, broken with innumerable lakes, each teeming with trout, pickerel, Northern pike, and giant maskinonges — some of the best fishing in Canada — this once posed a 600-mile-wide barrier between east and west Canada. Today it is still one of the emptiest parts of Canada, outside the Far North. Until the Trans-Canada Highway was completed, there was no continuous road across it, and in 1958 we still had to dip down into the States, south of Lake Superior.

Coming back into Ontario, we spent a pleasant fishing week-end at a place called English River, which was perhaps typical of the country. Well over a hundred miles from Fort William on the Lake, with absolutely nothing in between, we chose it because it appeared marked as a small town on the road map. When we arrived we found a motel on a lake, with a sign saying 'LOOKING FOR ENGLISH RIVER? THIS IS IT!' On the other side of the road was a pile of smashed-up cars, and a sign announcing 'ENGLISH RIVER — BUSINESS SECTION'. The motel was owned and run by a shy, quiet-spoken Canadian called Brown. He told me that he had 'laid the first tree' himself, some twenty-three years ago, and that he and his wife had since done most of the building themselves. In addition he functioned as post-office, store, bus depot, garage, breakdown service and first-aid post. The nearest doctor was a hundred miles away, either direction, and he told me that the previous year he had travelled 2000 miles on ambulance calls alone. He generated his own electricity, ran his own cinema and his own fleet of outboard motor-boats. He had to go to Fort William for all his food and supplies, yet each of his highly comfortable cabins — in their glorious wild setting on wooded promontories overlooking a glassy lake — had hot water, mod. cons., and central heating. After leaving with a full creel of fish, we felt that English River fully deserved its dot on the map.

Next to 'Soo' Ste. Marie, Northwest Ontario's biggest centre is the twin constellation of Fort William–Port Arthur, which started off life as the Lakehead depot for the Prairie's grain. Climbing the table mountain that looms over the two cities, we gazed down on row after row of grain storage houses in the great natural harbour of Thunder Bay, each looking like a row of giant pillars from some unfinished Roman forum, and together representing the world's greatest concentration of grain storage; an exciting panorama, especially when one reflected that through here had funnelled most of the wheat that kept Britain from starvation in two World Wars. Around the Lakehead, in plains from which low mountains abruptly thrust their flat heads, is a substantial area of good mixed farmland, farmed largely by Scandinavians who have seeped over from Minnesota. In the middle of the Shield, the country's midway point, and nearly two and a half thousand miles from the open sea, it is a lost, but attractive corner of Canada. Fort William–Port Arthur have expanded greatly in recent years, and some

respectable industries have grown up around them (notably
a sizable offshoot of the Canadian Car Company, producing
buses and trailers).   Near by, at Steep Rock, an iron-ore
mine has been developed with American capital; cheap
energy has arrived with the transcontinental natural gas
pipeline, and there is more hydro-electric potential still un-
tapped in this part of Ontario than elsewhere in the Province.
A big new cargo terminal is under construction at the Lakehead, and with the Seaway that will enable 25,000-ton
ocean-going ships to travel right to the door of Fort William–
Port Arthur, great things are predicted for all Northwest
Ontario in the next decade.

Despite all this rich, varied, tempting expanse of Ontario,
British immigrants still flood in their thousands, tens of
thousands, into one tiny overcrowded, often unreceptive,
corner of it — Toronto.   It is the one Canadian city every
Briton has heard of; heard of somebody who emigrated there
and made a quick fortune.   Few seem to have heard of the
thousands who have suffered the most miserable, soul-
destroying weeks of their life there.   It can't all be blamed
on Toronto.   A senior immigration official told me that
immigrants should reckon on spending an average of four
weeks before finding a job in Toronto.   (This was disregard-
ing 'abnormal' conditions experienced during Canada's
'little slump'.)   A Cockney plumber I met told me he had
been three weeks unemployed in Toronto when he first
arrived; they were the worst he had ever known.   'One
more week of it, and I'd have gone home in despair.'   His
story was one I heard repeated everywhere.   When I saw
the Governor-General, the Rt. Hon. Vincent Massey, he told
me he would like to advise British immigrants to 'try the
smaller towns of Ontario.   Life is very pleasant there, and
they have none of the mad rush of the big cities.'   After a
few days in Toronto, I think I understood what he meant.
   The first I saw of Toronto was during the war, at odd
moments when we were allowed to emerge from the bull pen
of the Agricultural Fair Ground, in whose copious mangers
some 5000 RCAF and RAF airmen in transit were quartered.
It would be impossible to exaggerate the warmth of the

Torontonians towards the RAF in those days, but otherwise it seemed a cold, formless and rather provincial city; dead as a door-nail on Sundays, our one day of complete release. 'Toronto the Good' it was known as then, and it is still sometimes called that today — though the title is getting perhaps a little ragged round the edges. Filling stations that open on Sunday are still hard to find, but the city now abounds in once-banned cocktail bars and night clubs. It is the only city I know whose leading newspaper (the biggest in Canada) has an entire section devoted to Church matters each Sunday, and where a church is named after one of its tycoons. But it is also the only city I know where you can watch a strip-tease during the lunch hour — or could, until demolition put an end to twenty-two years of service to the community. (Yet, when *Les Ballets Africains* came to Toronto in 1959, dancers were made to cover up their bosoms; whereas even fastidious Boston had raised no complaints.) 'Toronto the Good' must also be one of few cities where a large hotel exists, with little attempt at subterfuge, as a 24-hour-a-day brothel. (I forgot to ask our good friend Nathan Phillips, Toronto's energetic Lord Mayor, whether City Hall knew about it.)

By tradition Protestant, Loyalist, Tory Toronto has always been regarded in Canada as the antithesis, and frequently the antagonist, to Catholic, French and generally Liberal Montreal. Even today much of the emotional hostility towards French Canada seems to centre around Toronto, and her Press can seldom resist an opportunity of taking a crack at the rival city. When one of her papers published the headline — 'PRINCESS STANDS UP MONTREAL SMART SET' — during Princess Margaret's 1958 tour, it was hard not to detect behind it a gentle note of malicious glee.

Through the years, Toronto's diehard Protestantism has been associated with its vocal and closely-knit community of Orangemen. In the past, this has made many visitors feel that the city had more of Northern Ireland in its character than of either England or Scotland. It has also been remarked, with some truth, that Toronto was the only place in North America where the Battle of the Boyne had not been forgotten. When the nineteen-year-old Prince of

Wales (later Edward VII) visited Toronto in 1860, Orangemen tried to make his cavalcade pass beneath 'arches'
decorated with fervid anti-Catholic propaganda. Today,
although the Orange Lodges still wield an influence that no
local or provincial politician dare ignore, their power has
greatly declined. So has that of the sternly devoted ladies
of the Imperial Order, Daughters of the Empire, with their
motto of 'One Flag — One Throne — One Empire'. Instead of a Mayor of Orange or Loyalist background, Toronto
today has one of Jewish ancestry. Things have indeed
changed in Toronto since the days when its society modelled
itself so closely on that of upper-class Britain, that anyone
engaged in 'commerce' was excluded from its most prominent club. And today's changes are reflected by what
has been happening — to a lesser degree, but for the same
reasons — in many other parts of industrial Ontario.

Just over a century ago, a British visitor remarked that
'Toronto is a thoroughly English place in its appearance,
and in the habits and manners of the inhabitants'.[1] The
same might have been said with nearly as much justice less
than a generation ago, but it is no longer true today. In
the fantastic expansion that since the war has swept along
Canada's second largest city (still growing by 50,000 a year),
its character has undergone a remarkable transformation;
the huge influx of immigrants from Europe (including many
thousands of East European and Jewish refugees) has combined with the increase of influences from south of the
border to dilute all the old British features of Toronto. In
the past the Torontonian has been described by his fellow
Canadians as being, superficially, the carbon copy of a man
from Buffalo, New York; but, under present trends, within
a generation he promises to become the twin, through and
through, of a New Yorker. Already the new Toronto
reminds one of what New York City must have been like in
the 1870s and '80s, before the melting-pot had done its work.
There are the great unassimilated chunks of foreign communities, towns within a town; the bustling Jewish market
with its kosher stores and Hebrew signs, the women in the
shawls and aprons of Eastern Europe; the Italian quarter

[1] W. H. G. Kingston, *Western Wanderings*.

(120,000 strong) with its pasta shops and multitudinous children; the Germans, driving most of the cabs in Toronto (one Bavarian ex-Panzer man told me there were now over 100,000 of his countrymen in Toronto); and, most recently, the sad-faced Hungarians, huddling together in disappointment and often despair. Pressure of the immigrants has been slowly pushing the older Torontonians out into the suburbs; the more prosperous into the agreeably wooded sections of North Toronto, which made an Englishman once describe the Torontonians as 'a million people living in a forest'. To try to cope with the problem at its hub, one big department store has even installed an interpreter service. Its new polyglot life is what gives Toronto a colour and a fascination that it would not otherwise possess; but it is also what causes the native-born (those outnumbered few) to exclaim in disgust that 'one never hears English on Yonge Street these days'.

And here is the reason why the British immigrants find three weeks of unemployment in Toronto a purgatory they never wish to endure again — why Toronto has acquired a reputation of hard-heartedness among the 'New Canadians'. The facts are that Toronto has had too many immigrants, more than she can assimilate or take to her heart. Her attitude was, I thought, summed up in a tough little slogan behind the desk of a CBC programme producer: 'IT IS NOT ENOUGH TO BE HUNGARIAN — ONE MUST ALSO HAVE TALENT.'

With its inrush of immigrants and new prosperity, Toronto has also changed, physically, out of all recognition. I spent an hour or two, wandering up and down University Avenue, looking in vain for a familiar landmark of war-time days. I found none; gone were the low, higgledy-piggledy, private dwellings — in their place serried ranks of imposing concrete and glass office buildings. (This in itself is no serious tragedy; Toronto has never been famed for architectural delights.) Mrs. Nathan Phillips told me how when they had bought their house thirty-one years previously it had looked out on open fields; now there were 10 miles of city between them and the countryside. In many ways, Toronto has outgrown its own strength. Only a few years ago, Greater Toronto was administered by no less than 13 councils and a dozen police departments. Today it is run by one 'Metropolitan' council, but although it is Canada's only metropolitan area, it somehow just falls short of being a true metropolis. Only Montreal really fulfils all the requirements. Expansion seems to have left Toronto without any true centre, and one cannot help feeling that the majority of its inhabitants, too preoccupied in the hurried pursuit of happiness (I mean money) have forgotten the cultural obligations of a metropolis.

Yet there are many plus signs. Despite some cultural deficiencies, surprisingly enough printing and publishing form, next to aircraft manufacture, Toronto's second largest source of wealth. The new O'Keefe Centre lays claim to one of the finest opera-houses in the world (in it, in 1960, was produced the world première of Lerner and Loewe's new musical *Camelot*). Toronto's City Elders are highly aware of the dangers of youthful spread that have overtaken sprawling Los Angeles. As a result, Toronto now has earned a reputation of being the most heavily 'planned' city in North America. The benefits may not be apparent now, but they will in a few years' time. Among the aims of the city planners is the setting aside in all new developments of 10 acres of parkland per every thousand of population. One of Toronto's newest town-and-factory satellites is the $200 million Don Mills. With 25,000 inhabitants and designed so that no child need cross a road on the way to school, it is a model of intelligent development, and well deserves the cognisance of British town-planners. One outstanding departure from Toronto's conservative, rather gloomy architecture of the past will be the much-disputed new City Hall, a daring design incorporating two wafer-thin towers thirty storeys high, slightly curved, and holding between them a low building shaped like a monster oyster shell.

Just as I was about to leave, I found I was beginning to like Toronto. I had been taken round parts of it by an Irish poet and publisher. With a sensitive eye and more than a touch of Celtic cynicism, I expected him least of all to have anything good to say about it. Yet his summing up echoed my unformed feelings : 'It may not be a very beautiful city. It has a poor climate and a lot of drawbacks — but I wouldn't go anywhere else. You always feel that things are happening here, always an element of excitement.'

One doesn't need the Gordon Commission Report to know that in 1980, just as now, Toronto — and Ontario as a whole — will be an even more exciting place. Unfortunately perhaps for the rest of Canada, there is truth in the axiom that money breeds money where Ontario is concerned. It is almost unfair that Ontario should have so much wealth — potential as well as actual. When she begins to run out of hydro-electric power for her growing industries, she finds she has probably more uranium than any other part of the Western World; and now natural gas is being brought to her doorstep. With the opening of the St. Lawrence Seaway, Toronto all of a sudden becomes a major seaport — all Ontario becomes a great new maritime trading country. Whatever strides the rest of Canada may make, it seems inevitable that the Empire Province will always be to the fore.

CHAPTER FIVE

THE VANISHING PRAIRIE

Come again and bring the kids. (ARCHIE MACNAB, Lieut.-Governor of Saskatchewan to King George VI in 1939)

The Lord said 'Let there be wheat', and Saskatchewan was born. (STEPHEN LEACOCK, *My Discovery of the West*)

With the thermometer at 30° below zero and the wind behind him, a man walking on Main Street in Winnipeg knows which side of him is which. (STEPHEN LEACOCK, *ibid.*)

WHEN you leave Ontario and head towards Winnipeg, you experience a strange metamorphosis that happens with quite astonishing swiftness. To record it, I took three photographs through the back window of the car, over a period of only four or five minutes. In the first, the firs of the rockbound Shield stand thick, massive and overbearing; in the second, they have thinned out drastically, interlarded with scraggy birch and aspen, jostling each other for existence in a sandy soil; and finally, the third photo shows an empty, flat plain of rich black earth, with the trees receding rapidly in the distance. After travelling for days through the close country of northern Ontario the sudden shock of bursting out onto the Prairies gives you a curious sensation of nakedness, almost of defencelessness. One early explorer, William Blane, remarked that: 'Leaving the wood appeared like embarking alone upon the ocean, and upon again approaching the wood I felt as if returning to land.' An hour or two on the Prairies seems enough to alter your whole attitude to life, and make you realise that the people who inhabit them must be very different indeed to the eastern Canadians. They are.

The Prairies compose a block of three Provinces — Manitoba, Saskatchewan and Alberta — separated by geographically meaningless frontiers, and together representing a third

of the total area of Canada, exclusive of the northern territories, and with about one-sixth of the overall population.
Although they have a shorter history than the rest of Canada,
the roots of it lie far back in the past, closely related both to
that glorious illusion, the quest for a Northwest Passage, and
that remarkable commercial enterprise, the Hudson's Bay
Company.

From Elizabethan days men like Frobisher had been
penetrating into the icy wastes of Hudson Bay in search of a
route to the fabulous Orient; in 1612 the first white man to
set foot on what is now Manitoba, Sir Thomas Button, landed
on the west side of the Bay complete with letters from James I
to the rulers of Cathay. About fifty years later, two French
Canadian adventurers, Chouart — the 'Sieur des Groseilliers'
— and Radisson, reached Hudson Bay overland from Quebec
and returned with a crop of furs of immense value. But not
only did they receive no encouragement for a further expedition, they had their precious furs confiscated by the Governor
of New France, and in disgust turned to Charles II of
England. In 1670, backed by the great commercial sense of
the King's enlightened cousin, Prince Rupert, they were
awarded a Royal Charter to found what was to become the
Hudson's Bay Company. The Charter (once described as
'the most far reaching commercial document in British
History' [1]) made its owners 'Absolute Lords and Proprietors'
over an area of more than a million square miles, or a quarter
of all North America, including today's three Prairie Provinces, and much of Ontario and Quebec. One of the few
conditions attached to it was that whenever the reigning
Monarch visited its territory he should be presented with
'two elks and two black beavers'; a condition which was in
fact only fulfilled for the first time in 1927, when Edward
VIII (as Prince of Wales) visited Winnipeg.

For almost exactly two centuries, a succession of bold and
most enterprising Britons from the Hudson's Bay (sometimes
irreverently known from its initials as 'Here Before Christ')
explored, trapped furs over, and governed nearly half of
Canada. In the early years they included men like Henry
Kelsey, the first white to see the buffalo of Manitoba,

[1] Stephen Leacock, *Canada, the Foundations of its Future.*

and who recorded his findings in a kind of semi-literate calypso:

> And then you have beast of several kind
> The one is a black, a buffillo great
> Another an outgrown bear wch is good meat. . . .
> He is man's food and he makes food of man.

The activities of the Hudson's Bay 'Adventurers' behind the lines of New France caused the French great concern, and war was carried intermittently to their forts and supply lines within the Bay. As a last attempt to secure both the fur-trade and the back door of New France, Quebec dispatched westward the last of her great North American explorers, La Verendrye, a wounded veteran of Malplaquet, to erect a line of forts in the rear of the British fur-traders. But it was too late; the Treaty of Utrecht had already acknowledged British rights in Hudson Bay in 1713, and time was running out for the French all over Canada. Despite the capitulation of 1760, the French returned to fire one last parting shot in the Bay. In 1782 Admiral la Pérouse descended by surprise on Fort Prince of Wales on the site of what is now Manitoba's only seaport, Churchill. In a delightfully English fashion, the garrison was out shooting duck, and the fort — with its 30-foot-thick walls that had taken twenty years to build — surrendered without a shot. But from then on, after this small setback, the 'Company of Adventurers' prospered, feasting (from time to time) sumptuously within their log forts on such delicacies as smoked buffalo tongues, moose noses and beaver tails, interfered with only by rival fur-traders.

Although they constructed forts as far west as Edmonton, the trappers were essentially nomadic and no serious attempts at settlement were made in the Canadian Northwest until the beginning of the 19th century. Then Lord Selkirk, a philanthropic Scottish peer who had married into a family owning a block of Hudson's Bay shares, and who was deeply concerned at the plight of the dispossessed crofters in Scotland, entered upon the scene. After earlier attempts (attended by mixed success), to settle crofters in eastern Canada, he obtained from the Hudson's Bay a huge grant of untamed

G

land astride the Red River of Manitoba. To this day,
Selkirk is a much disputed character; to his admirers, practically a saint; to his detractors, a hysterical figure verging at
times on lunacy, whose actions verged on the criminal. Two
things are certain; he did not know enough about conditions
in Canada, and the venture cost him and his family over
£100,000 — a lot of money in those days. The first shipment
of the unhappy crofters arrived in Hudson Bay just before
the freeze-up, and they had to spend the winter of 1811–12
there. Some died of exposure and scurvy, others shipped
home in despair as soon as the Bay reopened, and by the
following spring only twenty-two effectives remained from
the original seventy. When they reached the Red River over
700 miles away — led by a Highland piper after a journey of
fearful hardships — all they had to clear the ground were
hoes and a single plough. To add to their misery, their
presence as settlers was bitterly resented, and eventually
resisted with force, by the nomadic trappers of the rival
'Northwest Company', which, based on Montreal, had sprung
up since the French capitulation. Things finally came to a
head when twenty-one settlers and Hudson's Bay employees
were massacred by *Métis* [1] in the employ of the 'Nor'westers'
at Sevenoaks (close to what is now the centre of Winnipeg) in
1816. This was virtually the *coup de grâce* to Selkirk's project,
and he died a broken man a few years later, aged 49. The
settlement, however, was ultimately re-established, and
French *voyageurs* working for the fur companies became the
founders of today's French-Canadian city of St. Boniface,
adjoining Winnipeg.

The direct result of the 'Sevenoaks Massacre' and the
collapse of the Red River Settlement was the assimilation of
the 'Nor'westers' by the Hudson's Bay, and for another forty
years the company thrived on an ever expanding trade, with
complete power of governance over its immense realms, and
under the remarkably efficient governorship of Sir George
Simpson — aptly nicknamed the 'Little Emperor'. But the
days of supremacy of the 'Adventurers' were also numbered.
The growth of Canada as a whole was reaching a state of
maturity where it was inconceivable that a trading company

[1] Indian half-breeds.

should have absolute sovereignty over so large a portion of its territory — especially when, by its very nature, it was anything but dedicated to the colonisation of the empty West. Negotiations continued for a number of years, and when Confederation was achieved in 1867 the time had obviously come to replace Hudson's Bay rule by the Crown. Two years later, in 'the greatest land deal in history', the Company was bought out of virtually all its land holdings for the modest sum of £300,000.

In 1870, the new Province of Manitoba was created. At that time the whole of the West (excluding British Columbia) numbered only 12,000, most of them half-breed trappers. Once again they saw their way of life threatened by the encroachment of settled civilisation and a serious rebellion broke out on the Red River, lead by a French-Canadian *Métis* called Louis Riel. It was finally crushed by British troops who, in three months, marched all the way through the Shield from Ontario. But in 1885, Riel tried again — this time farther west, in what is now Saskatchewan. He was caught and hanged on the site of today's Royal Canadian Mounted Police depot at Regina. The second Riel uprising had a triple significance in Canadian history; it was the last time Indians were to go on the warpath, joining the *Métis* in what has been described as the 'last ditch defence of the old forest life and fur-trade versus the new age of the locomotive and the farmer'; [1] it was the last time there was to be open warfare on Canadian ground; and it was the first time that an uprising of this sort was to be pacified entirely by Canadian efforts — as the last British regulars had sailed for home in 1871, the North West Mounted Police being formed two years later. The hanging of Riel also unfortunately caused considerable bitterness in French Canada.

With the crushing of the second Riel rebellion, and the almost simultaneous arrival of the Canadian Pacific Railway, colonisation of the Prairies went ahead at a great speed. In 1886 the first shipment of Alberta cattle was sold in Great Britain, and by 1901 there were 420,000 inhabitants in Manitoba alone. But it was in the ensuing decade that the great filling-up of the Prairies took place; by 1911 their

[1] J. M. S. Careless, *Canada — a Story of Challenge.*

population had soared to 1,328,000, and had brought into being, in 1905, two new Provinces of Saskatchewan and Alberta. Occupied land had increased from 2·7 to 17·4 million acres. For the first time in Canadian history, the influx of British-stock immigrants was strongly tempered with large numbers of Ukrainians, Austro-Hungarians, Scandinavians, Icelanders and Germans. (In alarm at the mass exodus in quest of *Lebensraum*, the Wilhelmstrasse issued a bleat of protest to London that 'the attempt to lure our fellow countrymen to this desert, sub-Arctic region is to be denounced as criminal'.) By the First World War, 40 per cent of the population of Alberta alone was non-British. Today, probably no city in the world — with the possible exception of New York — publishes more foreign language newspapers than Winnipeg.

After the war the flow to the Prairies began to dry up, and during the dreadful '30s, when drought and world-depression combined in a terrible conspiracy to drive farmers off the Prairies, the flow actually reversed itself. In 1931 the population of Saskatchewan had reached 921,000; twenty years later, despite revived expansion after the Second World War, it was only 831,000. At last, in 1947, a miracle hit the still depressed Prairies; a major oilfield was discovered at Leduc, in Alberta. From then on, aided further by an improvement in world prices for agricultural produce and government wheat subsidies, the Prairies have experienced a great new wave of prosperity and immigration — prosperity on a scale that they have never known before.

Although the Prairies stretch for a thousand flat, unbroken miles from the edge of the Shield to the foothills of the Rockies, the title 'The Prairie Provinces' can be a little misleading. Alberta, with its western frontier actually running along the crest of the Rockies, in fact has many square miles of mountain and hill country, and only a relatively small wedge of Manitoba is true Prairie; two-thirds being Shield, with a slice of barren tundra at the top. From Manitoba, the Prairies widen out northwestwards, so that nearly half of Saskatchewan and the greater part of Alberta is Prairie, though much of the flat lands to the north of it are forested parkland. But it is in the Prairie belt that the settlements and all the great cities have grown up.

It is, I think, impossible to be neutral about the Prairies; either you love them or hate them. My wife was actively depressed by that unsheltered endlessness, and it worried her until at last we reached the protective lea of the Rockies. I hovered between fear and exhilaration, and finally came out on the side of the Prairie. First it was the sheer beauty of the Prairie in late summer, then the people, that decided me. It was beauty on the biggest scale I had ever seen, sharply defined contrasts like great daubs of a giant's paint-brush between the huge black squares of fallow earth and the gentle blue squares of flax, sometimes mingled with the bright illegitimate saffron of the ragwort; between the frantic green of the pasture — the grass looking as if it were cramming in every atom of chlorophyll to compensate for its long hibernation under the Prairie winter — and the dazzling gold of the ripe wheat; each splash of solid colour probably a mile square. In the background, the limitless horizon broken only by the red, slope-shouldered grain-elevators, and over it all the pure pale blue of the dry Prairie sky. Driving across it, the Prairie was far less monotonous than I had expected. The landscape was constantly changing, however undramatic those changes might be. Even the small towns and hamlets had their marks of individuality; there were those that were dusty, dingy and dejected, and there were those sparkling with optimism, new paint and miraculous garden plots, reflecting that marvellous Canadian talent for extracting the maximum from a difficult situation. But it was summer-time; when I thought of the wind howling unchecked from the polar regions across the bare land, driving first the dust then the thin, fine snow through every crack of the frame farmhouses, I thought I might perhaps be less keen about the Prairie after a long, cruel winter there. Any potential immigrant to the Prairies would, I am sure, be well-advised to spend, if possible, several weeks there (preferably in winter) to test his psychological reaction to them before irredeemably committing himself.

One thing, though, is certain; those born and bred on the Prairie love it with a fierceness that you will seldom find

elsewhere.   Take them away, and they pine for the fresh
smell of straw of its invigorating early morning, for the
doleful 'whooo-whooo' that the great grain trains send
sounding across the plain, and above all for the feeling of
absolute, unbounded freedom of a domain where nothing
separates man from his God.   At a mining town high up in
the Rockies, in a uniquely attractive setting, we met a young
woman, born and bred in Regina, but married to a mine
executive.   She longed to get back to the Prairies; 'I
can't see the beauty of these mountains; they oppress
me and they're useless — you can't even grow anything
on them!'

For all the drawbacks to life on the Prairies there is no
greater compensation than the people themselves; hospitality,
a deep spirit of 'help-your-neighbour' and a fundamental
honesty to go with it, a fine sense of humour and an unexpected consciousness of the outside world, were characteristics that we came across in full measure on the Prairies.
Here 'Western hospitality' really means something; nowhere
else in Canada did I feel, universally, quite so warmly welcomed.   If fortune turns against you, on the Prairies you will
always find people willing to go to quite astonishing lengths
to help — as we ourselves discovered when we had a blow-out
in the middle of nowhere.   The knowledge and interest of
these Prairie farmers in the world at large was one thing that
constantly took me by surprise — a notable contrast to their
opposite numbers in the American Midwest.   One wheat
farmer explained to me: 'American farmers can sell all
their produce at home, so they don't have to worry about
what's going on across the sea.   But we sell our wheat to
a hundred million people outside Canada.   How can we
help being concerned about what the rest of the world's
doing?'

We visited two farms in the 'Regina Plains', the great
wheat-growing centre of Saskatchewan, the Province that
still accounts for 60 per cent of all Canada's wheat.   The
owner of the first was a man called Zinnkam, whose father
had emigrated from Central Europe at the beginning of the
century.   He had been a stone-mason and had erected the
only stone house in the Plains.   His son now farmed just

under two sections [1] of land, a largish farm even by Prairie standards. (Prairie wheat farms are, in fact, smaller than one would think; an official of the Saskatchewan Wheat Pool told me that two-thirds of the farms in the Province were under 300 acres, there were only two over 10,000 acres — average size was about 550 acres.) The farm was highly mechanised, and rationalised down to the last degree; for an area of over a thousand acres under crop, he employed just one labourer during the summer (who worked as a plasterer in Regina during the winter). In addition, Zinnkam kept 30 dairy cattle which he milked himself in a most ingenious, semi-automated open-stall system; he had an elaborate workshop in which he overhauled all his machinery himself; had designed and built his own grain elevator, and his own barn. He owned a bulldozer, and when winter put an end to farming he turned into a one-man roadworks concern, operating for the municipality. He was a man of enormous ambition, which was clearly exhausting him. But he still remembered all too well the lean years of the '30s, could remember when wheat was 25 cents a bushel — if the 'drowth', as they call it on the Prairies, and the 'hoppers' had left you any to sell — when the Churches were collecting old clothes from the rich in the East for the nearly starving Prairie farmers, and those memories were what drove him on in the fat years, when wheat was fetching $1·50 a bushel. His face took on a haggard look as he talked about the Depression, it was still very real to him: 'They were terrible, terrible days. Often we didn't know where the next meal was coming from. For years we didn't know whether we could hang on to our farms — lots of farmers couldn't.'

Things had greatly improved since the '30s. Co-operative organisations such as the Saskatchewan Wheat Pool, with its vast storage facilities and 100,000 members, helped tide the farmer over times of surplus; the stabilising influence of the Canadian Wheat Board and the various international Wheat Agreements give him an assurance of reasonable prices, free from wild fluctuations, that he never had in the days when speculation on grain prices was rampant and unchecked.

[1] A 'section', the standard Prairie measurement, equals one square mile, or 640 acres.

And then the 'drowth' of the '30s had not returned — but on the Prairies you never quite knew just what might be around the next corner.

The second farmer, a cheerful soul called Copeman, had 600 acres, which he tended single-handed, and no cattle. It wasn't too difficult, he explained. You didn't bother to plough any more, because the scientists had discovered that was what made the soil 'blow' in a year of 'drowth'; you sowed in the spring and reaped in the fall. That was about all there was to it — it wasn't worth fertilising the soil; either you had a good crop or you didn't. Sometimes there were catastrophes; inside an hour your whole crop could be wrecked by a midsummer hailstorm, with stones so big they even killed the chickens and broke your windows. But you had to take the rough with the smooth; the main thing was that the life was good, wonderfully good. When winter came, some people simply boarded up their farms and took jobs in Regina — in these days of prosperity, the wealthier farmers took off to Florida, some of them even had their own planes. They called it 'wheat mining', not farming. But he stayed on the farm all year, he didn't need the extra cash, but, principally — 'the great thing is that you are your own boss out here'. He was concerned about American farm surpluses piling up: 'The trouble is that with us a year of *drowth* hits all the Prairies, but the Americans with their better climate always have some farmland that'll produce a good crop. Then they grab our customers and we have a struggle getting them back.' He wondered why Canada didn't open up the enormous markets of Red China, but otherwise nothing much worried him. Now he had TV and all the comforts of civilisation on the farm; he wanted nothing more out of his farm, or out of life as a whole. He seemed the epitome of Pope's contented man. The only cloud on his horizon was that he knew his 16-year-old son would not carry on the paternal acres; intelligent and alert as both his parents, he was studying architectural engineering.

The younger Copeman's decision to strike out from the farm is part of the pattern of change that has been taking place all over Canada. In the Prairies it seems particularly paradoxical, at a time when for years the farmers have 'never had it so good'. But the truth of the matter is that the grain farmers at any rate are still, financially, an under-privileged class in Canada. Despite the fact that the enormous degree of mechanisation on the farms has increased overall productivity at twice the rate of the rest of Canadian industry, farm incomes have far from kept pace. In 1956 Canada's average net farm income was $1090, compared with $1350 for all industries. Between the boom years of 1951–6, when Canada's gross national product was moving upwards every year at record rates, the total net income from farming actually dropped, quite sharply. With Mr. Copeman's aid, I worked out that he, as a fairly typical wheat-farmer (if anything more prosperous than the average), could hope to earn little more than a net 5 per cent return, after paying taxes, on his capital outlay — even in a good year. As the President of the Canadian Federation of Agriculture, Dr. H. H. Hannam, remarked in *The Times*, in 1957 — 'the farmer sees an era of unprecedented prosperity by-passing his farm'.

In 1901 46 per cent of Canada's total labour force was employed in agriculture; a little over a decade ago, the figure had slipped to 25 per cent, but since then, in this very short period, the number on the farms had sunk as low as 15 per cent. In Alberta the average age of farmers today is said to be over 55. Driftage was part of the explanation; a more important factor was mechanisation. Between 1941 and 1951 the numbers of trucks and tractors on Canadian farms trebled; combines quintupled. As a result, the Zinnkams and Copemans could operate by themselves larger and larger farms; by 1956 the number of hired labourers per farm (throughout Canada) had reached the absurdly low figure of one in four. Farms were becoming bigger — and fewer. From 1951 to 1956 alone the total of farms in Canada dropped from 623,000 to 570,000, although, through mechanisation, produce increased greatly. One tragic victim of mechanisation has been the native horse; there are now 800,000 fewer on Saskatchewan farms than in 1926. The beautiful wild herds whose fine stallions were once valued by farmers are now looked on as pests which, in the Rockies, are said to eat up the grazing of the protected elk, and in some parts of British Columbia $5 bounties are paid for a pair of wild horse ears. Perhaps saddest of all the changes on the Prairies has been the disappearance, between 1936 and 1956 of some 50,000 of the pioneer 160-acre and 320-acre 'homestead' farms in Saskatchewan alone. By 1951, for the first time in the Province's history, its rural farm population accounted for less than half of the total. The Prairies of the old days were vanishing rapidly.

Today there are no easy fortunes to be made farming on the Prairies; there never were. In central Alberta we visited an English peer who ran a 1000-acre pig farm. He had come out in 1919 with virtually no capital; had spent the first year in a tent, with his wife and a young child, through a – 30° F. winter, working as a paid hand to another farmer. Now he had his own farm, and 300 high-quality porkers — quartered in houses of straw like the indolent Little Pig, but designed to keep out the cold, not the Big Bad Wolf! Pigs were far more profitable than wheat, yet it was obvious that life was still a hard struggle for him, and while we were there he was hoping against hope that gravel — with an infinitely greater value in Alberta than pork — might be found on his land. For new immigrant farmers the various warnings contained in the Gordon Commission Report are well worth heeding. The Report foresees only a slow expansion of Canada's share in the world wheat market up to 1980, and estimates that agriculture's overall share of the labour force will slip further from 15 to 7 per cent. There are still millions of acres of new farmland available for settlement in the West (notably around Alberta's northerly Peace River district), and interested bodies (particularly the railways) only too anxious to help immigrants settle there. But — apart from the fact that the cream of the best land has long since been skimmed off — the Report is eminently sensible when it warns that, because of growing productivity of existing farmland: 'We are fairly sure that not much new land will be brought into cultivation to meet the rise in demand.' Finally, and most pointedly, it says that it would be 'sceptical of any immigration programme to bring agricultural workers to Canada which did not show itself fully aware that the agricultural labour force is declining and that welfare of those left in agriculture depends in large measure on that process not being impeded. . . .'

One exception the Report admits to these *caveats* is livestock farming, which it expects will increase further in importance over the next generation. Probably the most prosperous men on the Prairie today are the successful Alberta cattle ranchers, and they are likely to become more prosperous. In the decade that followed the war, Albertan wheat production slipped back slightly, in terms of income, while income from cattle increased by over 70 per cent. There is a growing world-wide demand for meat; in a lean year, even Texas cannot meet United States demands for steak, and Canada today is herself a deficit beef producer. In 1958 Albertan ranchers were getting between 22 and 30 cents per lb. on the hoof for one-year-old calves, compared with the 3 or 4 cents per lb. realised by mature cattle during the Depression. Few places are better suited to large-scale ranching of first-class cattle (especially Hereford, Shorthorn and Aberdeen Angus) than Alberta.

Alberta's great cattle country lies in the southeastern ranges (which the cowmen share with their despised rivals, the sheep ranchers), but notably to the west and south of Calgary, in the foothills of the Rockies — where even the roadside pubs are apt to be called 'Moo-tels'. We spent two glorious days on one such foothill ranch, belonging to a charming young couple, Jim and Mary Cartwright. One would like to think that 'D-Ranch' (lying just above the Duke of Windsor's, the 'EP') were typical, but in the beauty of its surroundings it must have been above average, and I knew at the time that I would have difficulty describing it in anything but fulsome superlatives. The ranchhouse itself was 4800 feet up amid hills sprinkled with fragrant bull-pine, juniper and wild geranium, and valleys of stirrup-high grass and shady aspen forests. Below it, you could see the hills diminishing into the hot, golden Prairie; above, they grow in great sweeps to the rugged skyline of the high Rockies, whence come the rushing cold trout streams, checked occasionally by small lakes that the industrious beavers have created. It was a real demi-Eden, one of several things that left me with a feeling that Alberta might be the best place to live in Canada. Here the cattle ranches run far larger than wheat farms; the Cartwrights' 30,000 acres was about average in the neighbourhood, and at near-by Nanton the Cross 'A–7' ran to some 70,000 acres. In the difficult country of the foothills the mechanical revolution has made little impression and the horse is still king. Relatively isolated in their splendid empires ('D–Ranch' is about 40 miles from the nearest small town), each rancher has to be entirely self-contained. The Cartwrights kept supplies for six months, generated their own electricity. Their sole link with the outside world was a radio-telephone, 'on the air' only in the early morning and evening. Once a month — an important occasion — comes 'Church Sunday' when the parson visits the little church built by the hands of the surrounding ranchers. Each owner has to be a complete jack-of-all-trades; Jim Cartwright, a skilled vet, did all his own gelding and branding; broke all his own horses (they had recently gone into rearing Arab thoroughbreds as an important sideline); as well as running a large herd of Herefords, haying, repairing, constructing, chasing rustlers (it still happens, costing 'D–Ranch' sometimes thirty head in a year), and carrying out the thousand-and-one tasks of a ranch. Mary, a qualified nurse, had set several broken bones on the ranch, and seemed equipped to cope with anything short of a major operation. Yet, somehow, between them they managed to find time for other things; he, to organise local 'cutting contests', take an active part on the Western Stockgrowers Association, and keep remarkably well abreast of world affairs; she, to keep abreast of music and modern poetry.

The worst, perennial headache of Albertan ranch life, Jim told me, was labour. You had to have manpower that the wheat farmers can do without; 'and the good ones want to own their own land as soon as they can afford it, and the rest are worse than useless'. Work is hard, but the life is unbeatable and the pay usually good — ranging between $100–$160 a month, plus board and lodging.

Of the big cities of the Prairies, the biggest, oldest and coldest (proverbially, it is the coldest in all Canada) is

Winnipeg. Germinated from the Selkirk settlement on the confluence of the slow-moving Assiniboine and Red Rivers, together with its city suburb of St. Boniface — French Canada's stronghold in the West — it now totals some 410,000. This is nearly half the total population of Manitoba; another sign of the shifting pattern of the Prairies. When we arrived in Winnipeg, on a Sunday evening, the Salvation Army was resoundingly on the march through empty streets, and I was reminded a little of Toronto fifteen years ago. Winnipeg is a God-fearing, highly conservative, grey, and rather stern city of immensely wide and draughty streets; its sternness relieved principally by the presence of lots of what seemed to be the prettiest girls in Canada, and gently pretty residential suburbs along the riverside. Its Chamber-of-Commerce blurb for tourists, with no desire to proclaim such marvels as the *First Anglican Cathedral Founded Since the Conquest*, the *Longest Corridor in the Commonwealth*, or the *World's Second Biggest Bridge*, merely claims modestly that Winnipeg's public buildings 'rank with any in the world'. For Winnipeg feels it has 'arrived' and has no need to advertise itself with the brashness of those upstarts to the West, Calgary and Edmonton. Certainly it has a solidity and feeling of permanence, lacking in some Prairie cities which make you think of tented encampments liable to up sticks and move on at a day or two's notice. Commerce and communications principally made Winnipeg grow to its present size; both transcontinental railroads pass through the funnel of its freight yards, and it is, of course, the headquarters of the still mighty Hudson's Bay Company. Of late, it has grown greatly as a manufacturing centre, producing heavy machinery both for mining and agriculture, motor buses and nuclear measuring devices. It is a little difficult to see, though, just what the future holds for Winnipeg. With huge expansion in mind, its Parliament Buildings — their entrance flanked by two magnificent symbolic bisons — were built large enough to be the capital of an entire nation, yet it may well be that Winnipeg will be overtaken by Edmonton within the next decade, just as Manitoba has already been overtaken in prosperity and population by Alberta.

Regina, Saskatchewan's capital, is a city that demands admiration. In theory it shouldn't be there at all. Somebody apparently stuck a pin in the map along the CPR route, and decided it was time for another depot, but forgot to find out whether there was any water there. When it was chosen as the capital of the Northwest Territories in 1882, it was nicknamed 'Pile-of-Bones', because of its only landmark of any size, and the *Winnipeg Free Press* snootily predicted that it would 'never amount to anything more than a country village'. Since then Regina has defied its detractors and, despite a 'twister' that destroyed half of it in 1912 and the crippling effects of the Depression, has grown into a thriving and spirited city of 90,000. Once its sole water supply, a stagnant creek called the Wascana has been miraculously transformed into a beautiful lake by which sit the handsome legislative buildings and a really creditable new natural . history museum. But most remarkable of all are the massed flower-beds outside the Parliament, which I have seldom seen excelled anywhere. You feel that people who can do this can do almost anything. In recent years, stimulated by near-by oil and gas discoveries, Regina has attracted a considerable number of small industries, but its future growth must be somewhat limited by shortage of water. Its rival to the northwest, Saskatoon, on the banks of the broad South Saskatchewan River, has no such problem and is likely to overtake Regina as the Province's chief industrial and manufacturing city. It is already the transportation centre, and since 1951 its population has risen from 53,286 to over 75,000. A pleasant, dignified city with a fine university, Saskatoon was founded by Nonconformist 'Temperance' men from Ontario, who made settlement conditional upon a pledge of temperance. They failed (though it is still one of the hardest Canadian cities to get a drink in), and ironically enough Saskatoon has been chosen as site of a big new distillery.

One of the things which makes Regina different from the rest of Canada is that it is the seat of the country's only Socialist Government, the Co-operative Commonwealth Federation (CCF). A product of Depression days, it has been constantly in power since 1944, led by Scottish-born

T. C. Douglas. Although the British Columbia branch of the party has threatened some extreme left-wing legislation, should it come to power there, the policy of the CCF Government in Saskatchewan has been moderate, perhaps more reminiscent of the Lloyd George style of Liberalism than true Socialism. It has administered the Province well, has done a great deal to safeguard the interests of the farmer and develop natural resources, and was one of the first Provincial Governments to organise some kind of health service.

In Alberta (and, at the time of writing, in BC) the Province is ruled by the most unusual Government of the lot — the Social Credit Party. The Albertan 'Socreds' came to power in 1935, and have been in ever since. Like the CCF, they had their roots in the Depression, but they claim (sometimes it is a little hard to see how) to be a right-wing party. Their founder was a remarkable man called William ('Bible Bill') Aberhart, the Principal of a Calgary school and leading light of the 'Prophetic Bible Institute'. Aberhart's principal theme was that in the West 'money gets too much and man gets too little'. He promised to strike at the private control of credit facilities, and re-distribute a 'dividend' of $25 a month to every man, woman and child in the Province. His was a popular platform in the grim days of Depression, when fixed interest rates had become particularly hard to bear, and Aberhart was swept into power. But in 1937 Ottawa moved in and disallowed three of his more spectacular pieces of legislation (they included the issue of Albertan paper money and forced conversion of the public debt), and the following year two more. Since then, the Socreds have ruled more or less like any other party. Probably the first time they came anywhere near fulfilling their original programme was in 1957, when they issued one $20 'oil' dividend from the Government's vast accumulation of oil royalties. Like the CCF in Saskatchewan, they too have done much to improve the lot of the Albertans and defend them against those unsympathetic men in Ottawa, and the greedy Easterners as a whole. Before the coming of Canada's 'National Health Scheme', Alberta was the only Province to have a free maternity service, and its 'family support' cheques are generous enough to make large families worthwhile (once,

I was told, recipients were somewhat taken aback to find their
monthly cheques in envelopes franked by the Post Office —
quite coincidentally — with the slogan : 'RECREATION PAYS
DIVIDENDS !').

When 'Bible Bill' died, he was succeeded by Ernest
Manning, the present Premier of Alberta. As Aberhart's
successor at the Prophetic Bible Institute as well, he too was
an active evangelist.[1] A large part of the Socred creed is, in
fact, mystical in origin, exerting a powerful emotional appeal,
particularly in rural Alberta, where religion (notably evan-
gelical) is a most important influence. As a recent British
immigrant in Calgary discovered : 'The Power of the Lord
to smite the Amalekites is the real thing in Alberta.'[2] There
is an unmistakable similarity between the Socreds' 'religion
plus funny money' and the gospel of the American Midwest's
William Jennings Bryan — as the editor of an Albertan
newspaper (not a Socred man) remarked to me : 'There
seems to be something about the harshness and isolation of
Prairie farm life that leads to the need both for easy money
and mysticism.'

Calgary, Alberta's second city, capital of the cattle kingdom and headquarters of the oil industry, to me has more
warmth and charm about it than almost any other city in
Canada. Calgary started life as a Mounted Police post in
1875. Ten years later when the Canadian Pacific arrived it
was 'just a poor place, a few shacks. They moved it a mile
or so, on ropes, rather than move the railway line.'[3] Yet
today Calgary gives the impression of having developed the
character of a much older city. I liked the little I saw of it
during Stampede Week in 1956, and I liked it even more two
years later. The Stampede, a combination of rodeo, car-
nival and Royal Agricultural Show, justly called 'The Greatest Outdoor Show on Earth', is the nearest thing to a *Fiesta*
in North America. Its symbol is the white stetson that the
genial Mayor of Calgary hands out liberally to distinguished
visitors. Even when Stampede Week is over, the cheerful
signs of 'Howdy folk !', 'Welcome !', now apparently left on

[1] The present CCF Premier of Saskatchewan, Mr. T. C. Douglas, was also
ordained a minister in the Baptist Church.
[2] Ernest Watkins, *Prospect of Canada.*
[3] Stephen Leacock, *Canada, the Foundations of its Future.*

Grain elevators in Alberta with the Rocky Mountains in the background

ON THE PRAIRIES

Harvesting on a one-man farm near Regina

Chuckwagon race at the Stampede

CALGARY

Street scene

Calgary's lamp-posts all year round, the cowboys and
Indians hovering round the saloon of the Queen's Hotel in
their stetsons and tight jeans, the antique saddle and boot
shops, are all there to remind you that the Stampede is never
very far out of people's minds; that Calgary is still first and
foremost *the* 'cow-town'. A wonderful situation, just within
sight of the snow-capped Rockies, and a dry exhilarating
climate, also contribute to the special character of Calgary.
Alberta claims more sunshine than any other Province —
an average of six hours a day — and, among the cities of
Canada, Calgary lies right in the mean of hot-cold, dry-
humid extremities. In winter there is also the miraculous
Chinook wind, with its feathered clouds in the sky, blowing
from the Pacific and capable of raising temperatures 50° F.
within an hour (an old Albertan joke is that farmers have to
use sleds with runners in front and wheels behind to keep up
with the *Chinook*!). Its population has doubled since 1946
(now just under 200,000), and despite the current oil recession,
in 1958 it was still very much a lively, expanding boom-town,
with construction reaching an all-time record. Constantly
growing in importance as a manufacturing city, its principal
industries include oil refineries, flour mills, meat-packing
plants, chemical and storage battery industries (it is now the
battery manufacturing centre of Canada), fertiliser plants,
and a new cast-iron pipe factory. In 1956, for the first time
on record, Calgary stockyard sales beat Winnipeg's.

If Winnipeg has substance, Regina spirit, Saskatoon
dignity, and Calgary character, it is a little difficult to decide
just what is the salient characteristic of Edmonton. Perhaps
it has grown too fast to know what it is itself. Many of the
streets of its mushroom outer suburbs are still unpaved; the
day we arrived a cloudburst had turned their dust to gumbo,
and, rolling down the car window to ask the way, I got a
mouthful flung up by a passing car. It was the essential
rawness of Edmonton that made it seem to conform more
to my idea of a new Siberian city than anything else I had
seen in Canada. It has a mixed, still unassimilated population, as testified by its Russian Orthodox cathedral and
Moslem mosque (the only one in Canada), and the Jewish
and Armenian second-hand shops clustered together on the

H

wrong side of the chateau-esque Macdonald Hotel. From across the river comes an occasional sulphury whiff of the great chemical plants and oil refineries. The operations base of the oil industry (whilst more opulent and polished Calgary is its executive HQ), it still has something of the raw, rough-tough, and slightly brutal atmosphere of a frontier town about it — more so than any other of Canada's major cities. Dust-covered men off the Alaska Highway with tall stories of the North, fishermen from the Great Slave Lake on a summer blind, uranium miners gambling away the high wages they couldn't spend at Port Radium, and 'roughnecks' from the oilfields in their yellow helmets, all add to this aroma of the frontier-town. Exciting, perhaps even colourful, but tough ; a city I would not like to be unemployed in. From fur-trading post to Provincial capital, Edmonton has recently had the highest growth rate of any city in Canada, probably in all North America. Between 1951 and 1956 it grew nearly 45 per cent, and it now numbers over a quarter of a million. This is its main trouble — it has the worst case of Los Angeles spread in all Canada. Even Edmontonians seldom claim theirs is a beautiful city, though some of its latest development — like the handsome Jubilee auditorium, the new Government Buildings and the flowery residential area that looks across at it over the chasm of the North Saskatchewan — promises better things for tomorrow, as does the mellowing influence of its excellent university. Whatever one may think of Edmonton at present, there is little doubt about its future. Its City Fathers certainly have no doubts, and have laid out the city grid system on a scale that would appear to dwarf Manhattan ; well out into the bush, we came across an isolated telegraph pole with '69th Avenue' daubed on it. Edmonton has the cheapest electricity in Canada, and sits upon vast reserves of low-cost natural gas, oil and coal (in seams 30 feet thick, with just a 5-foot overburden, yet unexploited because of lack of market). It already has some of the largest industrial plants between Southern Ontario and Vancouver ; it is becoming the centre of Canada's petro-chemical industry, and when markets finally warrant the setting up of a basic steel industry in the West, Edmonton will probably get it. It is the gateway and supply point to Canada's newest and rapidly growing settlement area, the Peace River, and it will also be the 'rear base' for the next frontier about to be opened up, the Great Slave Lake and Mackenzie Basin of the Northwest Territories. Within the next generation, Edmonton may well become one of Canada's leading industrial centres.

As noted earlier in this chapter, it was the discovery of the Leduc oilfield in 1947 that started the transformation of the Prairies. Leduc sparked the discovery of other fields, in all three Provinces, and the by-production of natural gas as a cheap and convenient source of energy. In Alberta, value of crude oil production rose from $14·3 million in 1946 to just under $360 million in 1957. Through a shrewd system of leases and royalties, between '47 and '58 the Socred Government collected some $716·3 million in revenue; a few years prior to Leduc they had actually defaulted on payment of bond interest, but by '57 they had reduced the Provincial Debt to the lowest in Canada, as well as being able to buy Alberta two of Canada's finest auditoria. For a time, nearly everybody had a share in the oil boom; in the afternoons, the proprietor of our motel in Calgary became a part-time drilling operator. Between 1939 and '56, the Albertans' *per capita* personal income had risen 311 per cent. Saskatchewan in 1945 had only 5 oil wells; twelve years later, she had 3000 capable of production, and her Government's revenue from oil was $2 million more than its whole budget twenty years earlier. By 1957, Manitoba, the least fortunate of the three, was producing half its own petroleum needs.

But the illusion that the Prairies' 'liquid gold' will make a millionaire of whom ever touches it is a dangerous one. Firstly, there are very few highly paid jobs in the industry itself (fewer than ever now) for any but skilled technicians. Secondly, the great overall prosperity in the Prairies has resulted more from the secondary industries stimulated by oil and gas discoveries rather than from the industries themselves. Thirdly, Canadian oil (though not so much natural gas) is seriously in the doldrums at the moment, and likely to remain so for some time. When I visited an Albertan oilfield not far from Calgary, foreman-drillers were still earning $700 a month — but two thousand were out of work; only four in every five of the oil rigs were working, and many wells had been 'capped in'. The small producers, I was told, were getting desperate, and even some of the larger companies were worried. It was hardly surprising, for each well costs (lease included) about £100,000 to drill, and only about one in seven finds oil or gas in sufficient quantity to cover costs. Every year since Leduc, the total expenditures of the Albertan oil industry have exceeded income. And yet, in 1956 alone, Canadian oil *imports* amounted to well over a third of her huge total foreign trade deficit. Why?

Once again the answer lies in those ubiquitous bogies of the Canadian economy; markets and distance. The three Provinces number only 2·9 million consumers; including British Columbia, the whole Canadian West has only 4·3 million. Unlike Ontario with her populous American neighbours totalling 65 million, the six American States nearest the Prairies are among the emptiest in the Union, offering a further market of little more than 6 million. Because of its oil, cattle and new prosperity, Alberta has sometimes been compared to Texas. In fact, in many things Alberta is richer than Texas; it has mountains, forest and great rivers that Texas lacks, and greater overall resources of power and raw materials. But, apart from population (Texas is rising 10 million), Texas has one vital advantage over Alberta — tidewater; for the cheapest way to ship oil, or any other bulk commodity, is by sea. To get Albertan oil to eastern markets, the world's longest pipeline (1772 miles) has been built, but by the time it arrives it still costs up to 25 cents a barrel more than crude shipped in from Venezuela, or even the Middle East. (Saskatchewan has a slight edge over Alberta in that its wells are 500 miles farther east, but it is not a decisive factor.) A further threat to the Albertan industry lies in the active exploration now going on near tidewater in Alaska, which may soon result in oil delivered to Vancouver and the US West Coast cheaper than Alberta can pump it through the Trans-Mountain Pipeline. Recently Russia too has been tempting Eastern Canada with cheaper oil, and one day even the islands of the Canadian Arctic may prove awkward competitors. Only natural gas, hissing through great pipes to the Far West, the Far East, and southwards to the United States can compete unchallenged wherever it reaches, but its reserves are limited.

The Gordon Report predicts (perhaps a little optimistically, compiled as it was before there was a world surplus of oil) that by 1980 Canadian oil production might have multiplied ten times over 1955. But meanwhile, to get over their immediate problems, the Prairie oil producers are faced with two alternatives. One is to extend the Inter-provincial Pipeline to the Montreal markets, which, to make it pay, would involve a tariff or quota being placed on crude imported from overseas. Here the small producers, who want the extension, are up against the ponderous weight of the big international companies whose parent bodies have still bigger interests in Venezuela, the United States and the Middle East, and who by cutting their deliveries to help increase Albertan production would simply be robbing Peter to pay Paul. (Albertan oil, it should be noted, is in fact predominantly controlled by United States interests and no fewer than 14 out of 20 members of the Body of Governors of the influential Canadian Petroleum Association are Americans.) A second alternative is to pipe oil to the expanding regions of the US Pacific Northwest. But apart from import quotas the United States has placed on foreign oil, Ottawa is also hesitant to enter into any long-term arrangement that might lead to serious depletion of her gas and oil reserves. It has some reason for this ; reserves of oil so far proven in Western Canada are in fact considerably less than is generally thought, only a fraction of known Mideast reserves. In terms of heat equivalent, Alberta's available oil and gas combined only equal 3·5 per cent of its coal potential. By far the greatest oil potential known in Canada at present is the famous Athabaska tar sands, a unique formation in the northeast of Alberta. These are believed to contain perhaps 150,000,000,000 barrels of oil (compared with other proven Albertan oil reserves of about 3,000,000,000), but as yet nobody has discovered an economic process of getting the oil out of the sands. Schemes of distilling it by setting off an atom bomb under the sands were temporarily postponed when an international ban on nuclear tests seemed in the offing.

Perhaps the next best solution for the Canadian oil industry lies in a major expansion in Alberta of chemicals production, based on petroleum and coal. Already the chemical industry there has shown the greatest growth of any, multiplying five times between '49 and '57. By manufacturing products with a high price/bulk ratio — such as polythylene plastics and synthetic chemicals — it is able to get over the bugbears of transportation, and, with all the raw materials at hand, Alberta could easily become one of the world's most important chemical centres.

Oil is not the only resource to enrich the Prairie Provinces since the war. At Flin-Flon, 500 miles northwest of Winnipeg, Manitoba has the second largest copper producer in Canada. Farther up into the Shield, at Mystery Lake just off the lonesome rail route to Churchill, International Nickel has recently built a town for 8000 to exploit what is claimed to be the world's second biggest nickel mine; in size, the biggest project in Canada since the start of work on the St. Lawrence Seaway. Saskatchewan, at Estevan in the same area as its main oilfields, has a vast open-cast lignite pit; the lowest-cost coal producer in Canada. Its Uranium City on Lake Athabasca produced some 60 per cent of all Canada's uranium in 1956 (the percentage has dropped since Ontario's Blind River–Elliot Lake mines came into production). The Province has the only potash deposits in Canada, now just starting production, and her first pulp mill began operations in 1957. In Alberta, the wood products industry had also achieved some importance in recent years; a further, and virtually costless by-product of the petroleum industry, is sulphur and it is estimated that by 1975 Alberta's production of it will amount to some $40 million a year.

In all three Provinces, boosted by the Albertan oil boom, manufacturing industries have made great strides. In Manitoba, they overtook agriculture as the leading income producer soon after the war. In Alberta, manufacturing showed the biggest increase in Canada between 1940–57; a more than sevenfold expansion, in terms of gross values.

Iron ore is a resource of which Alberta has substantial, fairly high-grade deposits, and the next step in both her development and that of the West as a whole must be the foundation of a basic steel industry and its manufacturing subsidiaries as soon as markets warrant it. The absurdity of the Prairies' transportation problems is nowhere more clearly displayed than in the fact that it costs $2·65 to freight 100 lb. of steel plate from Hamilton, Ont., to Edmonton — but only $1·20 to Vancouver via the Panama Canal. In some cases, it is even cheaper to ship it to Vancouver, then pay return rail charges from Vancouver back over the Rockies to Alberta, than pay the single rail charge from Ontario to Alberta. Although a steel rolling mill started operations in 1955, and the value of steel and iron products tripled between 1949 and 1956, they still amounted to little more than a third of the value of imports; and Alberta's imports of agricultural machinery (nearly a half of which came from the United States) exceeded her own production by some twenty times.

From what I have said here and elsewhere it might be deduced that I favour Alberta's prospects most among the three Provinces. And I do. In the summer of 1960 when unemployment in some Provinces had reached 8 per cent of the labour force, the Prairies jointly had the lowest rate at only 2 per cent. In Alberta alone, despite the setbacks of the moment, raw materials and energy resources alone promise it a great future. (An indication that transportation headaches are not insuperable is shown by the fact that it has been considered economically sound to build a $25 million nickel refinery at Edmonton, bringing to its cheap natural gas nickel ore 900 miles from northern Manitoba, then shipping the finished product thousands of miles east again.) Alberta has one of the most pleasantly exhilarating climates in Canada — better than that of either Saskatchewan or Manitoba — and most of its centres are within a stone's throw (on the Canadian scale of things) of some of the world's most glorious scenery, in the high Rockies of Jasper and Banff National Parks. One final point, and an important one for a would-be immigrant; an Englishwoman in Calgary told my wife that nearly all the British wives she knew locally were very contented — a situation she attributed largely to Albertan warmth and kindliness.

CHAPTER SIX

SOVEREIGN STATE ON THE PACIFIC

Tramp! Tramp! Tramp! the New Dominion
Now is knocking at the door,
So, goodbye dear Uncle Sam
As we do not care a dam
For your Greenbacks or your bunkum any more.
(Chorus of Cariboo song, Barkerville, 1869)

Such a land is good for an energetic man.
It is also not so bad for a loafer.
(RUDYARD KIPLING, 1908)

From Gastown to Kitimat is only the life of a man
Under the sweet rich rain, the mountains and the sea.
(LISTER SINCLAIR, 'Eulogy')

NOBODY quite knows who was the first European to 'discover' British Columbia. The indefatigable Drake may possibly have caught a glimpse or two of its Olympian coastline, peeping through the Pacific mists that lost him the entrance to San Francisco Bay. Then a pause of nearly two centuries, until Juan Perez, sent northwards from Mexico to bolster a tottering Spanish empire with new conquests, sailed up the British Columbian coast as far as the Queen Charlotte Islands. Four years later, in 1778, Captain Cook (who had begun his climb to fame twenty years earlier when he had navigated a way up the St. Lawrence for Wolfe's expedition) made a much more detailed survey and actually landed on Vancouver Island, before sailing to his death on the Sandwich Islands. On the basis of his findings the British Government decided that this immense new territory might be worth being tough about with Spain, and in 1790 (after a Spanish-provoked incident the previous year which nearly led to war) the Spaniards were persuaded to abandon their claims. The following year, Captain George Vancouver was dispatched with orders to take formal possession.

It is symbolic of the dominant role played throughout in

the exploration of Canada by that hardy perennial, the quest for the Northwest Passage, that Cook's chief instructions from the Admiralty were to find the western inlet to the mythical waterway.   Meanwhile, on the same quest, the trader-explorers of the Northwest were thrusting ever farther from the East.   In 1789 a 26-year-old Nor'wester called Alexander Mackenzie made a remarkable journey to the mouth of the river that bears his name, the second longest in North America; but, because it led into the Arctic and not the 'Western Ocean', in bitterness he christened it 'River of Disappointment'.   Four years later, however, and a few months after the advent of Captain Vancouver, he stood on the Pacific Coast near Bella Coola inlet — the first white man ever to cross the North American continent overland.   Mackenzie was knighted for his feat by George III, and his 'Voyages' even attracted the attention of Napoleon, who apparently hoped to derive from them some imaginitive scheme for attacking the British Empire from the rear.

At various times in its short history, British Columbia could easily have slipped into Spanish, Russian or — particularly — American hands.   More than a generation before Perez or Cook had arrived on the scene, Russian explorers under Bering (in fact a Dane) had established a foothold in Alaska, and the fur-traders that followed pushed far down the Pacific Coast.   As a result, when the Americans bought Alaska in 1867 — at a bargain price of twopence an acre — a large slice of coastline that should logically belong to British Columbia, the 'Alaska Panhandle', went with it; still a source of irritation to more xenophobe British Columbians.   By the end of the 18th century, the United States were travelling westward at a far greater rate than Canada. Repeating Drake's misfortune at San Francisco, Vancouver in 1792 had missed the mouth of the Great Columbia River in a fog, and two weeks later an American Captain hoisted the Stars and Stripes there.   In 1805 an official US expedition under Lewis and Clarke reached the Columbia overland, and John Jacob Astor founded a fur-post, beating the Nor'-westers to the draw.   Within a few years many Americans were taking it for granted that all the West Coast as far as Russian Alaska naturally belonged to their 'Manifest Destiny'.

The fact that British Columbia became and remained British was largely owing to the presence of a handful of these Nor'westers, and later Hudson's Bay employees. Most of them were Scots — hence the BC mainland's first name of 'New Caledonia', and the remark that 'the names of the North-West Company partners sound like the roll call of the clans at Culloden'. For tenacity of purpose, endurance and sheer courage men like Mackenzie, Fraser and Thompson have few rivals in the annals of history (except perhaps Mrs. Thompson, who gave birth between shooting rapids on the Columbia and survived to raise a brood of fifteen more). At the BC Centennial Celebrations in 1958, a team of international kayak champions attempted to emulate Fraser's feat, shoot the rapids of the Fraser Canyon and travel all the way to Vancouver. They covered 30 miles, then had to admit defeat.

In 1850 Vancouver Island was proclaimed a Crown Colony, although its total white population numbered only a couple of hundred, with that of 'New Caledonia' fewer still. Then, suddenly, news of the discovery of gold up the Fraser River brought in a flood of 31,000 fortune-seekers in a single year, 1858, and the price of flour rose to $30 a barrel. The great majority of this influx came from the United States, including many toughs from the California gold-fields, and fears that so overwhelming a 'minority' might revive talk of annexation made Britain hasten to proclaim the mainland a new colony, entitled British Columbia. At the same time, 165 Royal Engineers came out (around the Horn) to build roads and keep the peace. It was thanks to them, to the prompt decisiveness of the new Governor, James Douglas of the Hudson's Bay Company, and the iron-handed justice of Judge Matthew Begbie, that — compared with California and Nevada — British Columbia's gold-rush went off about as peacefully as a Sunday school treasure-hunt. Complete Americanisation of the new colony was further avoided by the arrival, in 1862, of the 'Overlanders', a group of gold-miners who made an epic cross-country journey from Eastern Canada.

In 1871 the gold-rush had collapsed, and, although at one time Barkerville in the Cariboo had claimed to be the biggest centre west of Chicago (now it is just a ghost-town), the total population of BC then consisted of only 10,000 whites and 25,000 Indians. That year Hudson's Bay sold out its rights in the West, and the two colonies merged into one Province to join the new Dominion of Canada — on the promise that within ten years it would be linked to the rest of Canada by a transcontinental railroad. As a result of delays caused by financial scandals in high places and the immense difficulty of finding a route through the Rockies — which cost many lives — it was in fact fifteen years before the CPR arrived. In their disgruntlement British Columbians seriously considered casting off and joining up with the United States; on his visit to Victoria in 1876, the Governor-General, Lord Dufferin, was confronted with placards demanding 'OUR RAILROAD OR SEPARATION'.[1] In London, *Truth* magazine grumbled: 'British Columbia is a barren, cold, mountain country that is not worth keeping. . . . It will never pay a red cent of interest on any money that may be sunk in it.' But the railway came through, and later two more. In 1914 the Panama Canal brought BC two-thirds closer by sea to Montreal and the Old World, and since then the Province has never looked back. In the 1950s the Rocky Mountain barrier was conquered twice again; first by the 700-mile-long Trans-Mountain oil pipeline from Edmonton, and then by the multi-million dollar Trans-Canada Highway. By its Centenary in 1958 the four or five hundred who had launched the Colony had grown to a million and a half. *Truth* had expired the previous year.

Bruce Hutchison, an ardent British Columbian, speaks of his province and its people as '. . . almost a sovereign state, themselves a chosen people'.[2] Insulated from the rest of Canada by the mountain barrier, living in a rugged country devoid of limitless horizons — except the Pacific — with a totally different climate, the people of BC look on themselves as different to other Canadians; perhaps just a cut above them. Geography has tended to make BC grow in patches. Through the patches the two main historical influences of BC, British and American, shine through with

[1] Marchioness of Dufferin, *My Canadian Journal*.
[2] Bruce Hutchison, *Canada, Tomorrow's Giant*.

lights of purer contrast than perhaps anywhere else in Canada. Few Canadian towns strike one as being so integrated into the 'American way' as the mining and smelter centres of Trail and Kimberley, close to the US border in the interior. Yet, sandwiched in between, the Kootenays, with their apple orchards, cottages and names like Josiah Wedgwood and Baillie-Grohman, could be a slice of rural Britain. Take away its surrounding mountains, and Nelson, the Kootenay capital, with its sleepy main street and chestnuts (the first we had seen in Canada) could be an English county town. And so could pretty Kelowna, in the Okanagan Valley, on Trail's other flank. At the lumber camp I visited in the forests of Vancouver Island, every man had his ear glued to the two-way radio system, listening for results in the US 'World Series' relayed from New York; yet Victoria and Vancouver are the shrines of cricket in the New World ('flannel'd fools', its players are dubbed by the baseball enthusiasts), and complaints flood in to any newspaper that omits British soccer scores. The pleasant garden suburbs of the two cities were the only places in Canada where we found the tea ritual religiously observed.

On the other hand, in many ways the Rockies and the Pacific create a natural affinity between the British Columbians and the Americans of the Northwest. Vancouver is closer to Seattle than Calgary, and — atmospherically — San Francisco is its twin. When they think of the outside world, both Canadians and Americans on the Pacific look inevitably out across its vast expanse. But the things they see are not at all the same. With the capture of the Aleutians and the shelling by submarine of a lighthouse on Vancouver Island, physically the Japanese came closer to BC than California, and at the backs of their minds British Columbians always have a sneaking fear that their great empty valleys will one day present a powerful enticement to the teeming Chinese. However, instead of being, like their neighbours, worried stiff at the menace of the 'Yellow Peril', they see an urgent need for BC with its tiny domestic market and vastly expanding industries to widen trade with the Orient. After the United States and Britain, Japan has since the war become BC's principal trading partner, and trade is growing at an ever-

increasing rate between the two ; most significant of all —
in both government and industrial circles in BC — the
desire to open up trade with Red China is far stronger than
anywhere else in Canada.

BC is almost a sovereign state in another sense. Though
only third in size among the Provinces, it covers a huge area
— nearly four times that of the British Isles. Unlike most
of the other Provinces, BC has depth as well as breadth.
Two-thirds of its population are concentrated within a hundred miles or less of Vancouver, nevertheless, its northern
half, from Williams Lake upwards, already has over 120,000
inhabitants, and is likely to grow at an even greater rate —
if the many promises for its future materialise.

Scenically and climatically, BC seems to have a large
bit of everything, and nearly all of it very powerful. It
certainly has more than its share of mountains. Travelling
through from the East they seem to go on and on for ever ;
first the Rockies themselves, then the Selkirks, the Monashees
and finally the Coastal Mountains — and in between them
an uninterrupted mass of hillocks four or five thousand feet
high that nobody bothers to give a name. Little wonder the
overall Provincial speed limit is 50 m.p.h. ! An unimpressed
Scot remarked over a century ago that he 'would not give
the bleakest knoll on the bleakest hill of Scotland, for all these
mountains in a heap.' But he maligned the BC mountains ;
they may not be as high as the Alps, but the various peaks
do not jostle each other for *Lebensraum* as they do in Switzerland. The Rockies stand majestically and unapproachably
apart, as if aware, like the giant firs that cover their slopes,
that they had all the space in the world to grow in. Between
the mountains lie great open valleys where you could lose
half a dozen Swiss *cantons*, with mighty opal-green rivers
several Rhônes wide. In some ways, it is what Switzerland
might have been like a millennium or so after the Ice Age,
before men began to hew down the forest and move up the
mountain slopes. No meadows, no chalets, no cow-bells ;
for hundreds of miles the emptiness and silence is uncanny —
switch off the motor of your car and you can almost hear its
last gasp echo back at you across the mountains. By comparison, the Great St. Bernard is suburbia. Innumerable are

the malachite-coloured lakes where you can fish for days
without hearing any sound but the crazy quavering of a loon,
the rising of the fish, or the splashing of moose grazing in the
shallows. Here, tucked away in the mountains and fjords of
BC are some of the last few pleasant corners of the earth
where you can still lose yourself — by intent or otherwise —
and where you can still live off the land. The country
abounds with wild game, duck, pheasant, goose, quail and
willow-grouse, salmon and trout — and, for the more ambitious hunter, cougar, wolf, elk, moose, caribou, deer, moun-
tain-goat, big-horn sheep (one of the world's most difficult
animals to stalk), as well as the ferocious grizzly.

After crossing two or three hundred miles of Rockies at
the southern end of BC the first major inhabited valley you
come to is where the Columbia River forms the Kootenay
lakes; as beautiful as the lake country of Italian Switzerland,
but, oh, so empty. In the Kootenay country lie Nelson, the
orchards of Creston, and the mining towns of Trail and
Kimberley. Nelson is a charming small town of about
10,000 tucked away on a lake arm, as if hiding itself in
embarrassment at the notoriety the troublesome 'Sons-of-
Freedom' Doukhubors have brought it. Visiting a Doukhubor village — with its squalid streets and battered log huts
it might have been lifted from some poverty-stricken corner
of the Ukraine — I arrived in the middle of what seemed to
be a Cyprus-like small war. A few days earlier, two 'Freedomites' had blown themselves to pieces experimenting with
dynamite for some un-pacific demonstration, and heavily
reinforced Mounties were carrying out frequent road-checks
for cars carrying explosives. Earlier that year a ray of hope
for the Canadian authorities had begun to shimmer, when
Russia offered to take all the Doukhubors back again. When
we were there, Doukhubor leaders were busily meeting in
Nelson to decide whether to go or not. By some ironic
coincidence, a cinema in the town was showing a film called
This is Russia, with — as the next attraction — *Between
Heaven and Hell*. It seemed to sum up the choice facing the
Doukhubors; the paradise of the Kootenays, or Omsk.
Eventually only a few dozen opted to go, but meanwhile the
Russian offer — probably only a propaganda gesture in the

first place — had fallen through. Nelson was left with her problem children.

'Silica Street' and 'Carbonate Road' sloping steeply up the hillside in Nelson remind one that this is also the centre of one of Canada's major mining areas. At Kimberley is the fabulous Sullivan Mine, virtually a mountain of solid ore, which, although worked intensively since the beginning of the century, is still the world's largest lead-zinc-silver producer. BC accounts for about 80 per cent of Canada's lead production, most of which comes out of this one great hole. Apart from incidentally producing valuable quantities of other such trivialities as gold, tin, indium, bismuth, antimony and cadmium, the Sullivan Mine 'tailings' have a 25 per cent iron content. This has all been stacked away in a lake-bed, millions of tons of it, waiting for the day when, combined with the plentiful coal from the near-by Crowsnest mines, it could form the basis of BC's first steel industry. At present, like Alberta, the Province has to import all its steel from Ontario, 2000 miles away. Nothing at all is wasted from the Sullivan Mine; in the '30s poisonous gases from the Trail smelter killed vegetation over a vast area of the State of Washington, and the American Government sued COMINCO, the owners, for many million dollars. Chemists brought in to see what could be done declared that the gases could be turned into ammonium sulphate. The result; a valuable sideline in the form of one of Canada's biggest fertiliser plants — and, in an experimental garden at Kimberley, some of the most magnificent blossoms I have ever seen, with dahlias a foot across and gladioli nearly seven feet high.

Westward over the mountains from Trail, about 100 miles as the crow flies but twice that distance by road, lies the glorious Okanagan Valley. There could hardly be more of a contrast between the two areas: the Kootenays have winters of continental cold, cool mountain summers (except Trail, which is a hot-box), and all the rain they want; the Okanagan has a warm winter, roasting dry summers, and so little rain that without irrigation it would be a semi-desert — its parched, eroded hills seem to belong more to the American Southwest. In fact irrigation has turned it into one of the world's greatest apple-growing countries; if you descend on it from the barren mountains in late summer, the delectable smell of ripe apples reaches you several miles before you can see the orchards. Almost anything will grow in the Okanagan Valley, it is Canada's Little California. The interior dry zone extends on up across the middle reaches of the Fraser River, the scene of the first BC gold-rush, and farther north into the Cariboo, where it all ended. Much of this area was colonised by Britons, often well-to-do second sons, early in the century. Several such colonies, like Walhachin on the Fraser, ended in tragedy. In 1914 the men of Walhachin left in a body for Flanders. None returned. You can still see the remains of the irrigation ditches they had laboriously dug, the untended runaway apple trees — for, perhaps out of superstition, no one has tried to revive the ghost colony.

In the dry, open grasslands from Kamloops to the Cariboo lie Canada's biggest cattle ranches. One of them, the Gang Ranch, of over a million acres, is said to be even larger than the famous King Ranch of Texas. For all their size, they are not generally as successful as those on the other side of the Rockies. They tend to be much farther from railheads, and as North American eating habits at present favour grain-fed steak, BC cattle often have to be shipped over the mountains to Alberta for final fattening. Something like three-quarters of the beef consumed in BC is actually shipped in from Alberta.

Several hundred miles due north of the Cariboo, where the Rockies begin to dwindle, is BC's own stretch of Prairie — the Peace River country. Shared half between Alberta and BC, this is Canada's most northern wheat-growing area, her latest frontier. Short as the Peace River summer is, its long hours of daylight grow more bushels of wheat per acre than almost anywhere in Saskatchewan, and as a result this is rapidly becoming a major cattle-raising country. It also has large resources of oil and natural gas, the latter now being shipped all the way to Vancouver via the Westcoast Transmission pipeline. Altogether this is a fast-growing area; from a population of 20,000 in the '20s, it has reached close to the 100,000 mark, and the recent extension of the Pacific Great Eastern (once known as the railway from

VANCOUVER

*Looking north
across
Burrard inlet*

Barkerville in the gold-rush days of the 1860's

PAST AND PRESENT IN BRITISH COLUMBIA

'Boom-scooters' replace the log-roller on Vancouver Island

nowhere to nowhere) now links it to Vancouver as well as to Edmonton.

There is promise of growth on a really unheard-of scale for both the Peace River and the Cariboo if a project that has been under consideration for a number of years is ever carried through. This is the scheme of Dr. Wenner-Gren, the Swedish multi-millionaire, and under investigation by British Thomson-Houston, to dam the 'Rocky Mountain Trench' formed by two tributaries of the Peace River. Creating a man-made lake some 200 miles long, the largest in the world, the dam would produce 4·5 million h.p. of electricity. This is 25 per cent more than the present installed hydro-electricity capacity of all BC. Intentions are to transmit the power over the 400 miles to Vancouver, but the $611 million project will also transform the surrounding country. The impact will be particularly strong on Prince George, the chief town of the Cariboo, and right in the centre of BC. Once just a sleepy lumber town, dwelling on distant memories of the gold-rush, Prince George has already become an important communications centre, with a fast-growing population of some 13,000. The 'Trench' scheme and its ramifications would make it an industrial hub perhaps second only to Vancouver. It may rival in cost the hydro-electric side of the St. Lawrence Seaway, but it seems almost certain to go through eventually — for at least one good reason. The Peace is the only river of BC to run into the Arctic, as opposed to the Pacific. Although it is estimated that the Pacific rivers of BC could produce the staggering total of nearly 20 million h.p., the greatest undeveloped power potential in the world, they are also the spawning grounds of one of BC's proudest and most valuable assets—the great Sockeye salmon. And nobody has yet discovered a way of getting millions of salmon safely over or around a high dam; either up or downstream. Some of the Pacific Indians showed great reluctance to allow Alexander Mackenzie to enter their villages — out of fear that the white man might drive away the precious Sockeye. They had remarkable foreknowledge; the white man's works have done the fisheries great harm.

An alternative scheme under consideration that would

I

not affect the salmon is one to increase power already derived from the Columbia, but for many years Ottawa and Washington have been unable to agree on the division of benefits. Yet a third hydro project, perhaps the remotest of the three, but the one that would produce the most power, is the Frobisher Company's scheme to repeat what was done at Kitimat, and reverse the flow of a tributary of the mighty Yukon River into Northwest BC. This would open up a huge area of both the Yukon and northern BC, at present almost uninhabited and little explored, but known to be rich in asbestos and many other minerals.

On my way back from the Yukon, I travelled to Vancouver via the inland waterways that run for a thousand miles between countless islands and the jagged coast of Alaska and British Columbia, aboard a freighter of the White Pass and Yukon railway. For four days and nights the Newfoundland skipper, quiet spoken and imperturbable like all his race, weaved his 10,000-ton ship as dexterously as a slalom skier through channels often no more than a hundred yards wide. At one point, on the erstwhile site of the deadly Ripple Rock, a thirteen-knot current actually forced us back; we had to turn around in the narrows and wait till the tide changed. One shuddered to think of the perils of this manœuvre had the rock still been there; having removed the bottoms of numerous ships, Ripple Rock was itself removed earlier in 1958 with the biggest non-atomic explosion in history. I felt I would remember the beauty of this coast for many years. So much like Norway, the huge tree-covered mountains fall abruptly into countless deep fjords, which every once in a while open up a little so you can see the snow-caps and glaciers of still higher mountains beyond. In the early mornings, narrow belts of autumn mist cut off the bases of the islands so they hovered substanceless as in a Japanese print; in the evening, the liquid sunsets merged the sea and sky into one, and small seiners approaching out of the sun seemed to float in a Turneresque explosion of gold and orange. And the peace, the silence. Hour after hour, sometimes a whole day, we would see no sign of life more sophisticated than the bobbing Helldiver ducks, the porpoises and seals, and the occasional languid tail of a whale, raised in slow motion — very occasionally, a log barge in the distance. To me it was the journey of a lifetime, to most of the crew it was monotonous and boring. Boring, I suspect chiefly because of the absence of human life. There can be no habitable coastline in the world quite so empty. In all the five hundred miles or more belonging to British Columbia, there is little more than a handful of small ports, logging camps and Indian settlements. The coast's principal town is Prince Rupert, the terminus of the CNR's transcontinental railway. Principally a logging centre of some 10,000 people, 'Rupert' has had a mixed past of boom and bust, and now that its thunder has been stolen by the new giant of Kitimat, just up the next fjord, it looks as if its future may be even more doubtful; although, as the nearest tidewater port, it too may get a boost from the Wenner-Gren project.

Northbound for the Yukon, I had made a brief call at Kitimat. The story of the creation of the huge aluminium smelter, one of the most inspiring feats of the century — the great river forced by the world's largest rock-fill dam to reverse its course and flow down a 10-mile tunnel into a power-house gouged out of the bowels of the mountains, the transmission lines strung by helicopter over a mile-high pass — is now so well known that it hardly needs recounting here. But the town itself deserves some mention. Where less than a decade ago only a small Indian village existed, today there is a handsome, thriving township of some 12,000, boasting the title of being the first completely 'New Town' built in North America in the 20th century. Already earmarked as the site of BC's next pulp and paper mill, it is expected to become a city of 50,000 in the not-too-distant future. In planning, Kitimat closely resembles Elliot Lake and the new model suburb of Toronto, Don Mills. It is divided into self-supporting 'neighbourhoods', each numbering about 6000, with their own schools, recreation areas and small shopping centre catering for, as Lewis Mumford, the arch-planner, demanded — 'a spool of thread or loaf of bread'. Between the neighbourhoods lies the usual, concentrated city centre, with its business section, main shops, cinemas, bowling alleys, municipal offices and vast parking lot. In the neighbourhoods, houses (each, in the modern North American style of things, set apart in its own small plot of land) are located on loops and cul-de-sacs to minimise traffic dangers. Their backs face on to interior parkways, giving direct access to the neighbourhood centres and schools. Where children have to cross any road, there will be usually an under-pass or a pedestrian bridge. As far as any new town can have, Kitimat has character. Its architecture is imaginative and pleasing, as one often finds on the West Coast of Canada; the $1·5 million High School, already with 500 students, was one of the finest I have seen anywhere.

Set at the end of a fjord, surrounded by great white-capped mountains and glades of giant Douglas firs, with a wonderful salmon river running through its centre, Kitimat is particularly fortunate in its environment. It also has a reasonably temperate climate. Connected to Vancouver 400 miles down the coast virtually only by sea and air, the settlement's worst drawback is its isolation. As a result, the cost of living there is over 5 per cent higher than in Southern BC; a house that would cost $11,000 to build in Vancouver would cost $15,000 at Kitimat. Even though, with production cut by about 30 per cent and numbers of workers laid off, there was a faint gloom of recession while I was there, through it it was possible to detect a very much better atmosphere than at Elliot Lake. Admittedly, Kitimat had been going just that much longer and had the advantage of being more mature and settled. Most of the streets were paved, and an elected municipal council was already functioning (whereas Elliot Lake was still governed by a company-appointed body; a source of some disgruntlement). Gambling, not crime, was its worst problem. But also one felt that people were happy at Kitimat and liked living there — despite its isolation. This was certainly the case with the dozen or so Britons I met. It was a good, healthy place to bring up children, and five hundred were born there in 1958 alone. Kitimat's inhabitants had obviously gained a sense of permanency from seeing that senior company executives were not stinting themselves on their houses. One, I was told, cost $100,000; and I could believe it. They were planning for a long stay in a community built to last and to grow.

When I left the Yukon at the end of September, snow was already settling on the White Pass, and on the way up, both at Prince George and the Peace River country, it had felt as if winter were just around the corner. But when the *Clifford J. Rogers* docked at Vancouver, there was still more than a promise of summer in the air. This wonderfully soft climate that the warm Japan Current gives to the southern coast of BC and neighbouring Vancouver Island resembles that of the British Isles more closely than anywhere else in North America; [1] if anything, it is even pleasanter and more reliable. It explains why two-thirds of BC's population huddle together in this one small corner, why so many elderly people head for Victoria on retirement, and why more than a third of all the Province's farms lie in the tiny, extremely fertile belt of the Lower Fraser River — except for the back-drop of mountains, for all the world like a stretch of rustic southern England.

Vancouver is the youngest of Canada's big cities, and few Canadians would dispute that it is the most beautiful of all; in its setting it is second only to San Francisco. It started life under the unpromising name of Gastown; in 1880 it had no population that the census of that year could find, six years later what there was of it was burnt to the ground by a spark from the newly established CPR compound. In 1931 Greater Vancouver had 308,000 people, today something over 650,000. Yet Vancouver is no parvenu; its wonderful position on the Fraser delta, sheltered by snow-capped mountains (which make it, I think, the only major city in the world that you can actually see from a ski-lift), was so obviously predestined to be the site of a great metropolis that one feels that at least something of it must have been there more than eighty years ago. And it seems to exist on more levels than many another North American city. There is the bustling business world of Hastings Street, full of the buoyant confidence you might find over the border in Seattle. There is the shady peacefulness of Stanley Park, with its cricket matches and elders playing chess beneath its giant cedars. There is the extra flavour provided by its

[1] It is the only part of Canada to have a January mean temperature above 32° F.

thriving Chinatown and all the smelly mysteries of a Pacific port.

Perhaps most significant of all, there are the sprouting seeds of an important cultural centre. About the first sight that caught my eyes in Vancouver was a stevedore propped up against the pile of a pier, listening to Beethoven's 'Pastoral' on a transistor radio. A recent book on the arts in Canada claims that Vancouver may be one of only two Canadian cities (Montreal being the first) with a public for concerts of Canadian works, whose curiosity about the music is beginning to outnumber the public which goes out of social or patriotic duty.[1] Doubtless inspired by its surroundings, Vancouver is producing some of the most original architects and architecture in Canada (its new skyscraper, the B.C. Electric Building, designed by a local architect and constructed by a British firm, is one of the most attractive — certainly the most striking — contemporary office designs Canada has produced for years). The Vancouver Arts Festival, which was launched the Centennial Year of 1958 with the importation of such international artists as Marcel Marceau, Bruno Walter, and the National Dancers of Ceylon, is now to take place annually and will undoubtedly give Vancouver a further cultural boost. In 1960, it brought the Peking Opera to the North American continent for the first time. Last but not least, Vancouver boasts a lively and go-ahead university — set out on a wooded point overlooking Vancouver Island, a site few other universities could rival, and with 1000 acres for expansion.

Yet, like most cities, Vancouver too has its black side. It has some nasty slums — such as 'Skidroad', a leftover from the rough past of the logging industry — on which clearance has only started. With its large Japanese and Chinese colonies, it probably suffers more from racial prejudices than any other Canadian city. Doubtless also because of these oriental colonies, it has become notorious as the narcotics capital of Canada. It has been said that there are more addicts in prison in Vancouver than are at large in the whole of Britain, and also that it has the highest addiction rate in the non-Asian world. In Chinatown, billiards saloons

---

[1] *The Culture of Contemporary Canada*, ed. by Julian Park.

display signs warning: 'Drug Pedlars Keep Out'. Closely connected with the narcotics problem, Vancouver has recently taken over from Montreal as Canada's leading crime centre.

In gold-rush days, Victoria, the Provincial capital, was once anathematised by pious San Francisco as 'the scandal of the coast'. Now it claims to be the 'biggest reading city in Canada'. A small garden city at the base of Vancouver Island, it is rightly renowned for its gentle charms and has long had a reputation for its almost aggressive Englishness. On arrival (in the tourist season) you will be taken on a sight-seeing tour in a pony and trap, through streets whose lamp-posts are festooned with baskets of flowers and whose shops are filled with tartans and shortbread, English tweed and 'English bone china'. It is the only part of Canada where the weather is problematical enough to be worth discussing at tea (or that even has tea-parties) and notices proudly inform you that it shares the same rainfall as Brighton, England. In its peaceful remoteness from the rough world, its sleepiness so much in contrast to its vigorous neighbour across the Georgia Strait, its retired Indian Army colonels and their ladies, it is perhaps the sole survival of the England of pre-1914. At least, that is what I thought when I had my first glimpse of Victoria in 1956; but after a second look two years later, I revised my opinions. Of all the great gloomy baronial piles that the CPR have scattered across Canada, the moribund interior of Victoria's Empress Hotel most resembles that of a Bournemouth hotel — but now its elderly clientele are almost exclusively retired Canadians. For with the demise of the Indian Army and the descent of the Dollar Curtain, reinforcements from Britain have been cut off. The legend of Victoria's Britishness is, one suspects, a doomed one. An English 'bobby' who used to meet tourist boats has now disappeared. Institutions like the 'Olde England Inne', with its 'Ingle-Nooke' and 'Duke of Windsor Room', are still there to offer you a bit of 'Tudor England in Canada', plus crumpets and trifle, but the thing is becoming a bit of a joke; not long ago, a Canadian merchant, bored with it all, hung a sign over his Victoria premises, advertising: 'YE OLDE WAR SURPLUS SHOPPE.'

Northwards from Victoria, over most of the 280-mile

length of Vancouver Island is what is reputed to be the largest 'stand' of lumber in the whole world. Forestry is still one of the leading sources of wealth in Canada; the pulp and paper industry alone is her largest single employer and, directly or indirectly, generates one dollar in eight of the income of all Canadians. Almost half of the world's newsprint comes from Canadian mills; about 10 per cent of all the timber used by the industries of the world originate from Canadian forests, and, as a delectable sideline, each spring they yield some two billion gallons of maple syrup. Of Canada's overall production, well over half its lumber and plywood and a large and growing proportion of its newsprint emanate from British Columbia. Few parts of the Province do more to earn BC its status as Canada's No. 1 forestry producer than Vancouver Island, where the mighty Douglas fir and hemlock, sometimes over a thousand years old, grow to the height of Nelson's Column and are often eight feet thick.

Not so very long ago, the Canadian lumberjack was a legendary figure said to shave himself with an axe, who disappeared into the woods for six months at a time. His bunkhouse quarters, a dilapidated, windowless shack might be more than fifty miles from the nearest road. There he would stay until the following year's spring thaw, living on a dreary diet of salt pork and baked beans. Women were rigidly barred from visiting the camps, because gaping loggers had been known to chop off fingers when distracted.

His tools were two-handed saw, axe (to cut down a 250-foot giant, two men would hack away interminably at its vast trunk from 'springboards', stuck into the tree 12 feet above the base), pike-pole, horse and sled. Accidents were frequent and appalling, and there was the ever-lurking menace of smallpox and typhoid in the woods. For all these hazards, the lumberjack was poorly paid, and generally out of a job half the year when gumbo and fire hazards drove the men from the forests. When he emerged to spend his savings, gambling, drinking and whoring in Skidroad, society regarded him as a separate and lower breed. 'There were 7 passengers and 12 loggers aboard the boat,' sniffed the *Victoria Times* of a generation ago.

Times have changed fantastically. As guest of Macmillan and Bloedel, the largest integrated timber concern in the Commonwealth, I spent a fascinating couple of days 'in the woods', at Port Alberni, towards the centre of Vancouver Island. Taking what seemed like a year to cover 200 yards (it is hard to describe just how difficult it is to move in the real 'forest primeval', over semi-rotten tree trunks 6 feet thick that have been piling on top of each other for thousands of years) I came across a Jugoslav and a Swede with a tiny pop-popping chain saw. Almost casually they set to work. In less than five minutes there was a chanting cry of 'Timbah toward the ro-ad', and a tree that had been growing since Chaucer was a young man came down with a roar like Niagara. There was something rather disturbing about the ease of it all.

The portable power saw is only part of the revolution that has struck the Canadian lumber industry within little more than a decade. Most important has been the new scientific concept of forestry, largely brought about by strict Government conservation measures that were introduced a few years ago. Their object was to end the appallingly wasteful methods whereby loggers would totally denude an area, then up sticks to devastate another stretch of virgin forest. These measures have now forced big companies to embark on what is aptly called 'tree farming'. For instance, Macmillan and Bloedel (their motto, 'Here Today and Here Tomorrow') have access to some 800 square miles — not, by Canadian standards, a very large area — immediately adjacent to its conversion plants, and this, it is reckoned, will suffice for all their future needs. Forestry scientists in BC think ahead in cycles of ninety years, now regarded as the optimum age for a Douglas fir, after which time the tree's growth begins to slow down. In their reserves they can 'see' enough timber today for at least another ninety years; and at the end of that time, they will come back to 'harvest' the crop being re-seeded today.

To carry out tree-farming on this scale requires stage-by-stage planning resembling a major military operation, with every stage controlled by two-way radio from 'Headquarters', which can thus switch equipment without delay from

sector to sector.   Hovering close at hand at every stage are
mobile fire-fighting crews, ready to combat the one emergency the woodsman fears most (in Canada fire, insects and
disease together consume annually as much timber as the
whole pulp and paper industry).

The impact that the new scientific 'tree farming' has had
on the life of the lumberjack is enormous.   At Port Alberni,
he commutes to work every day (as often as not in his own
last year's Chevrolet) 40 miles into the forest, and returns home
to his family every night, like any office worker.   Serious
injuries are rare, and unlike many industries in Canada, the
Vancouver Island lumberjack is now guaranteed year round
employment — that is, barring a phenomenally dry summer
such as all British Columbia experienced in 1958, when the
Government 'closed the woods' for two months.   Through
mechanisation, a 'side' with perhaps no more than a score
of men working on it can produce between 200 to 300
immense logs in one working day ; as a result, a skilful feller
(paid on piece work) can earn as much as £14 in a day.

At Port Alberni, the logs are dumped in tidewater from
seventy-ton trucks and towed in rafts down to the sorting
grounds.   Here a perilous job, formerly the lot of that
romantic figure, the log-roller, is now nimbly executed by
Indians mounted on motor 'boom-scooters'.   A cross between
a bath-tub and a marine Dodgem car, the 'scooters' tug and
buffet the great logs into one of eighteen different compounds.
After sorting, the logs go into either the plywood factory, the
saw mill — a terrifying inferno of a place, reminiscent of an
abattoir, where monster grappling irons fling the five-ton
logs about like matchsticks and howling saws rip them to
pieces in a matter of seconds — or, for the least worthy
timber, the pulp and paper mill.

Next to her forests, fish provide the basis for BC's second
most important industry.   The main difference between the
fisheries of Canada's East and West coasts is one of prosperity ;
in BC there is little or no 'subsistence' fishing, none of the
grinding poverty of the Newfoundland outports.   The reason
lies in the high value of the Pacific Sockeye, catches of which
total more than any other species of Canadian fish.   It makes
the Pacific Coast Indians as a group the most prosperous of

the indigenous Canadians; at Kitimat I was told by an
Indian leader about one of his tribe who had earned $30,000
from his salmon catch in that one bumper year. A huge
fish-processing industry has sprung up in BC over the years
and has recently become highly mechanised, employing such
gadgets as the 'Iron Chink' (so called because it can do the
work of thirty Chinamen!) that can gut and clean Sockeye
at the rate of one per second. Wages in the industry are
very good; but it is a highly seasonal occupation, limited to
the summer months when the great Sockeye runs appear at
the mouth of the Fraser.

Forced by high internal freight rates to become more and
more economically independent of the rest of Canada, BC
had developed her manufacturing industries at an exception-
ally rapid rate. In the generation since 1921, the value
of BC's manufacturing products rose from $141 to $1660
million; the number of employees from 23,000 to 101,000.
At present, nearly half of B.C.'s total output of wealth comes
from manufacturing, and this proportion is likely to increase
still further as the Province comes of age — always provided
she can find the markets.

Just prior to the war, Stephen Leacock praised BC as
'an ideal home for the human race, not too cold, not too hot,
not too wet, and not too dry, except in the hotels, a thing
which time may remedy'.[1] The 'dryness' of the hotels is
nearly a thing of the past, but there are a number of other,
rather more serious, factors that threaten to limit its idealness
in years to come. Firstly, like every other part of Canada,
BC badly needs population to provide markets for a stable
economy; not just pensioners from other Provinces, but
young people. However, although the boosters predict an
eventual population of 10 million for BC (and indeed the
Province has shown Canada's highest *consistent* rate of increase
over the past generation), over half of its 366,255 square
miles is in fact barren mountain and rock, not suitable for
habitation. A further 39 per cent is forest land; a mere 3-4
per cent is potential farmland, and (so Dr. Macleod, the
Chairman of the BC Power Commission told me) only an
estimated 5 per cent is ideal for settlement. Add to this the

[1] Stephen Leacock, *My Discovery of the West.*

fearful, expensive problem of communications. For all the blessings of tidewater, much of BC still consists of small, semi-isolated settlements, waiting patiently for the big world to join up with them. At a million dollars a mile (the cost of most of BC's section of the Trans-Canada Highway) it will be a long time coming. The aeroplane has made a big difference to communications, but it is seldom an economic form of transport. Geography and communications combined threaten to accentuate still further the lopsidedness of BC, with more and more of its population concentrated in the Southwest corner — a situation which must be bad for the rest of the Province, just as a top-heavy Ontario is bad for Canada as a whole. Then there is the nagging problem of power versus salmon, which will severely limit exploitation of the Province's enormous hydro-electric potential until a way is found for BC to have its cake and eat it too. It is also worth noting that, because of the difficulty of the terrain and high construction cost of hydro dams, power in BC actually costs the consumer more than in many other parts of Canada — and even the neighbouring state of Washington.

Still graver clouds hover over BC's beautiful horizon. In the recession, the Province has suffered probably more than any other. This was partly due to the fact that, despite the great increase and diversification of its manufacturing industries, nearly half of BC's earning potential, and 15 per cent of its labour force, were wrapped up in one commodity — trees — and as a result the Province was hard hit by the sharp world cut-back in newsprint and timber demand. At the time of writing, unemployment still appears to be more acute in BC than almost anywhere else in Canada. In November 1959 the Vancouver building trades council asked the TUC to discourage advertisements in Britain saying that Canada urgently needs all types of skilled tradesmen, on account of the number of unemployed in Vancouver even before the winter's seasonal layoffs began. There are certain serious inherent flaws in British Columbia's economy. The Province boasts the highest *per capita* incomes and the highest wages in Canada; but it also has the highest prices and the highest level of industrial unrest. In the interior of BC, I was taken round a boys' private school that had just been rebuilt after a fire. It was panelled with some particularly fine mahogany plywood. On enquiring, I was told that it was made from wood cut in the Philippines, converted into plywood in Japan, and shipped across the Pacific — where, because of BC's high wage rates and costs, it was still cheaper than the ordinary fir ply cut and processed on Vancouver Island. Anxious as BC is to increase trade with the Far East and the Commonwealth, there is a danger that she may price herself right out of the market with dollar-short trading partners.

For British Columbia, the Centennial Year of 1958 was also one of crippling industrial discontent. A strike of longshoremen closed seven major ports for over a month; the CPR steamship strike practically ruined Vancouver Island's multi-million dollar tourist industry for the year; a strike in the Teamster's Union spread to the carpenters and then to the plumbers. All this in a year when there were 20,000 unemployed in Vancouver alone. Unrest continued into the following year; in the summer of 1959 27,000 members of the Woodworkers Union struck for 66 days until they received a 10 per cent wage increase for the year, plus another 10 per cent for the following year. At Annacis Island, the huge British industrial estate under development near Vancouver, I was told that a train of strikes had set work back a whole year. Four clients had cancelled orders for the construction of factories; one was moving to Edmonton, another to Eastern Canada. Within six months Greater Vancouver lost seven large new industries; a US firm bought up a $5 million BC company manufacturing power saws, then transferred it lock, stock and barrel to Ontario — all because of the highly inflated wage rates, and particularly the unhealthy labour scene in BC.

British Columbia's labour problems peculiarly resemble those of Britain, more so than any other parts of Canada. Behind the demand for higher and higher wages, there is also a political taint. As already noted elsewhere, the CCF in British Columbia is the farthest left of all Canadian political parties, and in many cases its leaders are also local union bosses. Bearing little resemblance to Premier Douglas's moderate CCF Government in Saskatchewan, the BC CCF is pledged to carry out nationalisation to a more sweeping extent than anything hitherto achieved by a British Labour Government. With a solid 35 per cent following in BC, there is a reasonable chance that they may come to power one day; should the Liberals or Conservatives split the vote by challenging the tenuous rule of the present Social Credit Government, it would be a certainty.

There is no doubt that BC's unsettled labour scene has done, and is doing, the Province great harm. One of BC's most successful and shrewdest men confided to me that if he were younger he would 'move out', and expressed great pessimism about the future of the Province. I only hope he is wrong, and that — with the tough good sense Canadians have so much of — British Columbia will act before she sinks inextricably into the mess in which Britain has found herself.

CHAPTER SEVEN

REVOLUTION ON THE ST. LAWRENCE

Je me souviens. (Motto of Quebec Province)

'We bore oversea our prayers and our songs; they are ever the same. . . . Strangers have surrounded us whom it is our pleasure to call foreigners. . . . In this land of Quebec nought shall die and nought shall suffer change. . . .' ('The Voice of Quebec', from *Maria Chapdelaine*, by Louis Hémon, 1916)

The great question of today is how to preserve French Canadian culture, when the old pastoral, rural social order has been shattered by urbanisation; how to meet the new order, rather than merely to resist it. (Mason Wade, 1958)

THERE are many mistakes a Briton can make in Canada, but few are more foolish (or more common) than not bothering to get to grips with the French Canadians. The Province of Quebec is one of the most interesting — and remarkable — phenomena in all the Americas, and its influence on the national scene should never be under-estimated.

One of the truly remarkable things about it is that, the moment you reach the St. Lawrence travelling from the Maritimes, or cross the Ottawa River from Ontario, a hundred small things remind you of France. You will find it in the dark petiteness of the young girls, the sexual awareness in the walk of the women, the importance attached to good food (that you will not always find elsewhere in Canada), the carelessly Latin squalor of the slums of Montreal and Quebec, the doctors who ask to be paid in cash. The smocked 'habitant' ploughing his narrow strip of land down to the St. Lawrence with two massive-rumped percherons might easily be a peasant in Picardy; the gaudy *boîtes* with their pneumatic denizens on Montreal's St. Catherine Street could be on a turning off Pigalle. Get into a political argument (or better, don't) with a *Canadien*, and you will meet with that infuriating, beguiling, but invincible irrationality which Francophiles usually refer to as 'devastating French logic'. Get into a Montreal taxi and you will be as scared as on a circuit round the Étoile; when its driver is *légèrement accroché* (which happens perhaps oftener than with his more skilful Parisian counterpart — it befell me twice in ten minutes) the conversation and gesticulations that ensue, the crowd that accumulates, are well worthy of the *6ᵉ Arrondissement*. You may say it is fatuous to expect that French Canada should be anything but French; after all it was founded by Frenchmen. But what is really remarkable is that it should *still* be *so* French, when you consider that it had been deprived of all contact with the Mother Country for at least a century and a half before the first taxi rattled across the cobbles of the Concorde.

Isolated, encircled by a foreign race, and by the world's most aggressively vital culture, French Canada's survival is one of the most miraculous Toynbeean examples of a civilisation responding triumphantly to challenge. Its history has certainly had more than a fair share of challenge — and tragedy.

The New France pioneered by Champlain barely had a chance from the beginning. The two great French kings had little interest in it; Louis XIV was more concerned in the aggrandisement of his European territories; Louis XV in his infatuation for Pompadour, than in the development of what Voltaire dismissed as a 'few acres of snow'. Few serious attempts at colonisation were made. Cardinal Richelieu tried and failed. In despair at the stagnancy of the colony's numbers, one of its ablest administrators, the Intendant Talon, issued draconian edicts forbidding unmarried males to 'hunt, fish, or go into the woods'. Intransigent Benedicks among the '*coureurs du bois*' were to be branded. To aid the procreation drive, a thousand French maidens — hand-picked by Madame de Maintenon — were shipped out to Quebec in 1682. But it was all to no avail. Like Britons of a later age, Frenchmen preferred to stay at home rather than people 'the Empire' — and risk scalping or frostbite. There was indeed little enough attraction to settlement in New France; most of the land was divided into '*seigniories*', often the property of absentee landlords in France. Commerce was in the hands of monopolies in France; military advancement was limited to the favourites of powers at Court (during the final, and most crucial, period, those of Madame de Pompadour). It was administered, paternally, as a Province of France, with only a fraction of the power over its own affairs possessed by the British colonies of New England. 'New France was all head. Under King, noble, and Jesuit, the lank, lean body could not thrive', while in New England there was 'slow but steady growth, full of blood and muscle — a body without a head'.[1]

French-Canadian historians estimate that little more than 10,000 permanent settlers actually crossed the ocean to New France. By 1760 its population numbered only 60,000; [2] Britain's American Colonies then totalled somewhere in the region of 1,300,000. But for the incompetence of successive British expeditions, and the half-heartedness of British governments, New France should in fact have succumbed fifty years earlier than it did. When at last, riddled by the corruption of its administrators and overwhelmed by numbers, it collapsed before Wolfe and Murray, in France Voltaire threw a bonfire party to celebrate.

With their long memories, the French Canadians never forgave France the exultations of Voltaire and Pompadour; nor the cynicism with which French politicians wrote off the colony, arguing (with some foresight) that, unredeemed, it would prove more of a thorn in the side of Britain than an asset to France. After the French Revolution, devout Quebec finally turned her back on anti-clerical France. From that day to this, there has been hardly any contact between the two peoples; in 1957, the year of the last great European exodus, only 2 per cent of the 280,000 immigrants came from France. At a dinner-party in Los Angeles a few years ago, a French-Canadian diplomat with a French wife expatiated to me on his people's struggle to preserve their identity, then lamented that the trickle of new French stock immigrating to Canada tended to 'side' with the Anglo-Canadians rather than with its own kin. Later his wife took me aside

---

[1] Francis Parkman, *Pioneers of France in the New World.*
[2] Today the original 10,000 has grown to nearly 5,000,000 in Canada alone; there are another estimated 2,000,000 of French-Canadian stock outside the country, principally in the United States.

K

and said : 'Are you surprised ? The France they think of is
the France of the Bourbons. We hardly even have the same
language in common any more.' As she herself had discovered, for all the astonishing, small similarities, in big ways
there is a very, very wide gulf between the two ; in reality,
Quebec is no more modern France than English Canada is
an extension of Britain.

After the Conquest of 1760 Canada settled down fairly
comfortably under British rule. Many of Wolfe's Catholic
Highlanders remained, married local girls, and to this day
you can find in small Quebec villages Frasers and Macdonalds speaking only French, and perhaps still a smattering
of Gaelic. From Britain came some of the ablest administrators she has ever produced, and the terms they brought
were mild even by the standards of 18th-century 'reasonable-
ness'. Admittedly, there were political motives in the
background, nevertheless the early history of the French
Canadians under British rule makes an interesting comparison
to France under the Germans, or Eastern Europe under the
Russians, in the enlightened 20th century. By the Quebec
Act of 1774, French Canada was guaranteed 'conciliation
and toleration' and — above all — religious freedom ; promises that were faithfully kept by successive British governments. In fact, so generous were these terms that they
provoked a storm of indignation in New England, which had
had a vital stake in the campaign against Canada, and the
Quebec Act constituted one of the 'Intolerable Acts' that
sparked off the American Revolution a year later. The
Canadiens duly noted the thunderings from the Puritan pulpits
of Boston. When the Americans captured and held Montreal
for a few months, Benjamin Franklin set up a propaganda
press in the cellar of the Château de Ramezay, but, for all
his notable success in wooing Paris, he totally failed to win
the hearts of the French of Canada. In the War of 1812, as
in 1775, they remained loyal to Britain ; in their eyes, the
American Protestants a few hundred miles away presented a
far greater menace to their way of life than the remote and
laissez-faire British.

The post-1775 influx into what is now Ontario of thousands of U.E. Loyalists (still to this day looked upon by many

Québeçois as 'Americans') brought a new challenge to French Canada. This challenge was stated in black and white in the famous Durham Report of 1839 (compiled after rebellions in both French and British Canada two years earlier), when the author declared that the best way to achieve stability would be to 'swamp' the French by weight of numbers. Though the Report was one of the most far-sighted documents in British history, and eventually paved the way to Canadian Federation under the British North America Act thirty years later, for this one rash statement the name of Durham is still anathema to French Canadians.

To the threat of 'swamping', they retaliated with one of the most remarkable feats of sustained reproduction the world has ever seen, sometimes known as the '*revanche du berceau*'. As a result French Canada still accounts for nearly one-third of the whole country. Rallying round the Church as the focal point of 'passive resistance' (because it was the one institution they knew they still controlled), generation after generation the French Canadians pursued a deliberate policy of withdrawal — to protect their own culture behind barricades of '*nos institutions, notre langue et nos lois*'. For long years prior to 1867, French-Canadian fears of being 'swamped' in the Federal Parliament deadlocked talks on Federation. In 1899 there was bitter resistance in Quebec to participation in the Boer War, which it felt was purely a British affair. In 1914–18, though French Canada supported entry into the war, the cause of anti-clerical France had no emotional claims, and in 1917 one of the worst racial crises in Canada's history broke out over the conscription issue. Previously the heroic Canadian Expeditionary Force had been maintained entirely by volunteers, but after the fearful losses on the Somme, conscription became inevitable. It was badly handled by the Conservative Prime Minister, Sir Robert Borden, who had made the unfortunate appointment of an anti-Catholic Ulsterman, Sir Sam Hughes, as Minister of Militia. There were riots throughout Quebec, and the affair left a wound in French Canada that was a long time healing. Nationalist leaders urged that goods be bought only from French-Canadian firms, and there was talk about forming a separate state, 'Laurentia'.

During the inter-war period, French Canada was openly isolationist. When the Canadian representative to the League of Nations in 1935 proposed the stiffening of sanctions against Italy, he was disavowed by his Government under strong pressure from Quebec's Catholic hierarchy. In the Second World War the issues seemed even remoter to French Canada; as an American writer commented in 1942 — 'no one has yet succeeded in convincing the French Canadian that he would be defending Quebec if he would die in the sands of Libya'.[1] Again conscription raised its head, and opposition to it threatened to become even more violent; songs like '*A bas, la Conscription*' (sung to the tune of 'God Save the King') and '*L'Angleterre est en guerre, ce n'est pas de nos affaires*' made their appearance in Quebec. Marshal Pétain gained more sympathy than any French leader for a long time — because he had led France out of the war. In 1958 I could still make out the word 'DARLAN' painted in large letters on the wall of Quebec's Citadel. A plebiscite on conscription brought an almost 100 per cent 'No' from purely French-Canadian communities, and a Member of the Quebec Legislature, René Chaloult, went so far as to propose that the Province should secede from the Confederation if conscription were imposed. However, despite the resignation of his Minister of Defence, Prime Minister Mackenzie King managed to take the sting out of the conscription issue by a policy of compromise, not universally admired in English Canada, but one which history may record as being his greatest contribution to Canadian unity. Fortunately the war ended before King's policy was put to the breaking test.

It would be grossly unfair to the French Canadians to end this potted history without pointing out that there have been exceptions, brilliant exceptions, to the policy of withdrawal. Some of Canada's great statesmen have originated from Quebec, men like Louis Lafontaine, Georges Cartier and Ernest Lapointe who have put the interests of the nation above those of their own people; Sir Wilfrid Laurier, one of the very greatest, who did perhaps more than any other man to unite Canada into a nation, and at the same time was devoted to Britain; and, more recently, Louis St. Laurent,

[1] W. H. Chamberlin, *Canada, Today and Tomorrow.*

who was so largely responsible for the inception of NATO. In both World Wars, French-Canadian volunteers fought with unexcelled gallantry. I think my most moving experience in Canada was to watch the Retreat at the Citadel in Quebec carried out by the Royal 22nd Regiment, whose action at Courcelette was one of the great feats of heroism on the Somme. Up and down the Plains of Abraham, where Wolfe and Montcalm had fought each other to the death, they marched with the precision of Buckingham Palace drill, in red tunics and bearskins barely distinguishable from those of the Brigade of Guards, yet to orders given in French; a sight that symbolises all that is noblest in the British Commonwealth, all that it should be. And now the most distinguished soldier of 'Van Doos' has become the new Governor-General, the first time in exactly two centuries for the supreme post in Canada to be held by someone of French descent.

Since the war, a multi-pronged revolution has been creeping across French Canada. Gradual rather than sudden, its effects have been none the less drastic. For the first time in history, Canada's new industrial revolution has reached to the farthest corners of Quebec Province. War urgency gave the Province a big boost with the creation of a large aluminium industry. Today, Quebec also has about half of Canada's aircraft industry; is second only to Ontario in manufacturing and mining. It has the largest developed hydro-electric resources in Canada, nearly half the country's total horsepower, and the biggest pulp and paper industry. It has become the country's shipbuilding centre, and leads Canada in primary textiles (an industry that was already flourishing in 1760). High wages in industry have lured more and more French Canadians away from the farms; although Quebec still has the largest rural population in the country, it, too, has experienced the nation-wide driftage from the farms — between 1951 and 1956 alone numbers on the farms declined by 10 per cent and some 900,000 acres went out of cultivation. Of Quebec's five million inhabitants, well over three million now live in towns and cities; almost half a million are engaged in manufacturing, as opposed to less than 200,000 in agriculture.

In the cities, contact with other Canadian workers and the influence of the trade unions has opened a far wider world to the young French Canadian. Prosperity has even had its effect in the smallest St. Lawrence villages; at St. Justin (population 1583), for instance, a social-investigator[1] discovered in 1955 that for every three households there were two cars, one tractor, one television set and two telephones. Nearly each one had a radio, a washing-machine and a refrigerator.

To many *Canadiens*, the impact industrialisation has had upon the old social pattern is something of a blessing. A Quebec Rhodes Scholar remarked to me: 'I think it is a good thing that the isolation of the Province should be broken down. In my grandfather's day there was no railway, no roads outside the city; Quebec knew nothing of the outside world.' But this blessing is a mixed one. Within it lies also a double challenge, both cultural and economic, to French Canada's identity perhaps graver than any she has had to meet in the past. It used to be said that in Montreal 'the English own everything, the French do all the work'. There was much truth in the saying. After the Conquest, it was the merchants from Britain and New England who had all the capital; the *Canadiens* retreated to their farms, or went into the Church, law, medicine or politics — the only professions where they could really excel. A prominent Montreal professor told me that, although his people numbered a third of Canada's population, their share in the nation's economy was only 10 per cent — in terms of company control, it was perhaps less than 1 per cent. Since the war, the French Canadians have watched the great new dams and industries in Quebec being constructed by Anglo-Canadian and American engineers — because there was virtually no technical training for their own people. At the same time, they have seen their birth-rate dropping till it is no longer the highest in Canada;[2] in terms of numbers per family, Quebec now

---

[1] Philip Garigue, *St. Justin: A Case Study in Rural French-Canadian Social Organization.*

[2] A senior official in the Immigration Service, a French Canadian, remarked to me somewhat explosively in Ottawa: 'This . . . nonsense of *la revanche du berceau* is a thing of the past. If we wanted to base a society on sexual potency, I would go and live among the Zulus.'

comes only fourth among the Canadian Provinces, and all the time new and highly skilled hands are pouring in from Europe at the highest rate in Canadian history. The new, and deadliest, threat of assimilation was that the industrial exploitation of Quebec might be carried out *without* French Canada getting a share in it. The challenge was participate or abdicate.

There are diehard traditionalists in both Church and politics still dedicated to the course defined by Monsignor Paquet in 1902: 'Our mission is less to manipulate capital than to change ideas; it consists less in lighting the fires of factories than in maintaining and making radiate afar the luminous fire of religion and thought.' But the tide is now running strongly in favour of 'participation' and progress in Quebec. Within the last five years, in the teeth of strong opposition, new engineering, science and commercial faculties have been opened at Laval and Montreal Universities. The latter already has the largest engineering section in Canada. But in meeting the economic challenge, even the progressives among Quebec's intellectuals realise that French Canada may be exposing herself to the far greater danger of eventual cultural assimilation. They have watched the industrialisation of the rest of Canada bring with it Americanisation, and radio and TV spread its potent influence even to the farthest corners of Quebec; and they have watched prosperous peasants on the Ile d'Orléans bulldoze their centuries-old *habitations*, the last links with New France, in the interests of modernity. Where will it all end? In their eyes it is largely the existence of French-Canadian culture that gives Canada as a whole any distinctive character. There is indeed some force behind their arguments; as will be seen in a later chapter, French Canada probably contributes more than her share to the Arts, and indirectly the stimulus she gives them is even greater. If traditional French-Canadian values were to become totally submerged beneath the conformism of North America's materialist gods, Canada would undoubtedly lose something of immeasurable value. To protect it, to devise a modified philosophy to meet the challenges of the latter 20th century, a restless battle is in progress among the intellects of Quebec.

Since the war, French Canada's attitude to the nation and the world outside has also undergone radical changes. Or, rather, it has *been* changed by events. The atmosphere was different. Mackenzie King's compromise over conscription had ensured that there was none of the bitterness of 1918. Then there was the growth of Canadian nationalism as a whole, and the altered status of Britain as head of the Commonwealth. A French-speaking senior officer of one of the Canadian services commented to me: 'Some French Canadians never thought they were part of the British Empire. This was just a temporary measure they had to put up with. They did not want to fight *British Empire* wars, but now we are part of a marvellous organisation called the Commonwealth, not even the *British* Commonwealth . . . so French Canada is no longer on the isolationist band-wagon.'

But no single factor has contributed to hauling French Canada off the isolationist band-wagon more than the threat of Russia. For the first time since 1812, Quebec sees the threat of battle brought to her very door by the jet-bomber and now the ICBM. And in Communist, atheist Russia they see a far more insidious threat to their way of life than ever was presented by Puritan New England — let alone Nazi Germany. This has had a further effect of bringing French Canadians out of their shells. Since Korea, recruitment for the armed forces in Quebec has never been so high. In the RCAF, the proportion of French-speaking personnel is estimated to be well over the national ratio of 1:3. For the first time, the General Staff in Ottawa had a French Canadian, Major-General J. V. Allard, CBE, DSO, as its Vice-Chief.

In the past, one of the chief hindrances to recruitment in Quebec has been the lack of facilities for training French-speaking officers. Previously they had to go to the RMC at Kingston, Ontario, where they were doubly at a disadvantage in that all courses were in English, and the college itself run according to the educational system of Ontario, very different indeed to Quebec's. To get over this problem, in 1952 Mr. St. Laurent's Government founded the Collège Militaire Royal, expressly — but not exclusively — designed for the training of French-Canadian cadets. It is perhaps the most significant attempt ever made to bring together the two races.

The Collège is at St. Jean, some thirty miles from Montreal, on a site where a desperate battle was once fought against invading New Englanders, and housed in barracks (ironically enough) that were built for British regulars brought in to quell the French-Canadian rebellion of 1837. It is unique in being both tri-service and bilingual. Any Canadian, or British subject resident in Canada, can enter, but he will not receive a commission unless he can, by the end of his training, speak both languages 'coherently'. When I visited it, over 60 per cent out of a total of 364 cadets were French Canadian. All members of the staff have to be bilingual. The Commandant, Group Captain Archambault, AFC, was a charming and courteous French Canadian who had served with Coastal Command during the war. His Chief Instructor, Mr. C. A. Chabot, had degrees from universities in both Quebec and Ontario.

During the first fifteen days of the month, French is the 'language of the day' at St. Jean; for the remainder of the month, English. According to the date, everything takes place in the prevailing language; lectures, orders and all conversation. The rule is rigidly enforced; for the last fifteen days of the month, even the Commandant — he assured me — dictates to his French-Canadian secretary in English. Visiting speakers, often to their embarrassment, are also expected to comply. Each 'Squadron' of the Collège is composed equally of the two races, who, wherever possible, are made to room together. During their first summer, cadets are sent to visit units of their respective services right the way across Canada — thereby seeing places and people that only a few years ago might have remained forever foreign to a *Canadien* from a small St. Lawrence village.

The important thing about the Collège Militaire Royal is that, in its short existence, it seems to be succeeding remarkably well in dropping the barriers. During lunch at St. Jean, I asked the cadet sitting next to me — he was a Montrealer with a very English name — which branch of the services he was going to when he got his commission.

'To the army,' he replied. 'And I hope to the "Van Doos".
I've got a tremendous admiration for the French Canadians.
I think we're just as responsible as they for the barriers that
have grown up in the past, and its time we got rid of them.
It's up to our generation.'

I was impressed by the words of this 20-year old cadet;
his seemed to me the voice of Canada's future; I knew
exactly what he meant about French Canada not being
solely responsible for the 'barriers'. That same morning,
the RCAF driver who had picked me up in Montreal — a
Torontonian in his forties — had grumbled : 'I don't like
Montreal. These people are different to us. I don't understand them. I don't speak their language and I don't want
to.' As the editor of one of Canada's leading English-
speaking magazines remarked to me : 'There's more intolerance outside the Province of Quebec than inside'. His own
magazine was making its contribution towards breaching the
barriers by bringing out a French-language edition, a unique
experiment in Canada. But English Canada still has far
to go to meet French Canada half-way; throughout the
country I was astonished how few Canadians spoke any
French at all, how indifferently it was taught in most of the
schools. Of the genuine bilingualists, the overwhelming
majority, even in the Province of Quebec, are the French
Canadians. The *Québeçois* — outside the smallest villages —
who speaks no word of English is an exception ; the Ontarian
who speaks French is almost a freak.

Though to an outsider like myself the changes in French
Canada seem immense, many an English Canadian on the
spot remains sceptical. Edgar M. Collard of the *Montreal
Gazette*, historian and expert on French Canada, told me :
'I do not believe there has been any "revolution" in Quebec.
I have seen it said too often in the past twenty years.' He
referred me to a hysterical attack on the *Gazette* made that
very day by *Le Devoir*. The *Gazette*, which prides itself on
pursuing a policy of conciliation ('you can't change the
French Canadians by attacking them'), had published a
fairly innocuous political analysis of a rift between the Mayor
of Montreal and his party. In return, *Le Devoir* had scorched
it for treating Quebec political leaders with a condescending

tolerance normally reserved for the 'negro king' of a 'colony of exploitation'. Behind the one word 'colony' lay all the bitterness of two centuries.

But *Le Devoir* is *Le Devoir*, the last redoubt of rigid traditionalism in Quebec. And I strongly suspect that when French Canada — especially *progressive* French Canada — speaks to Canadians, it speaks with two voices. There is what it is really thinking, and there is the 'Voice of Quebec', the voice of unity, employed when speaking out across the barricades. One morning at Montreal University, I was treated to a brilliant discourse (in English, I am ashamed to say) on the problems of French Canada by one of her top historians, Professor Michel Brunet. Outspokenly he accused French Canada of 'refusing to face economic facts'. 'Over the past four generations,' he said, 'we have formed what psychologists might call a "compensation mechanism". We said, "we are more spiritual, we have a higher civilisation", as *compensation* for our economic failures.' That same morning, he told me, a student newspaper had accused him of going too far and being 'morbidly defeatist' towards the cause of French-Canadian 'Nationalism'. Yet, a short while later, I was reading a speech the Professor himself had just made to English Canadians at the University of Toronto, in which he expounded a theme as potently nationalist and traditionalist as if it had been made by the late Premier Duplessis himself.

Not everything has changed in the Province of Quebec. On the western slopes of Mount Royal there stands a huge white basilica, called St. Joseph's Oratory. It is one of the landmarks of Montreal, and its story is a remarkable one. Some seventy years ago, the porter at Notre Dame College, a humble lay-brother, developed a habit of praying to St. Joseph (the patron saint of French Canada) at a clearing in the undergrowth of Mount Royal. Later he placed a small statue of the saint on the site, with a collection box by it. By 1904 the offerings enabled him to build a tiny 18 × 15-foot chapel to house the statue. Six years later, reports of miraculous cures and conversions had begun to draw large crowds, and work was started on a three-storey rectory for priests serving the chapel. In 1915 the foundations of a huge crypt were laid, and today — though still unfinished — the Oratory, 316 feet high and 340 feet long, and already enlarged four times through the offerings initiated by Brother André, the college porter, is the largest sanctuary in the world to St. Joseph. When Brother André died, aged 91, over 500,000 people attended his lying-in-state. Since then, he has become looked on almost as a saint, his heart and other relics embalmed in places of honour within the Oratory, and showered with little notes of supplication left by the three million who visit the Oratory each year. The devout pilgrims climbing the 99 steps to the crypt on their knees, the racks of abandoned crutches and the museum attesting the miracles of St. Joseph within, are symbolic of the intensity of religious faith throughout French Canada. As ever, the Catholic Church is the supreme power of the land, exerting a greater influence than it does perhaps anywhere else in the modern world.

French Canada still clings as tenaciously as any Southern State to the 'Provincial Rights' granted her under the BNA Act. Though criminal cases are tried under British law, all civil disputes come under the Code Napoléon. Women's rights in Quebec (and this, of course, applies to English Canadians as well) are little in advance of what they were in Britain a century ago ; they cannot buy, sell or own property without their husband's permission. Until 1932 they were not even entitled to keep their own wages, and errant wives may still be 'corrected' by physical punishment. But first and foremost come Quebec's separate, religious schools ; a privilege that will be jealously guarded for as long as the Province exists. Since the war the interference of the ultramontane clergy in education has been greatly reduced, nevertheless the present Government in Quebec, in its determination to have complete autonomy over all education within the Province, still persists in refusing Federal grants to its universities ; a stand which has done McGill great harm. It has also declined to participate in such Federal projects as the Trans-Canada Highway, the national hospitalisation scheme, and Alvin Hamilton's plans for joint development of the North ; and in 1954 its reluctance to co-operate with the Federal taxation policy agreed on by all the other Provinces very nearly led to a crisis comparable to the lethal conscription issue.

Much of the rigidity that still lingers in official relations between Quebec and Ottawa can be traced to the past influence of one man; the late Maurice Duplessis. Politics are the *Canadien's* great love (perhaps rivalled only by ice hockey), he is a great deal more politically conscious than his fellow Canadians, and on only one occasion has a Federal Government come to power without winning a majority in Quebec. Foreseeing the landslide that was to sweep Mr. Diefenbaker into power in 1958, Quebec overnight switched from its traditional support of the (Federal) Liberals — so as to be arrayed with the side in power (a fact which French Canadians openly admit). Politician supreme in a race of politicians, Mr. Duplessis, the former leader of the Union Nationale and Premier of Quebec, was as astute and mobile in his tactics as he was inflexible and dogmatic in his philosophy. For nearly a quarter of a century — with only one interruption — Duplessis reigned over Quebec virtually as patriarchal dictator, unashamedly favouring friends of the Party in public contracts, and maintaining the cultural barricades as high as possible. In the official guide-book to Quebec City, his many re-elections are listed, along with Cartier and Champlain, as 'Historic Data'. At the opening of a new bridge some years ago, Duplessis expressed the hope that it would last 'as long as my Party'. The bridge collapsed the following year, but the ultra-Conservative Union Nationale carried on. However, the forces of progress were beginning to mount against Duplessis; even *La Presse*, one of the most influential French-Canadian papers, and the biggest French daily outside France, showed signs of turning against him. Then, in the summer of 1959, there occurred two events of great significance to French Canada; Major-General George P. Vanier was appointed Governor-General, the first French Canadian ever to hold the office; and Maurice Duplessis died of a cerebral haemorrhage. A matter of months afterwards, the man he had groomed for the succession also died in office, and a young Liberal, Jean Lesage, came in to bring an end to the Duplessis era and perhaps the beginning of a new one in the history of Quebec's relations with the rest of Canada. Given time they may grow from what a French writer, André Siegfried, once aptly described as 'a *modus vivendi* without cordiality' into something warmer; given time, racial acrimony may become limited to the hockey matches at Montreal's Forum.

Quebec is a huge Province, easily the largest in Canada, and nearly equalling in size British Columbia and Alberta combined. It is the only Province with a large chunk of territory above the 6oth Parallel, and only Ontario and a fragment of Nova Scotia extend farther to the south. Its great sweep of uninhabited, virtually unexplored Northland dwarfs even Northern Ontario — and it is full of riches. Within living memory the mining camps of Noranda and Val d'Or have grown into important settlements, and more recently gold and copper have brought men to the Chibougamau area, midway between the St. Lawrence and Hudson Bay. Aluminium smelters, including the world's largest at Arvida, have opened up the Lake St. John country, the 'wilderness' of *Maria Chapdelaine*. Little more than five years ago the Iron Ore Company of Canada established Schefferville, a town of 4000, on the empty marches of Labrador and New Quebec. But still, as ever, the great bulk of Quebec's population cling to the narrow, fertile strip along the valley of the St. Lawrence.

Even French Canada's ancient stronghold of Quebec City has been struck by the new industrial revolution. During the second quarter of the 20th century its population grew from a hundred thousand to a quarter of a million; though its English-speaking minority has remained at a steady 15,000. Many of them have been there a long time; its *Chronicle Telegraph* claims to be the oldest newspaper in the Commonwealth, founded in 1764. But, despite industrialisation, Quebec has retained its principal, traditional significance as a religious, intellectual and political centre. Henry James once described it as a 'small dead capital. . . . Its evenings must be as dull as the evenings described by Balzac in his *Vie de province*. . . .' The restraining hand of the Church still rests heavy on Quebec (there must be more nuns and priests per square inch of its narrow streets than in any other city in the world); night-clubs are banned, and the

leading paper, *Action Catholique*, refuses to advertise films —
deeming them immoral. If he could revisit Quebec today,
Henry James (his judgment always a little influenced by that
New England background) would no doubt find many things
that would give him no cause to revise his hard verdict of
eighty years ago. But I think he would be wrong. From
what little I saw of Quebec life behind the scenes, I felt there
might be much more gaiety and colour and zest to it than
appearances would suggest.

Presiding Olympically and aloof on its great rock, a city
of handsome monuments and terraces and charming high-
gabled houses, Quebec amply deserves all the eulogies that
have been poured forth on its beauty. But — to a European
— it is historically a little disappointing. Wolfe left little
enough of the old city, but much of what survived has
been destroyed subsequently by that peculiarly Canadian
hazard, fire, or by sheer neglect. It is depressing to discover
that Jolliet's house in the Lower City — one of the oldest
in Quebec — has been converted into the terminal of an
ascenseur to the Upper City. And everywhere there are the
intrusive signs of the Americanisation that the Quebec
traditionalists fear above all else; the Coca Cola signs, the
garage lighting up the historic Ursuline Convent with its
neon-lit 'Service With A Smile'.

Canada's great cities of the Prairies, could, one often
feels, have sprung up almost anywhere on that vast open
field. Even Toronto might have been planted elsewhere on
the flat shore of Lake Ontario, within a hundred miles of its
present location. But a great city inevitably had to grow
where Montreal now lies, on its island so strategically placed
amid the great waterway, with its seven-hundred-foot mound
of Mount Royal towering out of the lowlands. When
Cartier first planted his wooden cross on the summit of the
Mount, he must have appreciated the potential of the island
which was then the site of an Indian village called Hochelaga.
Cartier discovered Montreal Island in 1535, but, lying deep
as it did in hostile Indian territory, it was not until 1642 that
de Maisonneuve actually established a settlement there. For
many years, Ville Marie, as it was called, led an exciting but

precarious existence as a frontier outpost behind its strong palisades. It was from Ville Marie that the great French explorers of the 17th century, Dulhut, Cadillac and La Salle, set forth on their voyages. Lachine, one of the suburbs of modern Montreal and once La Salle's *seigniorie*, reputedly gained its name in derision at La Salle's attempts to find a sea-route to China. The early settlements on Montreal Island lived under constant fear of attack by the ferocious Iroquois, and a peak of horror was reached with the Lachine massacre of 1689. Some two hundred men, women and children were slaughtered; an act of vengeance for the treachery of a French Governor who two years previously had shipped off large numbers of friendly Iroquois to the galleys of the French Navy. At last, a regiment of regular troops was sent from France and for the first time the Montrealers could sleep in peace at night. Twice again Montreal, as it became known in the 18th century, found itself a front-line town; with its capture by the British in 1760, and by the American revolutionaries (for a brief period) fifteen years later.

It was after the capitulation of 1760, with the advent of the hard-headed Scottish fur-traders of the Northwest Company that Montreal, always an important fur-trading depot, began its transformation into a major commercial centre. The McGillivrays, McTavishes and Frasers laid the basis of the great city that Montreal is today; they also imparted to it much of its flavour, grafting a sturdy sprig of Scottish sobriety on to its volatile French stock.

The conflicting ingredients that compose modern Montreal are what make it one of North America's most exciting and intriguing cities; a 'sociologist's paradise', it has been called. The ingredients conflict, but they also overlap. In the 'down-town' business world of Montreal, the mighty Anglo-Scottish-Canadian counting-houses on St. James Street, heirs to the 'Nor'westers', rub shoulders with the Mairie and the ancient waterfront houses of the original Ville-Ste.-Marie. A few yards from the French-Canadian church of Notre-Dame with its lovely carved wooden screen and altar are the new law courts where criminal cases are tried by British law; near by, the old law courts where civil

French Canadian farmers tilling the ancestral way at Baie St. Paul

IN QUEBEC PROVINCE

French and American influences in the old city of Quebec

Helicopter view of the Labrador 'Shield' in mid-October

New school and church at Schefferville, Northern Quebec

cases are dealt with under the Code Napoléon. At each intersection, the carefully balanced street signs of 'Dorchester Street' and 'Rue St.-Maurice' proclaim the dual personality of Montreal and its spirit of (sometimes precarious) compromise. Under the shadow of towering North American office blocks, peaceful little squares with fountains lurk in hiding to surprise you with a pleasant reminder of a French city. Along St. Catherine Street, Montreal's smart shopping centre, great department stores bearing Anglo-Saxon names stand cheek by jowl with dress shops displaying an unmistakable neo-Parisian *chic* in their windows; up the side turnings that run into Sherbrooke, where the smart hotels belong more to Mayfair than either Paris or New York, restaurants with delectably Gallic menus coexist disdainfully with drug-stores and self-service lunch counters.

In the residential areas, divisions are more closely defined. Running down one side of the great barrow of Mount Royal, the straight edge of St. Laurent marks out a tarmac frontier. Eastward lies a solid section of Montreal's French-speaking two-thirds. Streets of characteristically subdivided houses, the first floors with their separate outside staircases descending to the pavement in graceful cast-iron swirls, eventually give way to over-populated slums as depressing as anything in Paris or London; defeated rows of square, painted-over brick dwellings, with decaying wood verandahs and huge washing-lines. Westward, gazing haughtily down on the city from the sylvan slopes of the Mount, where incomes rise according to altitude, lie the stately homes of the fur barons and today's tycoons. Local bye-laws are strict in this part of Montreal; you must have at least three trees in your garden and mow the lawn once a week (winter excepted). Past the mansions of the English-speaking elite trot the little *calèches*, bearing sightseers to the top of the Mount, whence, on a clear day you can see the green mountains of Vermont, away in the United States, beyond the great flood of the St. Lawrence. Like the taxi drivers, the *calèche* men are almost all *Canadien*; perhaps a tacit reminder to French-Canadian nationalists that there is still truth in the saying about who does the work and who reaps the benefits in Montreal. Yet, on the other side of the Mount, in the many prosperous-looking

L

French-Canadian villas at Outremont, there is evidence
for anyone who wants it that this is at best only a part
truth. Also on the far side of the Mount, beyond St. Joseph's
Oratory, is a large enclave of Montreal's Jewish community
(amounting to about a third of Canada's total Jewish population of nearly 300,000), which — together with a populous
Italian component — contributes greatly to the cosmopolitan
flavour of Montreal.

A hundred years ago, a visiting Briton wrote of Montreal,
'you cannot fancy you are in America; everything about it
conveys the idea of a substantial, handsomely built European
town, with modern improvements of half English, half
French architecture . . .'.[1] Today Montreal has become
more American, but it has still not lost its European flavour.
If Toronto bears resemblance to New York, architecturally
Boston is Montreal's counterpart. Technical innovations,
like Vancouver's BC Electric skyscraper and Toronto's new
City Hall, have, one feels, no place in Montreal. It is a city
of sober grey stone, quarried from the Laurentians; dignified
and imposing in the way that Boston is. When the first grey
skies of winter appear over the Mount one could wish the
city had more colour; but, beneath its austere Caledonian
surface, colour is there all right. Renowned for immorality
even in its earliest days as an outpost of the fur-trade,
Montreal has a reputation that still attracts the curious and
the meretricious from all over North America. Its strip-
tease *boîtes* are on a scale that rivals Montmartre, though
perhaps a little lacking in true Parisian light-heartedness, and
its pavement newsvendors can offer with impunity a selection
of forty sex sheets — all local produce. Few months go by
without a lively feud between rival newspapers, or news of
some scandal in local government; elections are often en-
livened by the mass invalidation of votes, caused by so-called
'goons' of a political faction raiding and carrying off the
ballot boxes from a polling station. Montrealers are seldom
left at a loss for a topic of conversation on local affairs.

Now overlapping its original island on all sides, Montreal
has grown hugely since the war, leaving its traffic facilities

[1] Lieut.-Colonel B. W. A. Sleigh, '*Pine Forests and Hacmatack Clearings*',
London, 1853, from *Early Travellers in the Canadas*.

far behind. The bridges leaving the city are hopelessly over-taxed, and driving out to the Laurentians one summer Sunday afternoon was the nearest I came to feeling over-crowded in Canada. Yet, for all its growth, Montreal has somehow preserved its character in a way that Toronto has not; perhaps helped by the fact that its Mount and its Dominion Square, watched over by a cathedral copied minutely from St. Peter's, lend it both a geographical fulcrum and a city centre of gravity that Toronto seems to lack. Montreal is, at least in my opinion, the only Canadian city (and one of possibly only half a dozen in all North America) that genuinely fulfils a European's notion of a *Metropolis*. With its two great universities, its thriving theatre and numerous art galleries, its wealth of excellent restaurants, it is an important intellectual, cultural and gastronomic centre. Its beautiful hinterland of the Laurentians, its French influences, and its own attractiveness as a city com-bine to make it possibly a pleasanter and more stimulating place to live in than Toronto.

Commercially, however — although with a population approaching one and three-quarter million metropolitan Montreal is still easily Canada's largest city — its position of pre-eminence is fast being challenged by its more rapidly growing rival. In some ways, traditional positions have been reversed. A century ago Montreal was the capital of the speculators — the railway builders and the fur-traders — Toronto the more conservative city. Today maturity seems to have given Montreal's business world a conservativism that matches the externals of its sober architecture and surface of Scottish respectability, more than its underlying French ebullience; Toronto has become the gambler's town. Its stock exchange has out-stripped Montreal's; it is the mining centre of Canada, and now also the banking head-quarters.

Montreal, however, remains — for the time being — the hub of the biggest manufacturing and industrial concentra-tion in Canada; in the last fifteen years, more than 5000 new enterprises have been added to this concentration, and future developments include $300 million worth of plants projected by Canada's two leading steel companies. It is still the headquarters of the two great railway companies, and its Dorval airport is among the busiest in North America. But above all it clings avidly to its reputation as one of the world's greatest inland ports; one ascendancy it will probably never cede to Toronto. Each year, early in April, ships' horns in the river interrupt the long winter silence, and skippers of ocean vessels from all over the world vie for the gold-tipped cane awarded to the first to arrive in Montreal when the ice breaks up. For the next eight months, liners from Britain carrying cargoes of immigrants surge up the thousand miles of the St. Lawrence, to share Montreal's ten miles of berthing accommodation with the great dachshund-like grain boats from the Lake-head and the red-dyed iron-ore boats from Seven Islands. Although nobody is quite sure yet how the new Seaway will affect the port of Montreal, on the assumption that trade will surely expand, vast new works of modernisation and expansion are already under way.

Apart from Montreal, the stronghold of the English Canadians in the Province of Quebec is the 'Eastern Townships', the slice of land lying southeast of the St. Lawrence with a population of about 350,000. It is lovely country, much like the New England states it borders, whence came the Loyalist ancestors of many of its present settlers. Most of it is fertile farmland, with the accent on dairy farming, and it enjoys the rare advantage for Canada in having large markets close at hand. It also boasts the world's richest asbestos mines, at Thetford, and has several quite large manufacturing centres — such as Sherbrooke and Drummondville.

To anybody willing to make the effort, and above all to speak French, life in the Province of Quebec (particularly Montreal) has a lot to offer. It is not easy to get on intimate terms with the *Canadiens*; even Catholic Italian immigrants who have tried to settle on Quebec farms have not found themselves readily accepted. And, of course, there are disadvantages; the disadvantages of being eternally a 'minority' (one which the French Canadians themselves understand so well). But for the pleasure of living among a people blessed with good humour, a quick wit, good manners, and much of the charm of their kinsmen in the Old World, of living in an atmosphere with perhaps more sophistication, more character and more excitement than is to be found in some other parts of Canada, it is worth paying a price; even if the price involves accepting the political brawls, the occasional corruption scandals and the tax-dodging, and — for women — having to furnish their husband's signature for every single business transaction.

CHAPTER EIGHT

HIGH NORTH

Men of the High North, you who have known it;
  You in whose hearts its splendours have abode:
Can you renounce it, can you disown it?
  Can you forget it, its glory and its goad?
            ('Men of the High North', ROBERT SERVICE)

This is the worst martyrdom I have suffered in this country . . .
the mosquitoes make such a noise that it distracts your attention
and prevents you from saying your prayers. (17th-century
Franciscan)

My Vision of the North. (RIGHT HONOURABLE JOHN GEORGE
DIEFENBAKER)

UP TO the end of the 19th century, the conquest of the
Canadian North — one of the most thrilling sagas in Commonwealth history — is once again the story of the quest
for a Northwest Passage. Exploration went on *pari passu* with
that of the West; many of its great names are the same —
Frobisher, Hudson, Button, Kelsey and Mackenzie — and
again and again the Hudson's Bay Company appears at the
head of its annals. But there were others whose efforts were
dedicated almost exclusively to the unrolling of the Northland. In 1769 the Governor of Hudson's Bay Company
dispatched from Churchill a young man called Samuel
Hearne to investigate reports of a rich copper mine far to the
northwest of the Bay. After two abortive attempts, with the
assistance of a remarkable Indian, Matonabbee (who killed
himself out of grief when the French captured Fort Prince of
Wales in 1782), he reached the mouth of the Coppermine
River on the Arctic Ocean. From there he turned south to
the Great Slave Lake, and then southeast again to return to
Churchill. Moving largely on foot, Hearne's triangular
voyage covered over 1700 miles as the crow flies across the
bleakest and most barren part of Canada, taking just 18

months and 23 days. It was a staggering achievement. He found little copper, but he became the first European to break through to the coast of the Western Arctic and to discover the Great Slave Lake, and his discoveries seemed to prove that there could be no Northwest Passage between Hudson Bay and the Arctic Ocean.

Less than twenty years later, Alexander Mackenzie made his great voyage to the mouth of his 'River of Disappointment'; apparently without realising that he had actually reached the Arctic Ocean until its icy tide came in and flooded his baggage. During the long peace that followed Waterloo, 'the search for the Northwest Passage,' as one writer has described it, 'became a Holy Grail for the British Admiralty.'[1] In 1819 Captain Franklin (later Admiral Sir John) made the first of three voyages, following Hearne's route in reverse and accompanied by Dr. John Richardson and Midshipman George Back, both subsequently to become famous explorers in their own right. On the return journey, reduced to eating shoes and the lichen of the rocks of the Barrens, the expedition nearly ended in tragedy — a forewarning of what was in store for Franklin a quarter of a century later. This time, equipped with two ships, *Erebus* and *Terror*, he disappeared into Lancaster Sound among the Arctic Islands. It was nearly fifteen years before the fate of Franklin was confirmed, and, as a result of the forty expeditions that set out in search, more was learnt about the Arctic than at any other time preceding the invention of the aeroplane. Then followed a lull in the tempo of Arctic exploration, during which time the fur-trade played the lead role in the North. At last, in 1903, the famous Norwegian, Roald Amundsen, sailed around the north of Canada, from East to West. He found the Northwest Passage; but it took him three years to navigate it, thereby apparently discounting for all time any commercial value it might have. Forty years later, under the necessity of war, a sergeant of the RCMP, Henry Larsen, sailed an 80-ton patrol vessel both ways through the Passage. He remains the only man to have achieved this feat, and he made the return East-West voyage in a single season.

[1] Douglas Mackay, *The Honourable Company*.

Meanwhile, at its western extremity an event had occurred which was to transform entirely both the purpose of exploration and the whole significance of the Canadian North. In 1896 George Carmack and two Indians, with the suitably romantic names of Skookum Jim and Tagish Charlie, found gold on Bonanza Creek, a tributary of the Yukon River. Although they were put on to the find by Robert Henderson who had been prospecting the area for two years, and promised to inform him the moment they made a 'strike', Henderson heard nothing of it until the whole creek was staked out. Between 1897 and 1904 more than $100 million came out of the Klondike, but Henderson died on a Government pension. Two years after the find a town of 30,000 — Dawson City — had sprung up. Countless amateur 'sourdoughs' and thousands of their pathetic horses died on their way up the deadly Chilkoot Pass from the Alaskan coast. Their equipment ranged from tennis rackets to a live cow somehow brought in by an enterprising miner, who sold its milk at $40 a gallon. Eggs fetched $16 a dozen, moose pies $5 a piece, and Jack London earned $3000 in a season piloting miners round the Whitehorse Rapids — though he missed the gold-rush himself. In 1898 construction was started on the first permanent means of transportation in the Far North, the 110-mile White Pass and Yukon Railway, from Skagway on the coast up to Whitehorse on the Yukon plateau. Probably one of the most difficult engineering feats ever undertaken, with workers deserting in droves on the announcement of each new gold find, the railway took two years to complete. By this time, the gold-rush was virtually over, and (although it is now one of the most important links in Canada's plans for future development of the North) the railway has rarely paid a dividend.

With the collapse of the gold-rush, Dawson City — at its peak three times the size of Edmonton — had sunk to a ghost town of two or three hundred. Once again the North lapsed into the slumbers of its long, lonely night. But the fortunes won on the Klondike had made men realise that there might be other treasure hidden away in the North, and with the advent of the aeroplane a new and determined assault was made. In 1929 Gilbert Labine, while pausing to cure a fellow prospector of snow-blindness, stumbled on a pitchblende deposit on Great Bear Lake in the Northwest Territories. For about ten years he produced small quantities of priceless radium from his mine, until the war closed it down. But when work started on the atom bomb, Labine's 'Eldorado Mine' suddenly assumed a far greater importance as one of the world's largest sources of uranium, and the Canadian Government took it over amid great secrecy. Shortly after Labine's discovery, a major gold-field was opened up at Yellowknife on Great Slave Lake. (Ironically enough, 'Overlanders' bound for the Klondike in '98 passed right over it, oblivious that here lay far richer reefs than any at their goal.) After Yellowknife, aerial surveys followed up with fabulous new discoveries of silver, lead, zinc, copper, iron, oil — and still more uranium.

Finally, with the stringing of the DEW-Line along the Arctic coast between 1955 and 1957, and the decision to supply as many as possible of the radar bases by sea, it seemed almost as if history had performed a full circle. Once again — at least temporarily — the Northwest Passage had assumed a real importance.

As emphasis on the North changed, so did the role of its former masters, the Hudson's Bay Company. In the days when the fur-trade was the sole economic mainstay of the North, the wild furs provided the company with by far the largest part of its vast revenues. But, even within the last decade, changing tastes and the impact of mink-farming and synthetic furs have struck a deadly blow at the trade. Immediately after the war muskrat pelts fetched $2·75 each; by 1954 they were worth only 67 cents. As late as 1951 Hudson's Bay trading-posts received 43 per cent of their income from furs; six years later it was down to 20 per cent. Particularly grave have been the repercussions on the Eskimos and northern Indians, to many of whom, for centuries, the fur-trade has been their chief livelihood. The company itself, however, with its huge resources (still over three-quarters British controlled), has not only survived but has seldom been more prosperous. Although it remains (next to the Soviet Union) the world's largest wild fur-trader, still maintaining 182 posts in the North, its trading profit of over £4 million a year now comes largely from other sources. Principal of these are the six giant Hudson's Bay department stores in the major cities of Western Canada, and — possibly the biggest long-term asset of all — its mineral rights to some 4·5 million acres in the oil-bearing parts of the West. Its eyes have never left the North, though; wherever a new town springs up, whether it be at Kitimat or Schefferville, the 'Bay' is likely to be there first with a bright new department store in miniature. Housewives praise it for bringing caviare and Dior dresses to remote places at southern prices; Eskimophiles curse it for the hard-headed differential between what its Scottish factors pay the Eskimo for his skins and carvings and what they charge him for essential goods in posts where the 'Bay' has a monopoly. But whatever people may think of it, there is no denying the influence the 'Bay' still wields in the North.

The story of the Canadian North seems to move in cycles of promise and disappointment, boom and bust. In the Second World War, once again the Yukon filled up with men; this time at work on the Alaska Highway. At Norman Wells on the Mackenzie River, some 25,000 men were employed (and probably more gold than ever came out of the Klondike was expended) on constructing oil-wells, a refinery and a 600-mile pipeline to Whitehorse to supply the Highway. After the war the men departed, the refinery and pipeline lay abandoned to rust away. Now, once again the limelight has been on the North in recent years, the air full of promise.

But just what is the North? It is not so easy to define. One notion is that it begins abruptly above the 60th Parallel, which marks the northern boundary of the four Western Provinces. But, in fact, Uranium City on Lake Athabaska to the south in Saskatchewan is every bit as northern in climate and inaccessibility as Yellowknife, and Ontarians reasonably enough reckon Moosonee on Hudson Bay to belong to the North — although it lies well to the south of Edmonton. The RCAF define the true Arctic as what lies beyond the tree-line. Yet the tree-line follows an erratic diagonal from the mouth of the Mackenzie right down to below Churchill in Manitoba. A definition based on mean temperatures would be even more erratic; for several States of the USA share the same summer isotherm as the Upper Mackenzie (where temperatures of over 100° F. have been registered, in contrast to the record low of −83° F. at Snag in the Yukon), and Knob Lake in Labrador has a considerably longer winter than Whitehorse at the other end of the country, with January mean temperatures 18° F. lower, even though it is 400 miles farther south. Conceptions are themselves constantly changing. Not many years ago the mining centres of Val d'Or and Chibougamau were considered 'up North' in Quebec; now the frontier has moved up to the new iron ore town of Schefferville, and in another decade it will probably have moved still farther north to Ungava Bay.

Perhaps the most satisfactory definition is that the North is what lies beyond the limits of Canadian commercial agriculture and beyond easy reach from the major centres. By this definition, the North falls broadly into six separate sectors.

The northernmost portions of the Provinces—In BC the true North today consists of perhaps just one mining centre, Cassier Asbestos at Watson Lake. In Alberta and Saskatchewan it is the new uranium complex around Lake Athabaska; in Ontario the forlorn, uninhabited muskeg and *taiga* south of the Bay. In Manitoba, which — next to Quebec — has the biggest slice of all, the North includes the rich mining centres of Flin-Flon (copper), Lynn Lake and Mystery-Moak (nickel), and the important Hudson Bay seaport of Churchill. The significance of Churchill is that it is actually closer to Liverpool than New York and a thousand miles nearer the West than the sea route via Montreal, so for three short months in the year its port and connecting railway provides a vital outlet for Prairie wheat. Since the war the new town of Churchill, all connected by roofed-over corridors, has also become the northern research centre for the Canadian armed forces, and now numbers about 3000 people.

Labrador and Northern Quebec—One of the most forbidding parts of the Canadian North, Labrador was aptly dubbed by Jacques Cartier 'the Land God gave to Cain'. Over much of it the Shield heaves itself up into giant furrows of rock as if the ground had been turned over by some Titan's plough. The furrows stretch almost endlessly towards an empty horizon, with a few dispirited firs huddled together in their lee and steely grey lakes lying in the troughs that are perhaps a mile wide. A grim country, where summer is little more than a brief buzz of a myriad monster mosquitoes. Prior to 1950, when the Iron Ore Company of Canada began its 350-mile railway from Sept Iles on the St. Lawrence and created a town of 4000 inhabitants at the other end, Labrador and its neighbouring area of 'New Quebec' were largely unmapped territory. Today this part of the North is estimated to contain one of the world's largest high-grade iron ore deposits. Plans are already well advanced between Cyrus Eaton, the US steel magnate, and a German consortium headed by Krupps to open a new iron ore operation at Ungava Bay on the Hudson Strait that would dwarf even the Schefferville undertaking. Krupps apparently look upon the Ungava deposits as eventually likely to become the chief source of iron for the huge demands of the European Common Market, but iron ore is only one of many treasures that Labrador may contain. Preliminary explorations in its untracked wilderness indicate there may be major deposits of uranium, copper, lead, zinc, titanium, nickel and asbestos. In addition to this, the British Newfoundland Corporation's project to dam the Hamilton Falls, with a drop greater than Niagara, could produce power equivalent to a third of all Canada's present capacity.

The 'Barrens' of Keewatin—On the other side of the Hudson Bay, the Labrador Shield runs on to form the eastern portion of the Northwest Territories, here devoid of trees or any vegetation but sparse lichen and moss. Across the tundra of these 'Barrens' Hearne made his epic voyage; still tenanted only by a few handfuls of Eskimos, they are the least promising part of the mainland North, and — with the exception of a nickel-copper mine at Rankin Inlet — are also least likely to see development in the immediate future.

The Mackenzie Basin—For two and a half thousand miles, most of them navigable, North America's second largest river sweeps relentlessly, majestically, down to the Arctic Ocean, through a huge plain that is really an extension of the Prairies. At its mouth lies Aklavik, the world's biggest fur-trading post and Canada's northernmost town, permanent population about 600. Around the corner, on the Arctic coast, lies the port of Tuk-tuk, open to shipping from the Pacific for two months in the year. Along the Mackenzie, from Waterways in Alberta to Tuk-tuk lies the longest and most viable transportation route at present existing in the North. Down it romp the little tugs in the few short months of summer, pushing their barges ahead of them. They bring in food for the whole area, then struggle back upstream taking out the steel drums full of uranium from Lake Athabaska and Port Radium on Great Bear Lake far to the North; gold from Canada's fourth largest mine at Yellowknife (population 3000); and millions of pounds of Whitefish that Indians and half-breeds have patiently caught by 'jiggers' under the ice of the Great Slave Lake during the winter. In the valley of the Mackenzie itself lie immense coal deposits, some of which have been burning away for uncounted centuries before even Alexander Mackenzie spotted them; it contains the only commercially worthwhile forests in the North, and the largest areas of potential agricultural land — plus, in parts, a winter that is little more severe than in the Laurentians of Quebec. The oil-wells that have already been producing for many years at Norman Wells represent huge reserves which — spread over wide areas of the North — are estimated by some experts to amount to perhaps ten times as much as those already proven on the Prairies. On the Hay River, a tributary of the Mackenzie, important natural gas finds have been made recently. At Pine Point, on the south shore of the Great Slave, Consolidated Mining have already staked out for early development what is said to be the biggest lead-zinc body in the world. And this may be but a prelude to the mineral wealth that remains to be discovered in the Mackenzie basin.

The Yukon—When Robert Service's savage Eden began to awake from its post-Klondike hangover, it was realised that the sourdoughs of '98 had mined in a thoroughly wasteful fashion. With the use of modern techniques and giant dredgers, the Yukon Consolidated Gold Corporation currently produces $3 million worth of gold each year; and, as a result, has boosted the once derelict population of Dawson City up to about 900. Some two hundred miles due east of

Dawson lies the only other major mine at present operating in the Yukon; United Keno Hill, Canada's largest source of silver and an important lead-zinc producer as well, connected to the outside world only by an unpaved road. The seat of government has now been taken over from Dawson City by Whitehorse, with a population of 6000 the biggest Canadian centre north of 60°. It is both a vital junction of the Alaska Highway and the terminus of the White Pass railway. Every morning a train, hauled by two powerful diesels, sets out from it over the impossible mountains that the sourdoughs staggered across fifty years ago, down to Skagway, the ghost gold-rush port on the Alaskan coast. On this lifeline of the Yukon, all cargo is now carried in great containers, some refrigerated for shipping perishables in summer, others specially heated as protection against the northern winter. At Skagway the containers are lifted bodily aboard a freighter, so their contents are never disturbed between Whitehorse and Vancouver, over a thousand miles to the south.

Whitehorse itself is a dynamic and colourful town, where past, present and future of the Canadian North dwell higgledy-piggledy together. The shanty-town of Whiskey Flats and its generations of accumulated debris shock the eye (the custom is to throw nothing away in the North, as any piece of old junk may come in useful one day). But across the river a splendid new hospital has just arisen— incorporating, with typical Yukon optimism, a spare wing for future growth — and elsewhere a fine indoor swimming-pool, new schools and a new housing estate are gradually replacing the relics of '98. Modern sewage facilities are beginning to oust the nocturnal calls of the euphemistic 'honey-wagons'. Whitehorse proudly remembers Robert Service and Jack London, boasts the only three-storey log cabin in the world, and makes little attempt to conceal the fact that it has the highest alcoholic and VD rate in Canada. Its cheerful paper, the *Star*, flies a banner above its portals proclaiming 'Published every Thursday — if the staff is sober', and during the Queen's visit in 1959 it advertised: 'Baths 50 cents. With soap 75. Royal Fambly Free. (This week only.)' The English-born owner of the comfortable hotel where I stayed was reputed to have won it in a poker game, but today poker is banned by the Mounties. Instead, someone had tactfully scattered pamphlets on 'How to Play Contract Bridge' around his lobby. Times change.

At Whitehorse is one of the saddest sights in all Canada. Sitting high and dry on the banks of the Yukon River are the superbly proud sternwheelers, the great white swans that — till only a few years ago — regularly churned their way to Dawson and back, winching themselves by cable around the torrential Five Finger Rapids. There they lie, like Byron's *Bucentaur*, unrestored, waiting till the Yukon frosts burst their timbers asunder, or the Indians pick out their entrails for firewood, a fading memorial to the glories and disappointments of the past. But disappointments are soon forgotten in the Yukon, which abounds with more optimism than any other part of Canada; great things are always just around the corner. Recent prospecting has revealed big deposits of basic metals and asbestos, and in 1959 a Canadian company made an oil strike reported to be one of the biggest in Western Canada. The only part of the North to be within easy access of tidewater that is ice-free virtually all year round, the Yukon might well be able to sell its oil to the outside world at prices lower than that of the Prairies. Coal is already mined on a small scale to fill the needs of Keno Hill, but seams are so rich and accessible that it is estimated that six miners could supply the whole Yukon! If the Taku River hydro-electric scheme is ever undertaken, the Territory would have limitless supplies of cheap power. It has probably the pleasantest summer in the North and some of the world's most magnificent, unsullied scenery; it is also perhaps the finest big-game country in North America.

The Arctic Islands—On a Mercator Projection they seem to dwarf the rest of Canada. In all this vast area (in fact equal to five times the United Kingdom) there are only 400 resident Canadians; of whom 34 Mounties, and 42 government employees look after the 3500 Eskimos on the islands. The remainder is comprised of factors of the 'Bay' posts, missionaries, weather men, research scientists and representatives of private mining companies, divided among some 13 principal outposts. Each brief summer another 300 'visitors' come to the islands, to leave before the ice-up. Since the advent of the US-sponsored DEW-Line, the Canadians have been greatly outnumbered by Americans; a constant source of worry to Canadians where sovereignty of the sparsely settled islands is concerned. Despite their total barrenness, isolation and the ice and snow that cover many parts of them all year round, even the remotest islands offer important promises for the future. Within the last few years, a major airfield has been opened at Frobisher on Baffin Island for planes flying on the Great Circle route from Europe to the Pacific coast. On the same island, fourteen different companies were exploring for minerals in 1958. At the extreme north of the archipelago on Ellesmere Island, 30-foot-thick coal seams have been found, and experts believe that the neighbouring Queen Elizabeth Islands may contain one of the world's major oil-fields.

It is safe to assume, however, that the 'future' for the Arctic Islands almost certainly lies further off than it does for other parts of the North. It is the Yukon, the Upper Mackenzie, and Quebec-Labrador's Ungava Bay that are earmarked for the next stage of development.

In 1953 Prime Minister St. Laurent — referring to the North as a whole — remarked in Parliament: 'Apparently we have administered these vast territories in an almost continuous state of absence of mind.' Short of capital and preoccupied with filling up the South, Canada has neglected the North in the past, so that today — despite the great expansion over the last decade — in the two Northwest Territories which comprise 40 per cent of the land area of Canada, there are only 32,000 people. Of these, some 12,500 are Indians and Eskimos. There are perhaps another 10,000 whites in Labrador and the northern portions of the Provinces, making a grand total of somewhere below 30,000 whites for the whole North (excluding the DEW-Line). By comparison, it is worth noting that in Siberia there are at least five cities north of the 60th parallel with populations over 50,000. (Admittedly, Canada has no system of forced labour to help fill up her North.) Murmansk, well above the Arctic Circle, has 160,000 inhabitants; Aklavik, the only Canadian town within the Circle has 600. Alaska, too,

General view across the Yukon River

WHITEHORSE, CAPITAL OF THE YUKON TERRITORY

New RCAF married quarters

*Mid-Canada Line helicopter with two British technicians
in group and author in centre*

FAR NORTH

Eskimo family at Great Whale, Hudson Bay

now has a rapidly growing population of nearly 200,000, with some 6000 at Fairbanks north of Dawson City. Of the little that the Russians have disclosed about the tremendous post-war developments in their North, it is known that they have recently completed a 1100-mile railway to open up mines near the mouth of the Ob, and over 1000 miles of highway in northeastern Siberia. Compared with this, since the war-time completion of the (American sponsored) Alaska Highway, just 356 miles of railway have been laid in Canada's North, and that largely with US capital.

Despite Mr. St. Laurent's warning, during the remainder of his government's stay in power little enough was done to remedy Canadian absent-mindedness about the North; a fact which contributed substantially to its downfall at the hands of the astute Mr. Diefenbaker. 'You can't get millions of young Canadians to switch Parties just by offering them $5 a week more,' he told me in an interview. With his mystic 'Vision of the North' and the messianic expression that comes into his eyes whenever he mentions it, he fired the imagination of countless voters who felt it was time 'something was done about the North.'

Whether the Conservatives will live up to their election promises, or whether they too will lapse back into absent-mindedness, still remains to be seen. Their present development plans are devoted almost exclusively to improving transportation, both the key to the North and at present its most seriously limiting factor. To keep one man in the North a year requires some sixteen tons of supplies; yet at a place like Keno Hill, for example, transportation costs may add up to as much as sixpence *per pound*. The biggest Government-financed project is to be a $55 million railway that will connect Great Slave Lake with the Alberta network. This would make possible the development of Pine Point and other new mines in the area, and cut transportation costs between Edmonton and Yellowknife by perhaps 25–30 per cent. Next on the programme is the construction of a network of 'resource roads' to be pushed from existing communications centres into mineral-rich areas of the North. 'Until we get these roads in, we don't even know just what we've got up there,' I was told by Mr. Alvin Hamilton, the

M

first Minister of Northern Affairs appointed by Diefenbaker. One of these networks will circumscribe Great Slave Lake, opening up promising areas at present out of reach of the summer boats or the tractor trains that traverse the ice in winter; another will connect Dawson City on the Yukon River to Fort Macpherson on the Mackenzie.

Somewhere between $145 million and $200 million are to be spent on these projects over about five years. But is this anywhere near enough, when compared with the enormous development that needs to be done in the North, and when one considers that at both Kitimat and Schefferville private industry spent twice this sum just to establish one single industry? Under the expanded Hamilton Plan, rather less than 1 per cent of the 1959 Canadian Budget was earmarked for the North — compared with a 4 per cent slice of a vastly larger cake being spent each year by Russia on her North.

Many problems confront development of the North. Building is one. Much of the North lies in the Permafrost zone, where the ground never thaws, and to drill foundations in the diamond-hard soil high pressure steam jets have to be used. Pipes have to be encased in huge ugly boxes, and carried above the ground. Inside these boxes, steam pipes are placed alongside the sewage and cold-water pipes to prevent them freezing solid. At Aklavik, heat generated by the houses melted the surface of the Permafrost, and the whole town began to sink into the mud. At a cost of $10 million, Aklavik had to be moved to a new site, its buildings mounted on stilts with an air space between the floor and the ground. To prevent penetration when blizzards rage buildings must be almost hermetically sealed; for the northern snow can be so fine that uninhabited quarters have been found almost completely filled with snow simply forcing under a loose door jamb. All this makes construction in the North an expensive business (as an example, a simple three-room house on Baffin Island recently cost the Government $48,000), especially when virtually every single item of material has to be transported from the South. At Yellowknife, with a climate mild by Northern standards, it is reckoned that 50 per cent more heating is required than at

Edmonton. All the fuel for this extra heating also has to be laboriously and expensively hauled from far away. The same is true of all food, which may cost 25 per cent more than in the South, because there is virtually no agriculture in the North.

'You won't find any Canadians in the North; only mad dogs and Scotsmen,' a Welsh scientist on the Defence Research Board had told me. After nearly being eaten by half-starved Huskies on Hudson Bay, I understood part of his remark; the rest turned out to be only a slight exaggeration. Senior officials of the Hudson's Bay admitted to me that most of their young factors were recruited from Scotland — because young Canadians, comfortably ensconced and earning good salaries in the South would not go North. At McGill University's Sub-Arctic Research Station outside Schefferville, of the four graduate students working there in 1958, three were British and the fourth Norwegian. The scientist in charge was a 26-year-old British geographer, and his wife told me: 'McGill can't get young Canadians to apply for this course; even though it's excellent field training, and they actually get *paid* $3500 a year here while studying for their MA. They just won't come up North.' On the Mid-Canada Line posts that I visited, something like a third of the personnel were Britons. In order to get people to work in the North, both Government and private industry have to offer huge wages. The driver of the 20-ton gasoline truck who took me from Whitehorse to Keno Hill told me that on piece-work he could earn between $7000 and $10,000 a year; miners may earn as much as 50 to 75 per cent more than in the South, and on the DEW-Line the Americans pay semi-skilled workers at the fabulous rate of $1500 a month. Even on the Mid-Canada Line, a carpenter or a plumber gets $700 (with overtime), and electronic technicians (many of them Britons in their thirties) between $900 and $1100 a month.

It has been calculated that it now costs $100 a day to keep one labourer in the North. Thus it may easily cost a private company more than twice as much to develop and operate a mine in the North as in any other part of Canada. This means that firms are naturally reluctant to risk capital, unless, like Knob Lake and Pine Point, deposits are of such

high grade as to more than balance out costs. Consequently,
the tempo of development of the North naturally suffers.
Northern *entrepreneurs* have pleaded frequently with Ottawa
to be allowed special tax exemptions to encourage development in the North ; so far in vain, despite the strength of their
case. But one thing is abundantly clear ; if Northern development is to be speeded up, Government must play a still more
active part.

So far its greatest, indirect, contribution to the conquest
of the North has been the construction of the two great
radar lines that stretch across Canada ; the Distant Early
Warning Line within the Arctic Circle and the Mid-Canada
running for over three thousand miles from Labrador to the
Pacific along the 55th Parallel. Thanks to the RCAF and
Defence Research Board, I was one of the first 'foreigners'
to be taken on a tour of the then highly secret Mid-Canada
Line. Whereas the DEW-Line is largely an American
undertaking, the Mid-Canada is entirely Canadian ; built
by Canadians (at a cost of $235 million), its detection devices
invented and operated by Canadians. Next to the St. Lawrence Seaway — although much less has been heard about
it — it is probably Canada's greatest single achievement of
the 20th century. Still only a blueprint in 1954, the Mid-
Canada Line actually went into operation some three years
later ; no mean feat, considering that work often had to be
carried out in inaccessible country where the working
season lasts no more than two to three months.

The 'McGill Fence', as its detection system is called,
consists of about half a dozen 'Sector Control Stations', each
manned by some 300 civilian technicians under the super-
vision of a handful of RCAF personnel, and each with a
score of 'Doppler Detector Sites' (DDS) under its control.
In the Second World War, before the heavy cargo plane
and the helicopter came into operation, both the construction
and maintenance of the line would have been an impossibility.
Each of the one-hundred-odd DDS had to be built entirely
from materials flown in by helicopter — and they are now
supplied the same way. This is quite an accomplishment
when one realises that even the big 'Workhorse' helicopters
can only carry a payload of 3200 lb. — including fuel, crew

and passengers — and cannot fly in bad weather. During
the short summer months (at Knob, ice leaves the lakes the
third week in June, and the first snows have generally fallen
by the end of August) the suppliers work like a feverish colony
of well-trained ants to stock up each DDS with a whole year's
fuel and frozen and canned food. First the amphibious
'Cansos' fly in to load up with food and machinery in their
hulls, diesel in their big wing tanks, at the base at Knob.
They discharge their cargoes at lake-heads nearest each DDS,
pumping the diesel from the wing tanks into barrels. Then
the helicopters move in, to fly the barrels and provisions
from the lake-head up to the top of the hill where the DDS
is situated.

The helicopters used on the line are run by a firm called,
appropriately enough, *Spartan Airlines*. The men that fly with
Spartan are some of Canada's most experienced bush pilots.
Before they can get a job on the Mid-Canada Line, they have
to have chalked up 1000 hours as captain of a fixed-wing
plane, and a further 1000 hours on 'choppers'. Unlike the
amphibian pilots, they must keep communications open
along the line all year round — flying in replacements,
repairs men and spare parts. Crews have to take sleeping-
bags, emergency rations and special clothing with them, as
they may be forced to 'weather it out' for a week or more in
the wilderness. At Knob alone several 'choppers' had been
lost — but no lives.

In the North today, man's greatest enemy is fire — not
cold. At Winisk, on the western shore of Hudson Bay, an
unexplained fire had wiped out three huts in the middle of
the night before we arrived. Forty men had lost their
accommodation and their belongings, and the last boat had
just left the Bay. With no building materials on hand, they
faced a cramped and uncomfortable winter — a generation
ago it would have been a matter of survival. Because of the
deadly menace of fire, each DDS has to have a complete set
of 'survival huts', equipped with emergency heaters and
generators, some 100 yards away from the main building.

Only a few years ago, long periods of isolation and hardship were the norms of life in the North. On the remote
DDS, two men may still be left for six months at a time. On

one, I asked a former RAF man from Ulster how often men broke down in this solitude. 'Seldom,' he replied. 'There was I believe a case when someone shot the cook. Since then we do the cooking ourselves, and no firearms are issued — except at one island in the Bay where, in winter, chaps literally have to fight for their lives against polar bears. Oh, and there was a fellow who began pestering Sector Control for permission to start up a *motel* out here.'

'What happened to him?'

'Nobody paid much attention — until next he asked for a parachute to while away the time by jumping off the 350-foot aerial tower. Then they decided it was time to move him.'

But even out on the DDS crews live in warm, comfortable quarters with electric light and hot and cold running water; connected by radio to the outside world and the frequent flights of the 'chopper', bringing in visiting technicians; and provided with a deep freeze, a year's rations and any other supplementary delicacy they care to radio for. One very well-fed young Canadian at a DDS was almost in tears when our 'chopper' had brought in Cheshire cheese, instead of the Danish Blue he had radioed for. At the main bases, there is little time for boredom or gloom. Once a week the 'Sched Run' Dakota arrives, with a load of new faces, news from the outside, and sometimes — as when I flew in on it —a cargo of frozen oysters and Scotch. On the night it arrives, the messes erupt into a conviviality that is typical of the North, a little recalling the rollicking '*Ordre de Bon Temps*' in which Champlain's settlers whiled away their first Canadian winter. Each camp has a large 'Community Centre', consisting of a magnificent gymnasium, equipped with every kind of sporting equipment; indoor tennis courts, ping-pong rooms, a library, reading and recreation rooms off to one side.

Like the frustrated sailors of *South Pacific* the men of the Mid-Canada Line might well adopt as their theme song:

> We've got volley ball and ping-pong
> And a lot of dandy games.
> What ain't we got?
> We ain't got dames!

The biggest drawback to life is that on most of the stations there is not yet any accommodation for families. At Great Whale on Hudson Bay, in a settlement of about 350 people there were only four women; the wife of the Northern Affairs representative (who acts as nurse at the RCAF hospital), and the wives of the RCMP constable, the Department of Transport radio operator, and the young English missionary. With the exception of the larger centres, such as Whitehorse and Schefferville, this is a formula that is still fairly common to the North as a whole; hence, no doubt, the numbers of happy bachelors and unhappy husbands who seek refuge north of 60°.

Today the ICBM may already have made the DEW and Mid-Canada as obsolete as the Maginot Line, but the experience they have provided on how to come to grips with the terrible North has been invaluable. How such military experience can be utilised by private enterprise has been admirably demonstrated in recent years by the Iron Ore Company of Canada. The ore deposits they wanted to develop at what is now Schefferville lay in the middle of some of the most forbiddingly inaccessible terrain in Canada. To build a large hydro-electric dam needed to supply the project with its power, the company used the biggest airlift since the Berlin blockade; men landed by helicopter cleared a runway for planes which then flew in every single piece of equipment to construct the dam. Working all through the Labrador winter, bulldozers carried a relief driver prostrate in a sleeping-bag alongside the engine for warmth, towed houses for the gang crews on sleds behind and completed the 350-mile railway in three years.

Even when the first ore train came out in 1954, many Canadians were sceptical that the Company could ship out ore for enough months in the year to make it a paying proposition. To prevent ore freezing inextricably during transportation in winter, at Schefferville monster dump-trunks are used with their exhausts ingeniously ducted around their containers. At Seven Islands, the shipping terminus on the St. Lawrence — a few years ago a fishing village of two or three hundred inhabitants, now a town of some 10,000 — batteries of giant blow-torches play up and down the sides of the railway trucks to free the ore before tipping it into waiting ships. In the extreme cold of Schefferville, the huge steel booms of the excavators sometimes snap off like rotten sticks; to meet this kind of emergency, 700 miles away from the nearest machine shops, the company had to set up what amounts to a small factory on the spot at Schefferville, capable of virtually rebuilding anything from an electric motor to a 500-ton dragline. It is now able to operate its mines for about 180 days in the year — from beginning of May to mid-November. A little over five years after the first railway contract was awarded, ore was being shipped to the steel plants of the American Midwest at a rate of 12 million tons a year; proving what, with determination and the aid of modern science, can be done in the North.

Schefferville itself, once just an encampment of a few Montagnais Indians, is now a town of about 4000 (three-fifths French Canadian) with well-designed comfortable houses, schools, bowling alleys, shops and — of course — 'the Bay', and a cathedral-sized Catholic church. Once the merciful snow covers the unfinished construction and all-pervasive red ore dust, it seems as pleasant and established as any town in Southern Quebec. Huge American cars prowl about its streets — even though these abruptly end in the Labrador wilderness within a radius of fifteen miles or so. Like most of the new company towns in Canada, Scheffer-ville is run along highly patriarchal lines. In fact, the Iron Ore Company's rule struck me as being the most total of all. It owns all the land and all the houses in Schefferville, and if a loose woman, a chronic drunk — or even just a philanderer whose activities have upset the work of another company employee — come to its attention, the company can (and often does) give them the proverbial twenty-four hours to leave town; the order enforced by the simple means of denying the miscreant any accommodation within 350 miles. At Schefferville the company is the law, and a very law-abiding and well run town it is.

As a sample of life in a mining centre in the North, Schefferville is perhaps more typical of the future than the present. With its railway outlet, it is too well connected to civilisation. At Keno Hill, the most remote point I visited

in the North, 180 miles south of the Arctic Circle and the
second most northerly mining community in Canada, most
of its 500 inhabitants still lived in bachelor bunkhouses.
Within the last few years, however, a number of ingeniously
constructed prefabs, called 'Panabodes' had been brought
in by truck for the senior married families. In design somewhere between a Swiss chalet and a log cabin, these 'Panabodes' are only prefabs in the sense that their timbers and
fittings are cut to size in Vancouver, 1500 miles away.
Inside, with two or three bedrooms, a large basement play-
room, steam heating piped from a central plant, a self-
contained laundry, and deep freeze (this last has to be
particularly capacious as housewives order their provisions
from Vancouver, through the company, on a *once a year*
basis), they seem every bit as comfortable as houses in the
South. Outside, so typically Canadian, each one has a
greenhouse full of magnificent blooms and huge tomatoes,
and brave attempts are being made to grow lawns on the
Permafrost.

In the third week in September, the overhead conveyer-
cables were already crackling with hard frost at Keno.
Within a week or two winter would have begun in earnest;
a winter that would last until the end of May and bring
temperatures that might sink to $-70°$ F. Nobody tried to
pretend that the winter was anything but brutal, and particularly hard on women. Yet a young Canadian wife
described to me the experiences of her seven winters at
Keno — how, with a child about to arrive, she had ridden
into the tiny hospital at Mayo, 40 miles away, in a bus full
of drunks, to find the doctor clad in pink ballet tights and a
T-shirt — just as a housewife in Toronto might recount the
vicissitudes of her life. Women found themselves particularly
depressed between November and January, she said: 'Because you never see the sun then; it just goes around behind
the mountain. And you have to be constantly worrying
about the children. If their shoes don't fit exactly they can
get frostbite in a few minutes, and they don't even realise
it until it's too late. And a white patch on their cheeks can
turn into frostbite even quicker.' Once, when the family was
driving to Whitehorse, she told me, 'it was sixty below, and

suddenly the motor just seized up. We are always supposed to carry oily rags in the back, so you can light a fire at once, and to travel in convoy; but this time we had forgotten the rags and got a good way ahead of the rest. We were less than an hour waiting for them to catch up with us, but it was long enough for it to get really cold in the car. The children began to go to sleep, and then — for the first time up here — I got really frightened.'

When the car broke down they had actually been on their way to Mexico for a month's holiday, for up North most people take their vacations in winter and travel far south. On their high salaries, even the mineworkers of Keno often fly as far afield as Hawaii. But many residents of the North in fact prefer the crisp winters to the summers, when the mosquitoes and black flies (nicknamed 'no-see-ems', because of their tiny size, but with a bite like a *piranha*) can make life unbearable, and when in the towns dust from the unpaved roads can fill the air with a stifling grey smoke-screen as soon as a breeze comes up. Science, however, is gradually combating the insect-scourge, too. Although in Whitehorse the only postcard I could find was one depicting a terrified 'sourdough' lying on his back with a monster mosquito astride him, an air-spray of the area with DDT each spring does in fact keep the insects down to tolerable levels there and at the other larger communities of the North.

In one of his more nostalgic poems, Robert Service writes:

> You may recall that sweep of savage splendour,
> . . . And feel in memory, half fierce, half tender,
> The brotherhood of men that know the North.[1]

This great 'brotherhood' of the North, more than anything else, makes up for the last remaining discomforts of hyperborean life, and all the innovations of the modern world have done little to change it since Service's day. Whitehorse may suffer from the highest consumption of liquor in all Canada, and some of its most pathetic human wrecks, but the lively congenial atmosphere around its drinking tables — as well

---

[1] Robert Service, 'Ballads of a Cheechako', *L'Envoi*.

as in the messes of the Mid-Canada Line — more closely
approximates that of a British pub than anything I found
elsewhere in Canada. There is a perpetual ozone of excitement in the Northern air, a mysterious indefinable extra
something to life that captivates and enslaves men to the
North, and that you cannot sense until you have been there,
and cannot explain even then ; but above all there is this
tight brotherhood between men of the North, as between
members of some secret order. A young girl from Southport,
Lancs., who had worked in Toronto, then in an isolated motel
on the Alaska Highway and was now receptionist at a
Whitehorse hotel, remarked to me : 'The loneliness in
Toronto was far worse. Up here the only unfriendly beings
are the dogs !' With the brotherhood of the North goes an
immense pride, and almost a contempt for those sad humans
who live on the 'Outside'. That is, anywhere that is not
North.

Nothing activates this contempt more than when 'outsiders' talk of the North as a rough-tough, uncivilised place,
or show their ignorance in other ways. (And even Canadian
ignorance about *their* North can, apparently, be really
astonishing. The publicity manager of the White Pass
Railway told me that a third of all his mail from the 'Outside' came addressed 'Yukon, Alaska'. Worse still, a Yukon
mine executive had recently wanted to send his daughter to
the University of Toronto ; but the Registrar's Office replied
that they were unable to accept 'any more *American* citizens'.
She went to the University of Alberta instead.)

It is the men of the North that make this brotherhood,
and that help make the North itself such a fascinating
country. Everywhere you go you meet unusual people,
each with an unusual story — sometimes true — to tell, and
generally willing to tell it. There was 'Wigwam Harry',
an illiterate white living all year round in the packing-case
of a grand piano in Whiskey Flats, but — when sober —
reputedly the fastest digger of foundations in the whole
Yukon. There was Sparkes, a young truck driver who —
accompanied by a Jehovah's Witness — had trekked 300
miles from the Yukon to Norman Wells over totally uninhabited country just as winter was setting in, in search of

work; then forded the mighty Mackenzie on a home-made raft. There was a former Lieutenant-Colonel of the Royal Marines running a petrol dump on Hudson Bay until he could save enough to retire in Canada; a middle-aged Canadian carpenter killing himself with overtime on remote posts of the Mid-Canada Line in order to put his sons through McGill; a French intellectual running away from Europe, men running away from women, ex-convicts trying to rebuild their lives, drunkards out to wreck theirs, fanatics in love with the North, and earnest technicians simply following their trade. And in many lost corners of the North, young British missionaries, unassumedly devoting their lives to the Eskimos, surprised that you should be surprised to find them there. Everywhere there were Britons. The North seems to bring out the best — as well as the worst — in men; it is there that you are most likely to find the characteristics that have made Canada what she is, and many of the Britons I met in the North seemed to have come to grips better with the country than those in the South. They complained less. It may well be that the North eliminates all but the Darwinian fittest among the immigrants.

Even in the most primitive of pioneering settlements of the North, conditions today are infinitely better than the pioneers of the Prairies experienced in their sod-huts of fifty years ago. But the benefits of modern civilisation have largely passed by the original inhabitants of the North. At Great Whale I watched an Eskimo sealing expedition move off into Hudson Bay in a rickety old motor-boat. They seemed in enormously high spirits, as Eskimos usually are, but the young English missionary, who had taken me round the settlement of clean but pathetically draughty tents, explained sadly: 'Don't let their smiles deceive you. They are probably the most cheerful race in the whole world, but these people here are literally on the brink of starvation. This particular community had to be forcibly evacuated from the Sleeper Islands by the RCMP, before they all died. Now they just have enough petrol for one day, if they don't catch a seal before it runs out, goodness knows what may happen. They may not even come back.' Today the average life expectation of the Eskimo is only 29, compared with 66 for males in the rest of Canada. All over the North the plight of both the Indian and the Eskimo is grave. Their traditional resources are no longer adequate to support them; between 1949 and 1957 alone, the precious caribou herds dwindled from 650,000 to 200,000, and whites are now strictly forbidden to kill any animal in the extreme North, unless it is a matter of sheer survival. The fur-trade the Indians depended on has collapsed, and the whale and seal industry that provided a living for most of the Eskimos has also been hard hit. The generally indolent Northern Indians have been only too happy to accept Government relief, but not so the proud and stoical Eskimos. Artistic and often highly intelligent, those that have taken jobs on the DEW and Mid-Canada Lines have astonished Canadians at the rapidity with which they have mastered mechanical equipment, and have made excellent workers. But after a while the lure of their traditional way of life proves too strong, and off they go — back to the existence that can no longer support them. Everybody who has ever had anything to do with Eskimos loves them, and when the Mounties and Northern Affairs administrators speak of their present plight, their voices become quite thick with emotion. Canada is now making great efforts to help the Eskimos (there is now said to be one civil servant occupied on Eskimo affairs for every ten of their population), but their future remains one of the gravest responsibilities in the North today.

The next big technical 'break-through' in the North that would benefit all inhabitants alike could well be in the field of agriculture. Strange as it may seem, low temperatures and the long winter are *not* the chief obstacles to farming today. More fundamental are the lack of rainfall (some parts of the North have no more than the semi-deserts of the Middle East), and the fact that — unlike Northern Russia where nearly a million acres are already under cultivation — the receding glaciers scraped away most of the soil. Nevertheless, experts reckon that there may be at least a million acres of good farming land in the Mackenzie Valley alone, plus another 500,000 acres of good ranchland on Great Slave Lake. At a staging-post at Minto, high up in the Yukon, I ate a delicious dinner of which all but the roast beef 'came

out of the garden'. Cabbages the size of footballs have been
grown under the midnight sun of Aklavik, and several vegetable gardens flourish at Yellowknife on soil laboriously
brought up from the South at $20 a ton. The Government's
experimental farm at Fort Simpson on the Mackenzie claims
to have succeeded with every vegetable crop grown in
Canada, except corn-on-the-cob. Even at barren Ungava
Bay, both sheep and geese have been raised successfully on
summer browse. But all this is still on a small, largely experimental scale. What is needed is both inducement (which
Government would have to provide initially at least) to make
it worthwhile for full-time farmers to operate in the North,
and the application of new scientific methods. It is perhaps
worth noting that at Fairbanks in Alaska, on the same latitude as Keno Hill, there are at least sixty thriving farms;
proving that full-time agriculture in the North *is* feasible.

On Hudson Bay I met an 'old-timer' called Fred Wood-
row. For over forty years he had been a Department of
Transport telegraph operator in the North, now he was
waiting for a plane to take him away from it for ever. 'The
North simply isn't the North any more', he grumbled in
language that would have blistered the walls of an igloo.
'I came North because I didn't care for being run into by
street-cars down South. Now the place is full of —— cars.
There's too much ruddy luxury; they're killing the soul of
the North' — waving his hand towards a new RCAF can-
tonment — 'it's become like any other —— part of Canada.'
Of course, he was right. For better or for worse, since the
war the Canadian North has changed out of all recognition.
For the first time, the Queen of Canada has visited it — with
as much ease as the Prince of Wales visited Winnipeg a
generation ago. Within the next decade, scientific agriculture and such technical innovations as 'pocket' nuclear
power plants could bring about even more revolutionary
changes in the North. Above all, there is the new and
wonderful invention of the Hovercraft, as yet unexploited,
but which, able to skim across muskeg, lakes and frozen
tundra alike carrying great loads economically and rapidly,
could finally exorcise the spectre of costly transportation that
has perpetually haunted northern development. A lot

depends on the world's demand for Canada's raw materials. With the thaw in the Cold War and a falling-off in the consumption of uranium, one or two mines are already scheduled to close down. Recession in the South has forced Ottawa to slow up on its plans for the North; Alvin Hamilton, the energetic young executive designated to make Diefenbaker's 'Vision' a reality, has been transferred to another post. But need for the riches of Canada's North must revive in the not-too-distant future, and ultimately it rests on the will and determination of the Canadian people and their Government as to whether the North will assume the role that is essential if Canada is to fulfil her destiny. Will Canada show this determination — the kind that pushed through the Canadian Pacific against seemingly impossible odds — or will their fabulously rich North simply be allowed to retrace the Yukon's cycles of promise and disappointment?

CHAPTER NINE

'NO CULTURE IN CANADA?'

The symbol of Canada is the beaver, that industrious rodent whose destiny it was to furnish hats that warmed better brains than his own. (ROY DANIELLS, from *The Culture of Contemporary Canada*, ed. by Julian Parks)

We can do with fewer level crossings and more museums. (Gordon Commission Report)

How often did you go to the ballet in Manchester, Mrs. Smith? (13-year-old Canadian)

'THE worst thing about Canada is the lack of *culture*.' The first time I heard this well-worn chant was from a group of Cambridge undergraduates who had spent a whole summer working in Canada. Some of them disagreed with it, quite passionately; several had widely divergent views on what constituted 'culture'. Of the forty to fifty undergraduates from both Oxford and Cambridge who went to Canada, and who subsequently wrote reports on their experiences for the Migration Council, only two were totally unenthusiastic (and they were the two who seemed to have been least successful in their jobs — but equally, only two had decided definitely to emigrate), but of all the various criticisms that were offered, 'no culture' easily led the field. Only one Oxonian actually declared himself impressed.

All the way across Canada I was to meet newly arrived Britons who took up the 'no culture' refrain. Just how valid a criticism is it? It is dangerous to accept all complaints at face value. An undergraduate from Cambridge, pampered by the easy accessibility of the Arts Theatre, the Fitzwilliam, the University Library, the Sunday Guildhall concerts, and innumerable university literary, arts and musical societies might, if he were to take a summer job in Glasgow, conceivably judge that it, too, was a little deficient in 'sweetness and light'. Among the British immigrants I met in Canada, I found that in an astonishing number of cases those who complained loudest about Canadian culture were those who had not done so well *materially* in Canada, and who seemed to be seeking a reason outside themselves to blame for their discontent; conversely, the successful were more prepared to accept cultural amenities as they found them. Also, when the immigrants complain, they often forget that they themselves are in a vulnerable position. How many decided to emigrate primarily to raise their *material* standards of life and not their *cultural* levels? And since they arrived in Canada, how many have actually 'done' anything to contribute to the world of culture there? In Toronto, an obviously intelligent Irishwoman, working as secretary in a big company, had just finished telling me how she found Toronto culturally deficient and materialistic, with 'everybody taking too much out, too busy to put anything back in'. Almost in the next breath, she then admitted that she and her husband had come to Canada *simply* because of the higher wages. Hers was, I thought, not untypical of attitudes among the immigrants. Finally there was the Canadian child's devastating question: 'How often did you go to the ballet in Manchester, Mrs. Smith?'

None of this, however, can quite disguise the fact that a Briton conditioned to a strong and regular dose of the Arts may genuinely suffer from cultural starvation in some parts of Canada. Polls taken among British immigrants almost invariably classify live theatre as one of the things they miss most in Canada; a Londoner accustomed to the choice and quality offered continuously by the West End could justifiably be depressed to find that only two Canadian cities support a permanent, professional theatre group. A music-lover will discover that in Toronto, the nation's musical centre, the opera season lasts a brief two weeks; a father with a son of outstanding intelligence may reasonably regret that there is nothing in Canada quite to compare to Manchester Grammar School or Winchester.

The really amazing thing is that Canada has any organised culture at all. Earlier in this book I have tried to stress some of the economic problems that confront Canada, but these are mere molehills compared with the mountains that

N

loom eternally over her cultural scene. Again the twin shadows
cast by distance and limited markets darken the foreground.
It has been said with some truth that Canada has never had
a real focal centre since the surrender of Quebec. Certainly
the Arts have none — with the capital, Ottawa, possessing
neither a national theatre nor concert hall. (Even Washington D.C., however, is hardly better off; up to two or three
years ago, its nearly one million inhabitants had only one
theatre worth the name and one newly created opera company.) In a country the size of Canada, each city, each
community even, has to be more or less self-supporting.
When one thinks of the varied fortunes of Sadler's Wells,
imagination quails before the idea of a city of only 400,000,
in the empty Prairies, being able to support a ballet company
at all, let alone one as good as the Royal Winnipeg. A
country of 17 million can only offer pathetically few openings for talent, and niggardly payment for these few. On
top of this, there is the (unintentionally) baleful influence
of the United States that with higher rewards and greater
opportunities can skim off the cream of Canadian talent all
too easily, and that with its incessant flood of magazines,
radio and TV across the border constantly threatens to
swamp Canada's vehicles of culture. Then, in all the Arts
there is a grave shortage of good critics. There are the
problems of creating a wide and enthusiastic support among
people who may have grown up to middle age without ever
seeing the opera, ballet, an art exhibition or anything but local
amateur dramatics. Last — but, alas, by no means least —
there is the sometimes crippling lack of self-confidence: 'It
can't be really good because it's Canadian.'

Cultural life has not developed at a uniform rate in
Canada. In the later years of the last century and the early
part of this, touring companies from Europe appeared
regularly in all parts of Canada. They included Henry
Irving, Ellen Terry, and Sarah Bernhardt (who was banned
by the Bishop of Montreal). Everybody came to see them;
an elderly man in Calgary told me how, thirty years ago,
he used to ride in from Drumheller — a trip that often took
eight hours in the roadless gumbo — whenever a 'travelling
show' came to town. Then a combination of an increase in

railway costs, the salary demands of the stars and the birth of Hollywood, sounded the death knell of the touring companies. The depression followed, and nobody could afford such luxuries as 'culture' even if there was any to be had. In the 1920s Toronto had seven theatres; only two now survive.

Since 1945, however, with the boom in material prosperity, there has been a great resurgence of interest, and activity, in all the Arts, right through Canada. Within two years of the end of the war alone, a dozen new professional and semi-professional dramatic groups appeared, but developments have been particularly marked in the last five years. Before leaving for Canada, I had a conversation with Ian Hunter, the former director of the Edinburgh Festival, who had just completed a trans-Canada tour at the invitation of the Governor-General. He had been amazed at the wealth of talent that he found, and on the strength of his discoveries recommended that an annual Festival [1] (on the lines of Edinburgh) be inaugurated to exploit this talent. He added, 'I think you will be surprised, too, at what is going on in the cultural world all through Canada'. I was, over and over again.

Every Canadian, from the recent Governor-General, Mr. Massey (who has probably done more to stimulate the growth of the Arts than any other Canadian of his era), down, is concerned about the state of Canadian culture. An immense amount of money is being spent on it. Everywhere one finds new structures dedicated to the Arts. either just finished, or under projection; the Beaverbrook Art Gallery in Fredericton, a new National Gallery for Ottawa, the Stratford Festival Theatre, the new Vancouver auditorium, the palatial twins at Calgary and Edmonton, and now the new O'Keefe Centre in Toronto seating 3200 in a hall which, it is claimed, acoustically will be excelled nowhere else in the world. Drama and ballet may have to compete for the stage in each of Alberta's 'Jubilee' auditoria with motor shows, cooking schools and the 'Calgary Crusade for Christ' (when the Canadian National Ballet came to Edmonton it played

[1] The scheme is temporarily in abeyance — because politicians could not decide on a permanent centre for the Festival.

to half-full houses, while the Baptist Convention packed the auditorium), but this is still a huge improvement on having to perform in a high-school gymnasium and has notably increased the incentive of local musicians and actors.

Neither facilities nor talent are evenly spread across Canada. The Atlantic Provinces are probably the farthest behind (but not necessarily in ambition — while we were in New Brunswick, Fredericton's 'Summer School Players' were putting over a repertoire that consisted of Shaw's *Passion, Poison and Petrifaction*, Fry's *A Phoenix Too Frequent* and Strindberg's *Miss Julie*). The traditional poverty of the Maritimes may well be a reason for this backwardness — yet, Saskatchewan, another 'poor' Province, seems to contribute more than its share. Jon Vickers, Covent Garden's brilliant young tenor who began life singing for charity performances in the small town of Prince Albert, is of course the favourite example of Saskatchewan talent, but there are many lesser known working their way up to fame — such as Arnold Spohr, the present choreographer and leading male dancer of the Royal Winnipeg Ballet and Frances Hyland, one of the stars of Canada's Stratford. At Regina, when I asked our host from the Wheat Pool how he had come to select the two farms he took us to visit, he replied: 'Actually I've never met either farmer before, but our children all play in the Junior Symphony Orchestra together.'

Repeatedly I was struck at the cultural endeavour going on in the smaller Canadian communities; it was from them that the Jon Vickers of the next decade would spring, to surprise the world. Sudbury, the forlorn nickel town in Northern Ontario, has its own symphony orchestra (it is also reputedly one of the best markets for pianos in Canada[1]) and a thriving theatre; Trail BC, another mining town, manages to organise four concerts a year for musicians 'of international repute'. At Kitimat a concert was to be given by 'World Famous Artistes' a few days after I left, and a recent appearance of the Vancouver Symphony Orchestra filled a 1500 seat hall twice, with a waiting list; meaning that more than half the adult population had wanted to attend. At Whitehorse, I just missed an apparently very

[1] According to Miriam Chapin, *Contemporary Canada*.

creditable performance of *The Mikado* (with the Bishop of the Yukon playing 'Pooh-Bah'!). Plays produced by the Whitehorse Drama Club over the long winter nights of the past two years included *The Lady's not for Burning* and *The Emperor's New Clothes*. In fact, there are probably few communities in Canada of more than a few thousand without an amateur dramatics society or a chamber music group.

Of the major Canadian cities, there has long been heated rivalry between Montreal and Toronto (as in many other things) for supremacy in the Arts, and today Vancouver is rapidly appearing as a potential challenger to the other two. The truth is that no one centre is supreme in all cultural fields. My own impression was that Montreal, if anything, had the edge on Toronto, and was the nearest to being a national capital of the Arts; but not every Torontonian would agree to this. Many English Canadians (including Mr. Massey) told me that they felt that the French Canadians — proportionate to their smaller numbers and greatly smaller financial resources — were more active in some of the Arts than themselves. This is perhaps truest in the theatre; Montreal boasts no less than three companies that regularly produce French classics, and at least ten smaller ones operating in so-called '*théâtres de poche*'. A higher content of 'live' television emanates from the CBC's French-speaking studios in Montreal than from Paris; there are four art museums and some twenty-five active art galleries in Montreal, which produces much of Canada's more experimental modern art. Montreal also claims a concert audience for works by Canadian composers that it is said Toronto lacks.

On the other hand, Toronto is Canada's musical metropolis; it is the home of the National Ballet and the Royal Conservatory of Music, and its symphony orchestra is rated one of the two or three best in North America. It is also the headquarters of Canadian publishing, and its Provincial Museum has one of the finest collections of Oriental art in the Western World. Ever since Toronto was the centre of the important 'Group of Seven' movement it has had a flourishing art colony, and a British immigrant told me that, whereas there had been only one art gallery when he arrived five years earlier, he now knew of sixteen. Nobody can say whether Toronto or Montreal has pre-eminence in the visual arts today; but both may well wake up soon to discover that the laurels have been grabbed for Vancouver by the increasingly active schools of artists and architects in the West. In drama, a few good repertory companies, such as Donald Davis's Crest Theatre, have sprung up in Toronto since the war. Nevertheless, one cannot help feeling that — for all its great wealth and resources — Toronto does not make the most of its cultural opportunities. The talent is there and now the theatres and galleries are there, but where are the patrons? While in Toronto we met a young couple, very well off and belonging to one of the city's most prominent families. They were active on countless cultural committees, gathering funds for the Stratford Festival Theatre and the Royal Winnipeg Ballet. But they had never actually seen the latter; had only visited Stratford once, during its first season, and had not taken tickets when the Stratford Players came to Toronto (where they failed — through lack of support). If every Torontonian followed their example, the city really would be the cultural desert many immigrants claim it to be (and which it is not), but their attitude was — we both felt — possibly more typical of busy, prosperous Toronto than any other Canadian city.

Let us examine briefly the state of the Arts in Canada by their separate fields:

Art—The visual arts are the least affected by general Canadian disabilities. They can survive without a focal centre, and can flourish (and have done) regardless of American influence. More than any other cultural field, they have succeeded in establishing a distinctive Canadian character; principally because of their ability to relate themselves most closely to fundamental Canadian values. Cornelius Krieghoff, her most famous 'classical' painter (though not really Canadian), devoted his talents exclusively to depicting life and customs in mid-19th-century Canada. His work has great charm, and — admittedly in a crazy world where it seems that buyers will pay anything, just so long as the artist is defunct — is currently fetching very high prices. Clarence Gagnon continued the tradition in his paintings of French-Canadian village life. Canada's 'great' school of modern art, the 'Group of Seven' which grew up during the First World War and the '20s, achieved its deserved fame through basing its work on the savage, and highly distinctive, mighty sweep of the Canadian landscape. I would give quite a lot to own an A. Y. Jackson (even though hackneyed prints of his work hang in every Canadian Government office) or a Lawren Harris; their paintings are excitingly vigorous — and unmistakably Canadian. Today's Canadian painters are turning increasingly towards abstractionism, away from the Canadian backdrop, towards the influences of Europe. Personally (and this is very much a matter of personal taste) I think this is a pity; as a source of inspiration the Canadian scene has still not been fully explored. I was little impressed by much of the abstractionist art I saw in Canada, but greatly impressed by the new work (particularly in the West) following on the realism of the 'Group of Seven'.

Most encouraging of all, though, is the immense activity and interest in art all over Canada. Canadian artists still suffer from the lack of markets for their work, but, with prosperity, these are probably expanding faster than in any other of the Arts. Galleries in many Canadian centres have evolved 'rental' schemes for pictures, which both help the artist and serve to spread further art consciousness. Next to markets, the most serious deficiency is in trained gallery personnel, art historians, and — particularly — critics. The least flourishing of the visual arts seems to be sculpture. With the exception of Ann Kahane and very few others there is a dearth of competent sculptors in Canada, and not a very strong market; the best works are perhaps still to be found in the striking primitive art of the Eskimo soapstone-carvers.

In architecture, Canada has had three main styles; the French 'colonial', its most original, of which, alas — due to that peculiarly Canadian scourge, fire — all too little remains; Canada's own adaptation of 'Scottish Baronial', ranging from the handsome suitability of Ottawa's Parliament Buildings and Quebec's Chateau Frontenac to the repulsiveness of the mansions of the late 19th-century Toronto tycoons and the Canadian Pacific hotels that defile the Rockies with their awfulness; and today's contemporary style. The new schools, churches and public buildings I saw in Canada made a strong impression on me, as did the clean and striking lines of the Stratford Playhouse and the Jubilee auditoria of Alberta; and I liked the bright and cheerful design of the modern bungalows that make up most of Canada's post-war urban expansion. The influence is strongly American; but here only a blind man, or at any rate someone who has never seen post-war London, could think that Canada would have done better to follow British example. Architecture has difficulty flourishing in the open nakedness of the Prairies, and the mild climate of the West Coast which permits the wide use of glass and similar materials that might not be so successful in the East partly explain why, as mentioned elsewhere, Vancouver has become Canada's centre of original architecture, and I should not be surprised if its so aesthetically pleasing surroundings also make it one day *the* centre for all the visual arts.

Literature—Of all the Arts, writing probably has the hardest time keeping its head above water in Canada. The problem is to create a truly Canadian writer and then to provide him with a truly Canadian market. Canadians are not, by and large, a book-reading people; their annual expenditure on books, papers and magazines of all kinds totals only $20 a head.[1] Sixth among the manufacturing nations of the world, Canada comes only tenth among nations of the West in terms of library books *per capita*. The shortage of good libraries in Canada varies from place to place. It is generally least acute in the more densely populated areas; although an isolated city like Kitimat already has a $1·5 million library with 10,000 books, and on the Prairies 'travelling libraries', or 'book-mobiles', and organisations like the Saskatchewan Wheat Pool, with its 'mail order library' for members, help conquer distance. Worst of all is the shortage of bookshops. At Trail BC, I was told that the nearest proper bookshop was 150 miles away, over the border at Spokane in the State of Washington. This is not untypical. As in the United States, publishers' costs are astronomic. The same book may cost 50 per cent more, or over, in Canada than in Britain. Yet a Canadian publisher

[1] According to *Working and Living Conditions in Canada*, put out by the Economics and Research Branch of the Department of Labour, 1958.

may have to sell more than twice as many copies before breaking even — and to a reading public perhaps only a sixth as large. Thus a Canadian, if he reads the book at all, rather than spend $5 on it, will borrow it from whatever library is available — which helps neither publisher nor author. As a result, for approximately every thirty-five new titles that appear in Britain each year, Canadian publishers produce one.

One of Canada's leading native [1] novelists today, Ethel Wilson, told me she considered that 'no young writer in Canada could hope to live on his writing alone, and I doubt if anybody could if he wrote just for the Canadian market.' At the University of Alberta, I had a long conversation with a Professor of English. He was very gloomy about the prospects for literature in Canada, and put the problems this way: 'Not so many years ago I had pupils who had come from sod-huts or log cabins. They had never seen a painting, let alone a stained-glass window — so how could one begin to tell them what literature was all about? But when you do get a pupil who has real talent, where can you get his work published? So many of our promising ones never get a chance to crawl, so they never learn to run, and become engineers or salesmen instead.' He told me that he had the greatest difficulty getting the few Canadian magazines to accept even 'the really excellent short stories', and when they did they paid badly. 'So anybody who does have the courage to become a writer ends up by angling his writing to catch the American market — with the result that sooner or later he becomes no longer a *Canadian* writer but just another American.'

The Professor was perhaps unduly pessimistic, and several Canadians assured me he was at least five years out of date. The demand for novels by Canadian authors has increased out of all recognition since the war, and these are now selling as much as four times as many copies in Canada as British and American novels. In the last decade alone, seven new magazines devoted to *avant-garde* prose, poetry and criticism

---

[1] I do not include writers like David Walker and Nicholas Monsarrat, whose writing is neither essentially Canadian nor directed principally at the internal market.

have started up, and during the same period the CBC has grown to be an invaluable patron to Canadian writers. The situation has vastly improved, yet still the disparity between what a Canadian and an American magazine can afford to pay tends to act as a siren song in the ears of young Canadian writers.

The Canadian magazines have their case, too. No single aspect of Canadian culture suffers from American influence more than they. Thousands of tons of reading material, ranging from *Confidential* to the *Saturday Evening Post*, pour over the border daily. Even the *New York Times* can reach Montreal and Toronto on the same morning, and for the same price, as the local Canadian papers. Browsing around bookstalls in these two cities, I estimated that slightly more than nine out of every ten magazine titles on display emanated from the United States. What possible chance could the native product have against this deluge ? If there was a case for tariff protection, here seemed to be one. Yet, when in 1956 the Federal Government decreed a tax on Canadian editions of US magazines, it was overwhelmingly opposed in Canada. The result is that to survive at all, magazines like *Maclean's* (the closest proximation to the *Saturday Evening Post*) has somehow to offer features written only by the top household names (therefore, no promising young authors), and at the same time items of purely regional — often downright parochial — interest not to be found in American products. How, fortnight by fortnight, *Maclean's* manages to incorporate such essentially homespun material as a series on the streets of Canada, or descriptions of small-town life, and yet almost always have something interesting, controversial and lively that appeals even to non-Canadian readers, is one of the miracles of modern journalism. It is a first-rate production and also (I do not know how) pays its contributors on a scale almost comparable to US magazines.

In one of the last books [1] he wrote before he died, and in one of his more sombre utterances, Stephen Leacock said: 'There is not yet a Canadian literature. . . . Nor is there similarly a Canadian humour, nor any particular Canadian

[1] Stephen Leacock, *Canada, The Foundations of its Future.*

way of being funny. We use English for writing, American for conversation, and slang for profanity, and Scottish models for philosophy and solemnity. *Maria Chapdelaine* may well be rated as one of the world's books, but it is only Canadian in the sense that it was written about Canada. . . .' [1]

He went on to doubt whether Canada would ever be able to develop an indigenous, characteristic literature.

'The times are against it. In all the British Commonwealth, and in the United States, speech, thought and language now amalgamate, not diverge. . . .'

I thought about Leacock's pronouncement all the way across Canada, and asked most of the intellectual leaders I met whether they thought it was true. Some, like the Edmonton Professor, said yes. At least one, the eminent President of another Western University, refuted it in unacademically strong language, and in terms that sounded almost like something from Leacock himself:

'You have to consider that that must have been written a very long time ago.'

'Actually I believe it was written as recently as 1941.'

'Well then you have to consider how old he was when he wrote it.'

It seems to me that — if nothing else — Leacock was being unfair to himself. If ever there was a truly Canadian writer, he was; his humour, with its gentle ridicule of the extravagant, a touch of the farcical but with underlying good sense and level-headedness seldom far away, was never entirely American or entirely British. In his portrayal of provincial life (*Sunshine Sketches of a Little Town*), even though written nearly half a century ago, and in his capturing of the earthly pleasures of the outdoor life (*Bass Fishing on Lake Simcoe*) he still seems to impart much of the essential flavour of Canada today (and his comparisons of British and North American education in *Oxford as I See It* remain as cogent in 1961 as they were in 1922) — which is why I have quoted him so frequently in this book.

Much of modern Canadian writing has humour, but

[1] Its author, Louis Hemon, was in fact a Frenchman — run over by a Canadian train before he had even heard of the acceptance of his book, which was to become the great classic of life in French Canada.

seems to lack wit. Yet, in ordinary conversation as well as in literature and journalism, satire — that quality Leacock possessed in such abundance — is a highly developed art in Canada. Pastmasters at balloon-pricking, Canadians give the absurd, the excessive and the pompous little chance of inflating to large dimensions in their country. Satire, as a Canadian playwright-director recently remarked, has always been Canada's 'most effective form of self-defence against the very British and American culture we borrowed and were swamped by'.[1]   While I was in Canada, a highly competent satirical revue called *My Fur Lady*, which had started as a McGill undergraduate show, was sweeping the country. Two of Canada's leading satirists today, Lister Sinclair and Robertson Davies, are also her most popular playwrights.

In the past, the best of Canada's literature has usually been closely related to her potent physical background, like the 'Group of Seven' in painting. *Maria Chapdelaine* and some of the poems of E. J. Pratt are preoccupied with the loneliness of humanity confronted with the savage forces of the Canadian scene; 'Ralph Connor' gained world readership at the end of the last century with his melodramatic tales of life in the Canadian backwoods. In some writers, preoccupation with the native land became a form of regionalism; Mazo de la Roche in her prolific saga of the Whiteoaks family seldom strays far from southern Ontario; or Ethel Wilson from Vancouver. Today poetry especially seems to be following the trend of Canadian art; away from the soil and towards experimentalism. Novelists have — like Hugh MacLennan — begun to concern themselves more with speculation about Canadian character, relations with each other and the outside world, and less with environment. Suspicious of *-isms* and abstract ideas, Canada's leading writers are, however, still strongly wedded to realism. Yet their works seem increasingly to possess a universality that was not always there; perhaps significant was the warm reception given by British critics to Mordecai Richler's most recent book, *The Apprenticeship of Duddy Kravitz*. Instead of

[1] Mavor Moore, 'Theatre in English-speaking Canada', from *The Arts in Canada*, ed. by Malcolm Ross, 1958.

exploring sexual and political behaviour like modern American novelists, Canadian writers — more moralistic in tone — tend today to be chiefly concerned in the search for a national identity. Perhaps when Canada herself has found this identity, her literature will also have found the national character that Leacock feared it never would. One of the most sensible of Britain's literary guardians has observed that almost more important than style or content is the personality of the writer; [1] where a whole literature is concerned, this might also apply to a nation.

Drama and Ballet—Probably the most remarkable artistic accomplishment in Canada since the war has been the birth of the Stratford Shakespearian Festival, which in a few short years has transformed the Canadian theatre, by its example if nothing else. The Festival originated in 1952 as an idea in the mind of an inhabitant of Stratford (Ont.), one Tom Patterson — then in his early thirties. He succeeded in passing on his enthusiasm to Tyrone Guthrie — former manager and administrator of the Old Vic, who came to Stratford as its first director — and at the same time he set about raising money to launch the opening season. No less than $40,000 of the total amount was collected from the small town of Stratford alone, within a space of two months — another example of 'cultural consciousness' in Canadian provincial centres. The first season opened in the summer of 1953 in a gigantic tent, and was an instantaneous success — with box office receipts averaging 99 per cent of capacity. Over its first four seasons the Festival gave 260 performances and attracted audiences totalling some 400,000. In 1955 Patterson and his supporters launched a campaign to finance construction of a permanent playhouse. Again Stratford itself rallied round, subscribing an average of seven dollars for every man, woman and child, and by the end of the following season sufficient funds had been collected to start building. By working flat out through the sub-zero winter, the theatre — a most imaginative circular auditorium designed by a Toronto architect, with none of its 2200 seats farther than 70 feet away from the stage — was ready for the next season.

[1] F. L. Lucas, *Style*.

Already, after so short a time, Stratford has established itself as a major institution on the cultural scene, not only of Canada but the United States as well. Its casts have included such international notables as Alec Guinness (its first star), James Mason, Eileen Herlie and Irene Worth. Each year the Shakespearian Festival is followed by an operatic season and a jazz festival, participants in which have ranged from Benjamin Britten, Peter Pears and Elizabeth Schwarzkopf, to Dizzy Gillespie. A two-week Molière season by Montreal's famous *Théâtre du Nouveau Monde*, which represented Canada at the International Festival of Dramatic Art in Paris in 1955, has also become a recent feature at Stratford. In 1956 its new British director, Michael Langham, established a notable precedent by producing *Henry V* with the parts of the Court of France played, in French, by the leading French-Canadian actors. As well as creating a new cultural bond between the two races, it was a great and moving success — one that only Canada with her dual nationalities could have achieved.

While we were in Toronto we drove out to Stratford to see *Henry IV, Part I.* We were both wildly impressed, and I cannot remember having enjoyed an evening at the Stratford Memorial Theatre quite as much. To begin with, the atmosphere is excellent. With its pleasant lawns, its languid Avon, weeping willows and swans this could easily be the real thing — with a dash of Glyndebourne thrown in. If anything, it is rather less commercialised than its famous prototype; the neon-lit 'American Bars' and tourist-trapping 'Ann Hathaway Tea Shoppes' that grate so in Warwickshire somehow seem less offensive in Ontario. The theatre itself is sheer genius. With its black dome, it manages to preserve something of the intimacy of the original tent, at the same time the circular stage and complete simplicity of scenery bring it closest to the 'Globe' of Shakespeare's day. It may not have so many trapdoors as that technically unsurpassable crematorium at home, but I think I preferred the flavour it imparted. And there were a number of small touches I liked — such as the fanfare of trumpets in place of the five-minute buzzer, and even the discreetly Elizabethanised programme ads. At first Prince Hal with a Canadian accent seemed strange, then I began to wonder whether that pleasantly robust inflection might not perhaps be more akin to the language of the Elizabethans than our own. Although the performance we saw may have been partly swept along to success by the tremendous enthusiasm that radiates from every inch of Stratford, and although some of the players obviously lacked the experience of the top-flight of the Old Vic, by any standards it was a first-rate production. After that night at Stratford, it was difficult to believe that prior to the Second World War there had been no real professional theatre at all in Canada.

I have dwelt on Stratford at some length not only because it is such an appealing 'success story' and a proof of what *can* be done in Canada, but also because in its setbacks nothing illustrates better some of the tribulations that the stage — indeed the Arts as a whole — have to face there. Although ever since its inception the Stratford Company has averaged houses between 85 and 99 per cent of capacity, when its travelling company, the Stratford Players, toured Canada in 1957 the results were 'disastrous' — ending in a loss of $55,000. The worst flop of all was in Toronto, which had supplied so much of the financial support for Stratford in the past. Harder still, despite the bestowal of what amounted to 'rave notices' in the usually hard-to-please *New York Times*,[1] and other US newspapers, by and large the Canadian Press (especially Toronto) remained coolly indifferent — even when, for the first time, productions had an all-Canadian cast and were largely Canadian designed and produced. Why?

I heard three separate reasons advanced. At Stratford itself both Michael Langham and Canadians on its administrative staff gave this analysis; there was a strong disbelief throughout the country that 'anything Canadian can be good'. This thesis is backed up by the fact that during Stratford's opening season no less than 40 per cent of its audiences came from the United States. As the Canadian public gained courage (and doubtless influenced by the encomiums of the US Press), the next season its proportion of the audiences rose to 80 per cent. This national diffidence

---

[1] Of Stratford's *Henry V*, it said: 'Something extraordinarily promising has happened in the theatre of Canada.'

about its own artistic prowess is also reflected in the fact that no Canadian actor can hope for acclaim at home until he has made a name for himself in London or on Broadway. The same is equally true of ballet and opera, and an obvious consequence is that of those who go to seek fame abroad a goodly proportion remain, and their talent becomes lost to Canada.

A second explanation, which has some bearing on the first, was offered to me by the Professor in Edmonton, as well as by a member of the Canada Council who had long been closely associated with the Royal Winnipeg Ballet. This was the really disastrous shortage of qualified dramatic critics on Canadian newspapers. All too often a young reporter assigned to the role passes out tepid comment on what is really good, simply through inexperience or in default of critical standards and out of fear of being slapped down himself. Or else, in the manner of the smaller British provincial papers, he distributes meaningless bouquets to all and sundry; or worse still, he becomes too closely involved with local artistic personalities and (as has happened with the Royal Winnipeg on past occasions) allows personal prejudices to lead him into damning a fine performance.

Finally, a Canadian stage producer in Winnipeg told me that, as he saw it, the real reason for Stratford's failure on tour was simply because 'Canadians rather resented the fact that Stratford seemed to have been taken over by Englishmen — both directors and players'. This resentment may have had less of an anti-British content in it than a feeling that Stratford was making itself out to be more Canadian than it really was; but on any score, this attitude — if in fact it existed — was largely unjustified. When Tyrone Guthrie accepted the invitation to be Stratford's first director, he insisted that it 'demonstratively be a Canadian scheme carried through by Canadians, but with help (indispensable and important help) from Great Britain.' And so it has been. Of the leading members of the cast of the *Henry IV, Part I* that we saw, I counted ten Canadians and only six Britons — and apparently this was an unusually high proportion of outsiders. The year that James Mason took the lead role, the sixty-member cast included only *one* other non-

Canadian. All the visiting artists, including the director, come only for a year or two, so there is little suggestion of any 'monopoly' keeping native talent out of jobs. Apart from this, Britain is — as of course she should be — still the fountainhead of Shakespearian theatre, and if Canada wants her Stratford to achieve the summit it is plain that, initially, she must turn to Britain for assistance.

Justifiably or not, there were probably elements of all three attitudes behind Canadian reactions to Stratford, and the reactions in themselves reveal some of the psychological problems confronting the development of the Arts in Canada. How, the Governors of an undertaking like Stratford could well ask, is one to please people — when some Canadians think a production can't possibly be any good because it's home-grown, and others boycott it because it's too 'foreign'? What is even stranger is that both apparently antithetical emotions can, and do, dwell simultaneously in the breast of many an otherwise rational Canadian. Here lies the nucleus of perhaps the most self-defeating of all Canadian traits (though rarely to be found in French Canadians, who, convinced of the superiority of their culture, are not so subject to the uncertainties that perplex the English Canadians). It needs further discussion, but this really belongs to a later chapter; let me here just mention two further instances of how it affects the Arts. At one of Alberta's 'Jubilee' auditoria, I met a young Englishman who was its stage director. He had had considerable theatrical experience in England, and was immensely keen about dramatic possibilities offered by the new auditorium. There were some very enthusiastic amateurs locally, and they had asked him to give them professional advice: 'They begged me to tell them what they were doing wrong, but the moment I did many of them became really huffy. Out came all the old saws — "What do you expect? This is a young country", and "If you don't think we're any good, why did you leave home?" They accuse me of being superior and some won't talk to me for weeks. At times it really makes one despair; I'm seriously tempted to follow the line of the local critics and say everybody was "wonderful" and it was a "lovely performance", but that's hardly going to create a decent theatre here.' In

o

Montreal, the vice-president of one of Canada's leading magazines took me out to lunch. He was a cultured, charming man, and struck me as being one of the most broad-minded and discerning Canadians I had met. But when I asked him what opportunities there might be for British journalists on his magazine, he replied: 'None. We've already got five Britons out of twenty-five on our editorial staff, and we don't want any more. Not that they aren't good — most of them are first rate — but we just don't want to get the stigma of being too English.' If an applicant happened to be the best possible literary critic available, it seemed to me to be perhaps just a little short-sighted to turn him down because he was born in London. And a little sad.

I have already referred to the activity of countless small repertory and amateur groups throughout Canada, but before leaving this section some mention should be made of the various schools and courses in drama. In a beautiful setting amid the Albertan Rockies is the Banff School of Fine Arts, holding courses in all the Arts each summer; the 'Extension Department' of virtually every Canadian university also provides drama courses for 'outsiders' — and they are usually among the most heavily attended of all. Each year since 1933 a 'Dominion Drama Festival' has been held, moving from one Canadian centre to another, and giving the Provinces a chance to show off their new talent. A post-war feature that has taken root all over Canada is the outdoor summer theatre, with all its advantages of low costs and large audiences. In a large park in Winnipeg, we saw a really creditable performance of *The King and I* (when I saw it in London it struck me as the dreariest of all the American musicals, and I should have thought it most difficult for a semi-professional group to put over, but the Winnipeg Summer Theatre succeeded nobly). In 1959 Quebec City — taking advantage of its unique setting — launched an open-air theatre with its stage in the Lower Town and the audience seated on the steps leading up to the ramparts, offering two plays an evening for 25 cents. There is also Vancouver's 'Theatre under the Stars' which has had several successful seasons. Another recent (1957) landmark has been the establishment by Gratien Gelinas — French Canada's re-

markably versatile actor, director, manager and playwright
— of the *Théâtre de la Comédie Canadienne* in Montreal. This
is the first professional theatre both to be bilingual and
dedicated primarily to the production of works by Canadian
playwrights. Yet a further factor that has made a big impact
on the Canadian stage within the last five years or so has
been the tremendous growth of television; a real godsend to
actors who, when the summer seasons were over, often had
nowhere to turn for theatrical employment over the winter.
The Canada Council is now devoting some of its energies to
aiding the emergence of native playwrights (of which there
has hitherto been an acute shortage), and a contest jointly
organised by the Stratford Festival and the Toronto *Globe
and Mail* recently brought in 185 entries, from which one
play was selected for production by the Festival Theatre in
the summer of 1961.

As in the theatre, interest in ballet has grown enormously
all over Canada since the war. There are several training
schools across the country, but there are only two regular
ballet companies; Toronto's National Ballet and the Royal
Winnipeg. Montreal has its Theatre Ballet, and its Television Ballet Company ranks as the first in Canada. Vancouver, which is said to have produced more dancers *per
capita* than any other Canadian city, still has no professional
company.

The National Ballet had its first season as recently as
1951. With a much larger supporting public than the Royal
Winnipeg, and consequently sounder finances (though, paradoxically, its deficits have grown with its audiences), it
has already earned a good reputation for itself during tours
of the United States. The Royal Winnipeg deserves note
particularly for its great courage in keeping going, against
heavy odds. It was founded in 1938 by two Englishwomen,
Gweneth Lloyd and Betty Farrally, and in 1949 became
Canada's first professional ballet company. In 1953 the
Queen (who had watched a performance in Winnipeg the
previous year) granted it permission to include the word
'Royal' in its official designation. The following year
triumph and tragedy struck the Royal Winnipeg; it reached
its peak of achievement during a coast-to-coast tour of the

United States when, for a week in Washington, Alicia Markova danced with the company in *Les Sylphides*. But that same June a disastrous fire wiped out its headquarters, all its properties and costumes. The loss would have spelt the end of most companies with as slender financial resources, but the Royal Winnipeg has made a remarkable comeback. Though it has only 16 dancers (or had in 1958) compared with its *corps de ballet* of 26 before the catastrophe, and can only afford to pay its dancers $42–$55 a week (or about what a stenographer would earn), the Royal Winnipeg still has a very high standard. Few cities of the size of Winnipeg anywhere in the world maintain a ballet company that can compare with it, and it is gratifying that its future survival now seems assured through the help of grants from the newly formed Canada Council.

That Canada is producing dancers of talent was evidenced in 1960, when, for the first time on record, a Canada-trained Canadian, 21-year-old Lynn Seymour from an Albertan small town, played the lead role with Britain's Royal Ballet.

Music—Before I went to Canada, experts at home told me that I would find her considerably further ahead in music than in other fields of endeavour. The high level of present activity is unmistakable, and it occurred to me that, of all the Arts, young Canadians seemed to have a greater interest in, and possibly aptitude for, music. There is also no disputing the quality of talent being turned out by schools like Toronto University's Royal Conservatory of Music. An outlet of growing importance for musically minded Canadian youth is the *Jeunesses Musicales*, started by a French Canadian, Gilles Lefebvre, some ten years ago and based on the French organisation of the same name. The Canadian *Jeunesses Musicales* now have their impressive headquarters at Mount Orford, a hundred miles from Montreal, with dormitories, huts for teaching and practising, and a concert hall on the site of what a few years ago was a swamp. The movement has about 40,000 members, with a number of English-speaking groups (notably in the smaller communities in the West) affiliated to it, and receives useful financial support from the Canada Council.

Canada has her own 'folk music' in the form of the often hauntingly sad songs of the French-Canadian *voyageurs*, and today there is more original music being written in Canada than ever before. The *Catalogue of Orchestral Music* lists some 233 works for orchestra composed by Canadians between 1918 and 1957; of which all but 36 have been performed publicly. Even Canadians are surprised by the present spate of activity. A lecturer at the Royal Conservatory, Mr. John Beckwith, comments: 'We have several composers . . . who have produced individual works of genius.'[1] Some of the most striking talent today belongs to the youngest generation of Canadian composers, aged 25 to 35, whose names, as yet unknown in Britain, may well bring world renown to Canada in the near future.

The opera in Canada has its centre in the Toronto company which sprang from the Opera School of the Royal Conservatory, formed in 1946. A kind Torontonian invited me to the opening night of the opera, and the company's performance of Verdi's *Un ballo in maschera* made an impression on even my unmusical ear. The production took place in the strongly Victorian confines of the Royal Alexandra Theatre (curiously marred by the substitution of a monster Coca-Cola machine for the Crush Bar), but removal to the new O'Keefe Centre will undoubtedly give the opera in Toronto a huge boost, by providing what is claimed will be one of the best opera houses in the world. In the last few years, Canada's opera world has been as busy as her composers; in his contribution to *The Arts in Canada*, Dr. Boyd Neel, Dean of Toronto's Royal Conservatory of Music since 1953, remarks that 'it is quite astonishing to read that in a season such as 1953–4, about two hundred public performances of some fifty operatic works of all types were given, employing 1200 performers'.[2] The CBC Opera Company has been particularly outstanding in its adventurous and often excellent productions.

In the last century, Calixa Lavallée, the composer of 'Oh Canada', had no sooner completed this tribute to his native land than he migrated to the United States. Like Lavallée, in music and drama especially, the cream of Canada's

[1] Writing in *The Arts in Canada*. [2] *Ibid.*

talent — the Jon Vickers and the Lois Marshalls — so often
in the past became lured away from her by dazzling opportunities offered by London and New York. But all the time
the openings, and audiences, at home are now increasing.
The ex-*Manchester Guardian* editor of a Winnipeg newspaper
told me he could think of no city of equal size with a symphony orchestra to compare to Winnipeg's; as mentioned
earlier, Toronto's (which celebrated its 50th Jubilee in 1958)
is rated one of the best two or three on the Continent, and
Halifax's is not to be despised. Smaller orchestral groups
are springing up all the time in every part of Canada; and
within the last five years two ambitious new journals devoted
to music have been started. Finally, there is that fairy godmother, the CBC, a relatively new and most important
factor in the life of Canadian musicians. Already the tide
may be turning in favour of Canada, with outstanding foreign
talent — like Herman Geiger-Torel, the director of the
Toronto Opera Company, Jan Rubes, its leading bass, and
Dr. Boyd Neel — actually coming to Canada, as counterbalance to the young aspirants who still leave the country in
search of recognition; though even their numbers may now
be waning. Canada seems well on her way to becoming a
force to be reckoned with in the musical world.

The Press—Because of the size of Canada, like the
United States, she has no such thing as a 'national Press'.
There are nearly a hundred daily newspapers published
across the country, and read by something over 4 millions.
Only nine (of which two are French Canadian) have circulations over 100,000 (*i.e.* one-fiftieth of the *Daily Mirror*). These
range from over 350,000 for the leading Toronto papers to
14,000 for the *Fredericton Gleaner* and 6000 for Quebec City's
English-speaking *Chronicle Telegraph*. In the West, circulations of the principal papers vary between 120,000 (*Winnipeg
Free Press*) and 34,000 (*The Albertan*). Because of these small
circulations, Canadian newspapers are expensive (generally
10 cents), and many of the weaker brethren have to derive
50 per cent or more of their income from job-printing.
Compared with what a truck-driver or miner can earn in
Canada, journalistic salaries are also poor on average. At
the top of the scale, the senior reporters on the biggest

Toronto and Montreal papers can sometimes earn as much as $10,000 a year (a Montreal editor claimed to me that salaries were only 10 per cent below New York levels, but I should have thought 25 per cent would have been a more representative figure). Lower down, the numerous small local papers like the *Elliot Lake Standard* (circulation 4000, twice weekly) can only pay its reporters (or reporter) about $4500. The worst feature of the salary scales in Canadian journalism is that, as in many other professions, there is a serious lack of differential. For instance, on most Canadian newspapers the Foreign Editor usually gets paid rather less than the top reporters, while the Editor-in-Chief of an excellent little paper like the *Chronicle Telegraph* would probably be earning as little as two-thirds the salary of the Chief Reporter on the *Toronto Globe and Mail*.

American competition affects dailies much less than it does the magazine world. Yet syndicated columns, such as that of the Alsop Brothers and even the London *Observer* foreign news service, are available to Canadian newspapers at a much lower price than similar Canadian features, with their much smaller markets. Result: fewer openings for Canadian journalists. Due to the proximity of New York, the Montreal (English) and Toronto papers are the most aware of American competition, and consequently have to provide a rather larger proportion of parochial news to keep up their readership.

Most of the leading Canadian newspapers tack the word 'independent' on to their banner somewhere. This does not necessarily mean that they are not diehard supporters of one Party or another (there is often one 'Independent Liberal' and one 'Independent Conservative' organ in the major cities) but it does impart an agreeable impression of flexibility, thereby gaining badly needed circulation that an otherwise rigid front might drive into the arms of a rival. Their endeavours not to antagonise, however, tend also to be accompanied inevitably by a certain editorial pallidness. There are few notable Canadian cartoonists and few columnists commanding a national readership. By and large, the linguistic quality of Canadian journalism is not high. This reflects of course the poor salaries offered by the profession, and perhaps, also, the long-term effect of the poverty of instruction in the English language at Canadian schools. But Canadians at least take the profession seriously; several of their universities now have their own separate 'Departments of Journalism'. The Canadian Press (with the exception of one or two of the sleazier sex-tabloids) has higher morals and is a good deal more scrupulous than our own 'popular' Press; devotees of the British 'Sundays' are hardly in a position to throw stones at even the very worst the New World can produce.

Despite all the forces against it, the Canadian Press does, in fact, manage to maintain remarkably high standards. (It is also somehow profitable to its owners.) Although essentially American both in make-up and style, in tone it likes to think of itself as being rather less flamboyant and rather more gentlemanly. In comparison to the American provincial Press (and one must remember that the Canadian Press is, by definition, largely provincial), its news value is, in general, several degrees higher. This is especially true of the Prairies, where, with a population much more concerned about the outside world than the American Midwesterners, a substantial portion of each paper is devoted to foreign news coverage and comment. Some of them also have quite excellent book sections. The *Winnipeg Free Press* could compare very favourably to the *Yorkshire Post* (once upon a time, in the days of a Titan called John W. Dafoe, it could have compared even to the *Manchester Guardian*). The most parochial of the Canadian newspapers seem to be on the West Coast (with the possible exception of Bruce Hutchinson's *Victoria Daily Times*), but this is the same in the United States. One of the contributors to *The Culture of Contemporary Canada* aptly remarks: 'We haven't any daily as bad as the *Chicago Tribune*, because we haven't any city as big as Chicago; but also we haven't anything as good as the *New York Times*.'[1] However, a paper like the *Montreal Star* is very nearly in the 'national' class in the way that the *New York Times* is — and with considerably higher standards than at least three-quarters of the British nationals. Another publication deserving particular mention is the *Financial Post*,

[1] Frank H. Underhill, *ibid.*

appearing twice weekly (from the same stable as *Maclean's*) but otherwise a genuine 'national' and one of the most informative (not only on financial matters) and well-edited publications produced anywhere.

Radio and Television—Few aspects of Canada's post-war revolution have had a more dramatic impact than the advent of coast-to-coast television. In 1952 Canada had no TV network at all, and only a few years ago visitors used to comment on the huge height of aerials on Canadian homes — all straining to pick up programmes from across the border. Native TV was either unobtainable or just not good enough. But by 1956 Canada had already become second only to the United States in its number of TV broadcasting stations and third (after Britain) in the number of receivers.[1] The year 1959 saw the completion of the world's longest TV network, 4200 miles from coast to coast, relayed along a chain of automatic micro-wave towers that resemble giant oil derricks; the 20th-century's successor to the CPR. National television has now been brought to some 82 per cent of all Canadians — a phenomenal achievement in a country this size. (In Alberta alone, for instance, there are five TV and sixteen radio stations.) Since the first programmes went over the air, expenditure on CBC television has risen from just over $3 million to over $50 million a year. About three-quarters of all Canadians now have TV sets in their homes, which they view for an astonishing average total of over $4\frac{1}{2}$ hours a day, and aerials are growing noticeably shorter — implying general satisfaction with home-grown programmes.

The day after I had made a brief appearance on a Canadian TV programme called 'Tabloid', I was stopped at least a dozen times on the streets of Toronto. 'Everybody watches TV in Canada these days,' an Irish bus-driver explained. Certainly nothing has ever linked Canada together quite like this TV network; never has the West been made so aware of what the East is up to, and vice versa. Its cultural implications have been equally great. It has multiplied the openings for actors, writers, musicians, singers and ballet dancers. In Britain· and other societies where the

[1] From *The Culture of Contemporary Canada*, ibid.

Arts are more highly developed, television has generally had the effect of emptying theatres. This is far less true of Canada, where a TV production may often spark off curiosity in people who would never in their lives have seen a ballet or an opera to go to watch it in real life, or to see what the Stratford actors look like on the stage. As the CBC report for 1958 remarked, probably more Canadians saw its one production of *Madame Butterfly* than 'if it had run at Toronto's Royal Alexandra Theatre for six months.' Thus, at this stage in her cultural development, Canada is one of the few Western nations where television is an all-round blessing.

Broadcasting in Canada represents an unusual combination of private and public enterprise, with all stations coming under the surveillance of the CBC Board of Governors. The CBC network itself derives about half its income from commercial advertising and half from the Government. There is no TV or radio licence fee, only a 15 per cent purchase tax on receivers, but the largest share of the public contribution comes from other Federal revenues. The CBC's vetting of both commercially sponsored programmes and advertising is very strict indeed, and there is a long list of 'unacceptable accounts' — such as laxatives, gargles, etc. (but nowhere does the list of proscribed references quite approach the silliness of US commercial broadcasting, where on one network recently the expression 'blind drunk' was deleted — because it implied an insult to the blind!). Everybody grumbles at the CBC, and it seems to be under attack almost constantly from one section of the country or another. Canadians perhaps do not realise how lucky they are; before they lambaste their own CBC, they should come to Britain and subject themselves to the barrel-loads of hogwash piped out daily by the BBC and ITV, as represented by the dreadfully unfunny comedians, the dull talks on meaningless topics, the same sugary light music squeezed as if from a cake icing-bag by indifferent orchestras, year in year out. In fact, the fundamental system of the CBC is an effective and highly intelligent compromise of the sort that Canadians are so good at. Its backing of public funds enables it to produce serious, high-level programmes that a 100 per cent commercial network might not be prepared to risk. But it has to walk a precarious tight-rope. If its programmes become too highbrow, it may lose listeners to the trashier private stations, or to the American networks — and with them, of course, go CBC's commercial backers. On the other hand, its dependence on commercial backing introduces an element of competition (that the BBC so often seems to lack) demanding that whatever goes out over the air is *good*.

And, by and large, CBC broadcasting is remarkably good. Its quality seems especially high, when one considers that the Canadians operate a programme schedule which is greater than any of the US networks, and on a budget of perhaps one-tenth as much; and that a station in Chicago alone can reach as large a 'commercial' market as the whole of Canada. Moreover, these limited resources, slender as they are, are reduced still further by having to cover the costs of two entirely separate networks, in two different languages, and extending over seven different time zones. It is hardly surprising that salaries suffer as a result; in the words of a Canadian producer and playwright: 'Nowhere in the whole of our artistic life is the difference so great between the earning power of star performers and directors here and abroad as it is in television.' [1]

Withme across Canada I carried a pocket radio which I turned on every night, or whenever we had a rare idle moment. It did not take me long to appreciate how vastly superior CBC sound transmissions generally were to most of the US programmes I could pick up at the same time. Commercials were far less tiresome, and more discreetly timed. I reckoned that on average I could listen through between three and four, sometimes five, programmes before being actively bored or repelled — about twice my staying power with the BBC. A sample Sunday evening's listening which I noted down in Edmonton went as follows:

1. 'Citizens' Forum.' This claims to be the only one-hour continuous current affairs debate on the North American radio. The debate that evening was on the state of the Liberal Party; other typical subjects had been

---

[1] Mavor Moore, in *The Arts in Canada, ibid.*

'The Death Penalty Should Go', 'Canada Should Recognise Red China', and 'Bright and Dull — Should They Be Segregated at School?'

Next came

2. An erudite dissertation on 20th-century classics of literature.

3. A string orchestra playing songs by Mendelssohn, and finally,

4. Two pieces for lute by Segovia.

A breakdown of CBC programmes for a typical week in 1958 showed that on TV 44 per cent were devoted to some kind of drama, and something more than 20 per cent to other serious or informative broadcasts. A notable feature was TV's 'Concert Hour' which in five years has produced 88 operas and 82 ballets. Another recent success has been 'Rawhide' produced by Max Ferguson, one of Canada's brightest Angry Young Men, which with rare acid wit sought each programme to demolish one of the more pretentious Canadian gods. On sound, serious music comprised 12 per cent over the same week, news and weather another 12 per cent, 18 per cent for other serious programmes, and 7 per cent for drama. Comparable to Britain's Third Programme, the CBC's ultra-highbrow 'Wednesday Night' provides three hours of un-interrupted theatre, music or talks; the regional and national school broadcasts are the most extensive in the world, and considered by many to be the best. Finally, in 1959, the CBC gained recognition of its merit by winning the cherished Italia Prize for *A Beach of Strangers*, a play for voices, in verse, written and produced by a 33-year-old British Columbian, John Reeves.

Under the latest regulations governing CBC television, from 1961 on, at least 55 per cent of the content of programmes are to be 'Canadian', as part of a studied effort to reduce American influence over the air. This will necessitate a great deal of original production; already the CBC claims to use a considerably higher proportion of 'live' television than even the BBC. This is still truer of the CBC's French network, which, isolated and determined to wage its battle for cultural survival even (or especially) over the ether, has to produce virtually all its own material. Some 14 per cent of its programmes originate from France, only 5 per cent from US sources; otherwise the rest is all its own work, representing the highest output of live TV of any network in the Western World. I spent an afternoon in the French CBC studios in Montreal, and was greatly impressed by the vitality and imagination of the productions I saw. Even English-speaking producers admitted that the French network reaches a higher level, generally, than their own.

A growing use is being made by Canadian TV of home-produced films, and brief mention should be made here of the film industry. It is in fact still very much in its infancy in Canada, and there is no Hollywood or Elstree. Virtually all film production is centred around the National Film Board, a Crown Corporation, which started life just before the war in an old saw mill on the Ottawa River. The Board produces exclusively documentaries depicting Canadian life, two to three hundred a year, and some of them of outstandingly high quality. Its *City of Gold* on the Klondike gold-rush won the 1957 Cannes Festival award for short films, and its serial on the Royal Canadian Mounted Police has been bought by British television. That Canada still offers an eminently exciting backdrop for fictional films was indicated by the recent revival in London of the brilliant war-time film *The 49th Parallel*; though dated, it was as enthralling as ever.

The Canada Council—In 1951 a Royal Commission set up to investigate the state of the Arts, Letters and Sciences, and headed by Mr. Vincent Massey, strongly urged the creation of a Canada Council. This was finally established in 1957 by Act of Parliament, with its object 'to foster and promote the study and enjoyment of, and production of works in, the arts, humanities and social sciences'. For its task the Canada Council was voted a grant of $100 million. Half of this sum goes to a fund of which both capital and interest are to be devoted to construction of university buildings, and allotted to each Province strictly on a basis proportional to its population (undoubtedly the only fair distribution, but in practice it means that Ontario, which can afford more, will also get more). The remaining $50 million is an Endowment Fund of which only the income, about $2·5 million a year, is available for distribution — a small sum compared with the enormous needs it has to cover.

Right from the start the Canada Council has been faced with monumental problems. The applications flooded in; they included one from an inventor asking help to patent a new brassiere, and another from a Californian who wanted to publish a song on the Dionne Quintuplets. Where should the Council start? Should it concentrate its funds on creating talent, by the liberal granting of scholarships; or on boosting the means for employing talent that already exists, by subsidies to theatres, ballets, and so on? Whom should it back; the British Professor engaged in research on the Canadian Eskimo, or the Canadian Professor writing a book about the manorial system in 14th-century Britain? In its short existence the Council has shown that it can achieve wonders with infusions of even small sums of money, wisely spent. For $5500 it was able to send the Halifax Symphony Orchestra to Newfoundland to give fourteen concerts to people many of whom had never seen nor heard an orchestra before; for less than $15,000 it took the Montreal Bach Choir to participate in the Edinburgh Festival; for only $600 it enabled Whitehorse in the remote Yukon to have a season of four concerts by visiting artists, as well as special concerts for children. By yearly subsidies it can assure the survival of such organisations as the Royal Winnipeg Ballet. By providing scholarships of only a few hundred dollars, it has already proved that it can save for Canada talent that might otherwise drift towards American centres of learning. By special grants, it can counter the paralysing costs of transportation that, for a Trans-Canada tour of eleven cities by the Toronto Symphony Orchestra, would result in an average deficit of $6000 per performance, even with full houses. Among its ultimate objectives, the Canada Council hopes to bring about the day when 'most of the larger towns or cities across Canada could average at least one first-class presentation every year of an orchestra, opera and ballet.' In its aims to establish scholarships for Commonwealth students at Canadian universities, Rhodes in reverse, the gratitude expressed by the Chairman of the Council, Mr. Brooke

Claxton, was particularly moving to British ears when he spoke of making 'some contribution to those others, like Britain and France, to whom we owe so much.' [1]

Education—This is perhaps the most cherished of all the 'Provincial Rights' granted by the BNA Act. Throughout Canada education comes under special departments within the governments of each Province, and is financed from Provincial revenues. As a result, both in form and quality it can vary considerably from Province to Province, and, not unnaturally, standards tend to be higher in the larger centres than in isolated rural communities. All Canadian children start school at 6, but leaving age varies between 14, 15 and 16. Public (in the North American sense) schools are free in most parts of Canada, but in Newfoundland and Quebec fees may be charged at both elementary and secondary schools. In Newfoundland, schools are still run almost exclusively by the various religious denominations, with the majority (and probably the best) in the hands of the Salvation Army. Quebec has two virtually separate systems; Catholic and Protestant. Ontario, Saskatchewan and Alberta also have some denominational schools. (In Alberta there is a curious system of financing them, whereby tax on a corporation may be assessed according to the religions of its shareholders!) One factor, however, that is almost universal across the country, applying equally to schools and universities, is that education is based much more closely — and increasingly so — on the American model than on the British. The emphasis is strongly on the practical and utilitarian, as opposed to the abstract; both in Canada as well as the United States, the hand of John Dewey still lies heavy on education.

The closest to the British system is to be found in the 'private' (or, as they now call themselves, 'independent') schools, the equivalent of both British preparatory and public schools. For boys, there are about seventeen such schools in Canada, some of which have British headmasters and still play rugger and cricket. Standards are often high, and so are fees. Between 3 and 5 per cent of Canadian

[1] From an article, 'Culture to Keep Pace With Prosperity', in *The Times Canada Supplement* of November 12th, 1957.

children of both sexes go to private schools (compared with 2 per cent for boys only at public schools in Britain). There is, however, no equivalent to the British grammar schools — which educate some 20 per cent of our male population. Thus in Canada the great majority of children attend the public elementary schools until they are about 13, and secondary or high schools until they are 18. As in the States, all these are coeducational.

Canada's educational problems tend to dwarf all others on the cultural scene. One-third of her population is now under 15, and some idea of what Canada's extremely high birth-rate means to her schools can be gleaned from the fact revealed in a 1954 census that, whereas there were only 71,004 students in Grade XI (*i.e.* 16–17 year olds), there were 375,934 in Grade I of Canadian schools. There is still a serious shortage of good teachers; although this has to some extent been mitigated by recent large-scale imports from Britain. Distance also plays its ineluctable role. A large proportion of schools in rural districts are still of the one-room, one-teacher variety coping with several grades, but the education authorities make great (and often ingenious) efforts to provide children in outlying districts with a decent education. In some parts of the Prairies, tracked Snowmobiles take the children to school in winter. In the remoter parts of Northwest Ontario there are more than 6000 children in communities too scattered to support a regular school. Now school is brought to them in the form of a railway coach converted into a school-room and living quarters for the teacher. There are three of these schools on wheels and they cover an area larger than Wales each school term; yet some children still have to make a 30-mile canoe— or sled — journey to reach the school coach. At an isolated company town like Keno Hill in the North Yukon, with a population of just 500, the local school goes up only to Grade IX (13–14), and subsequently children are flown, at company expense, to boarding schools in Edmonton a thousand miles away. For families beyond the reach of any school, most Provinces have extensive correspondence school courses.

Canada is spending an enormous amount of money on

Shakespeare Festival Theatre, Stratford, Ontario

NEW BUILDINGS FOR THE ARTS

Jubilee Auditorium, Edmonton, Alberta

Children's section in Vancouver's new public library

EDUCATION IN CANADA

Boys' choir at Manitoba Music Festival

education — roughly $1,000,000,000 a year, or 3 per cent of
her Gross National Product. In relative terms, this is about
twice as much as Britain. All the way across Canada I
was struck by the excellence of the new school buildings.
Whether it were in a small fishing village in Nova Scotia,
at Schefferville on the boundary of Labrador, at Trail BC
or Keno Hill in the Yukon, the new high school was almost
invariably the proudest building in town — generally followed by the hospital.

But what of the education inside ?

At Kitimat in the apartment of some British immigrants
I listened in on a heated argument between three British
teachers from the local schools. Two were very young, had
been in Canada less than a year, and found little good to say
about Canadian education ; the third, an Ulsterman, was
older and had been out several years, in various parts of
Canada. There were lots of aspects of Canadian education
that worried him, but he could find mitigating circumstances
for most of them, and he weighed his judgments carefully.
He found it difficult, he said, to get work out of his students.
They lacked interest and did no 'background' reading ; the
lure of fishing and the outdoor life of BC was too strong.
(On the other hand, the Canadian Principal of the high
school at Trail BC told me that he found the children of
the British immigrants in his school, though educationally
more advanced, tended to be 'less adult than Canadians,
lacking in a sense of responsibility, and emotionally in-
hibited'.) The Kitimat teacher taught geography and
history, and it depressed him to have to identify for 17-year-
olds the various countries of the world. The only disciplinary
measures permitted were a maximum of thirty minutes
detention each day ('What use is that with a great tough of
16 who's been fire-fighting in the bush all summer ?'), but
most of all he blamed the curriculum imposed by the Department of Education in Victoria, which, he said, 'did nothing
to encourage a genuine love of learning'. This was a complaint I heard frequently from teachers in other parts of
Canada. Then, too, his work was not aided by the ultra-
sensitivity of his students to any implied criticism from a
'foreigner'. He told me how, when he had remarked to a

P

particularly materialistic youth that earning dollars was not everything, that education in itself was a good thing, the reply came back: 'Well, what good has it done England?'

This teacher felt, however, that education was 'better organised in Canada'. Even as far afield as Kitimat, schools were frequently visited by inspectors; although this resulted in a much more rigid adherence to the set curriculum of which he disapproved. This insistence that a centrally ordained syllabus be followed to the word is a feature I found commented on in many Provinces. At times the conformism of Canadian education in its endeavours to 'teach the youth to be Canadians' verges on absurdity. A few years ago an Englishman visiting Aklavik on the Arctic Coast was shocked to discover that in the Anglican Mission School (directed from Ottawa, 3500 miles away) '. . . the first reader for the Eskimo and Loucheux children was in *Streets and Roads* . . . teaching them about cities they would never see, in terms beyond their comprehension.'[1] But, as the Kitimat teacher rightly pointed out to me, there were good reasons behind the conformist urge. In a country where in the same school you might have an Irish, a German, a Hungarian and a Swedish teacher — especially among a scattered and 'nomadic' population like that of BC (some of the Kitimat high school students had been to as many as 15 schools in 12 years) — you had to have some rigidly established norm; even to the extent of applying almost police-state measures to get recalcitrants like the Doukhubors to send their children to recognised schools.

A British scientist in another part of Canada complained to me about the 'Credit System', which, he said, encouraged children to select the easiest courses. At the local high school, they could (and obviously did) choose carpentry instead of French. His son had gained three credits, out of 120 needed for matriculation, simply for being in the Air Cadets. Apparently brighter than average, he wanted to take English Literature and Physics in his last year; but, as there was no demand for the more 'difficult' Liberal Arts' courses there were not enough students to form a class in English Literature, so he would have to take 'Industrial Arts' instead.

[1] Ritchie Calder, *Men Against the Frozen North.*

More than once I was struck by the poverty of the English language as spoken by the average Canadian (especially young Canadians). It seemed to me to point to one of the most serious deficiencies of Canadian education. No form of English is more pleasing to the ears than that spoken by a well-educated Canadian, but, whenever I listened to a radio debate or public speeches, perhaps four out of five participants appeared to verge on inarticulacy, fumbling and groping for words — and, as often as not, ending up with the wrong one. The fault lies at both school and university level; too little attention is given to spoken English in the schools, and far too little to the English Classics. For instance, in the reading list for the last year of English in BC schools, students apparently have a choice between *The Little World of Don Camillo* (English Literature?) and *Martin Chuzzlewit*. Very little encouragement is given to public speaking or debating; in fact, it is sometimes said that in Canadian politics a good speaker tends to be automatically distrusted.

To be fair to the Canadians, it is quite possible that the immigrants are themselves partly to blame for the debasing of English in Canada. In Calgary I used to have breakfast every morning at a motel counter run by a fat and sleazy pair of Liechtensteiners, recently emigrated. I noted that when anyone said 'I'd like a fried egg and a coffee, please', he generally had to repeat the order at least twice; but when a Ukranian oil-driller came in and barked 'sunny-side up, coffee, 'n quick' they knew exactly what he wanted. And so to cope with the hundreds of thousands of lunatic foreigners that have poured into the country since the war, a sort of Basic Canadian has sprung up. Deviate from any of its 120 impoverished words, and as likely as not you will be met with that infuriating 'Parrdon?' The girl behind the counter, the waitress, or the hotel booking-clerk will very likely have understood you the first time, but, just as an unexpected noise will stop a cow ruminating, so the strange sound of non-Basic English will disturb her conditioning and bring forth that inevitable, reflexive 'Parrdon?' It is not simply a nationalist conspiracy directed against the English of the English.

The biggest single difference between the Canadian and British school systems is that, whereas in Britain the sub-average students tend to be sacrificed in efforts to bring on the ablest, education in Canada is based strictly on the 'Convoy System', where the rate of progress of a class is geared to the pace of its slowest members. There is no 'streaming' in Canadian schools, no 'eleven plus', and, as already mentioned, there are no grammar schools. Instead of streaming, Canadian schools are experimenting with three different approaches. One is '*acceleration*', whereby an above-average student is simply made either to 'jump a grade' or do three years' work in two. This is not entirely desirable, as the student may suffer from being thrust into a class physically more mature than himself. A second alternative is '*enrichment*', whereby the above-average are given special and more advanced courses. But this has the disadvantage of placing an additional burden on Canada's already over-taxed teachers, and — unless the 'enrichment' course is most skilfully planned — the bright child may find that the only reward genius brings is having to work harder. Result: disillusion. The third method, and nearest to Britain's streaming procedure, is '*segregation*' whereby consistently bright students are skimmed off to special schools. 'Segregation', Canadian-style is, however, still in the experimental stage and the special schools for the talented have been set up in only a few cities.

This failure to develop the brightest brains appears to disturb the Canadians more than any other deficiency in the system. They have long prided themselves that theirs is a fair and 'democratic' one, but many are now beginning to agree with the late Dr. Sidney Smith, former Minister for External Affairs and one of Canada's leading educationists, that 'an educational system based on egalitarian principles is foredoomed to failure. The true democratic principle is equality of opportunity . . . [which] means that the best brains must be afforded just as great an opportunity to develop to their full capacity as the slow.' In 1956 a survey conducted in Toronto's secondary schools purported to show the disillusion that educational egalitarianism is causing the gifted; out of every five students with an IQ of over 130, three did not go on to university, and nearly half of them did not even complete their schooling.

But are the end results of Canadian education quite as bad, compared with our own, as Britons in Canada claim, and as indeed many Canadians themselves believe? On returning to England I was interested to read the views of a British expert, Mr. John Sharp, Headmaster of the Prince Rupert School at Wilhelmshaven, who had made a detailed study of both systems under a Nuffield Fellowship.[1] Mr. Sharp had some hard things to say about the effects of 'streaming' in British schools: 'To be classified as "B Stream" (or lower) by the age of eight — and thus in all probability to see the way to a professional, if not even a clerical, career already closed — is not an odd freak of injustice. It is the experience of thousands (one might say, of the majority) of English children.' He particularly condemned the 'mechanical device' of the psychological IQ tests that relegated them to places of inferiority at so tender an age (and, I must admit, I agree with him). At Canadian schools he had noted a better, more assured atmosphere than that in Britain — caused by 'the existence of a sense of failure on the part of English children (that is, we should remember, at least three out of every four) who have "failed the eleven plus" . . .'

Mr. Sharp agreed that British education was 'mainly superior' to the Canadian, noting that 'in the high schools I saw there, the work of Grade XII would seldom compare with that of an English Upper Sixth Form. Often it was more akin to that of the Fifth Form in a good grammar school.' But — and a vital *but* — he was surprised to find that, whereas 'the mass of the population leaves the schools of England at 15', the great majority of Canadians stayed on for a year or two after the permitted leaving age; by which time they would, in fact, have more than caught up with their British contemporaries. He estimated that of ten Canadian and ten English youths of 17, five of the Canadians would probably still be in school ('in Vancouver the figure would probably be seven'), while several of the rest would have not been long in employment. Of the British, 'one will

[1] John Sharp, *Educating One Nation.*

be in school, possibly two more may have recently left, most of the rest will be out of school some two years already.' He was also surprised 'to find how much more importance appeared to be attached by employers to the attainment of Grade XI or XII by a candidate for a job ; even when the job itself seemed to me not to require any special academic qualifications.'

The tendencies noted by Mr. Sharp also apply to higher education. There are at present somewhere over 86,000 young Canadians who have continued their education beyond high school and are now at college. This compares with only about 97,000 full-time students at universities in Britain in 1958, and within the next five years it is estimated that numbers at Canada's universities will have caught up and probably passed Britain's, despite her numerical superiority of three to one. This is a fact which should put a check to any smugness we may have about the superiority of our education.

There are 32 universities in Canada (Britain 20), ranging in size from Toronto University's 15,000 to 500 or less in some of the Maritime universities, and another two hundred and fifty 'degree-granting colleges', generally affiliated to the universities. There are no colleges exclusively for women, as there are in the States, and the ratio of women at Canadian universities is about one in three ; considerably higher than in Britain, but lower than in the United States. The three Maritime Provinces boast no less than 16 universities and colleges ; there are six universities in the Province of Quebec and seven in Ontario. Some of the older universities, such as King's College in Halifax which is Anglican, are sectarian. The University of Manitoba is unique in that it was formed in 1877 as a coalition between three existing colleges (Anglican, Presbyterian and Catholic French-Canadian), but is in itself non-denominational — as are most of the larger universities (with the exception of French Canada's Montreal and Laval) and the Provincial universities in the West.

Standards vary greatly, largely according to environmental needs. Some Canadian universities are very good indeed. Montreal's McGill (founded 1821), probably the best-known abroad, has one of the world's most distinguished medical schools, particularly renowned for its work in neuro-surgery. Until it was hard hit by Duplessis's cutting-off of Federal grants, its School of Physics, where Lord Rutherford once taught, was almost as famous. Yet it was still able, a few years ago, to father the invention known as the 'McGill Fence' which provides the warning system along the Mid-Canada Line. With some 8000 students of both sexes, it comes closest to resembling Oxford and Cambridge. The University of Toronto (1827) is perhaps the nearest kin to London University. Thanks in part to Mr. Duplessis, it has become Canada's No. 1 scientific centre among the universities; much of Canadian research on supersonics is now done at its Institute of Aerophysics. It was also at the University of Toronto that Sir Frederick Banting discovered insulin in 1921. Its Law School is probably the best in Canada, the School of Graduate Studies has a high reputation, and mention has already been made of its Royal Conservatory of Music.

In the West, higher education is centred around the four Provincial universities of which the University of British Columbia in Vancouver is the largest with some 7500 students. These Western universities come somewhere in between British 'red-brick' and American State colleges. Courses tend to be patterned along the American system of the general rather than the specialist; on the other hand they eschew 'exotics' such as the Faculties of 'Mortuary Science', etc., that thrive in some US colleges, and view with a wry smile Southern California's granting of 'Football Degrees'. In place of exotics, the University of Manitoba boasts one of the world's few Chairs of Icelandic Studies, the only school for Ukrainian Orthodox priests in North America, and the only Department of Judaic Studies in Canada. Its Law School has for some time experimented with the innovation of students being articled to local firms while still at university. It also has what is probably Canada's leading agricultural college. The University of Saskatchewan at Saskatoon has a high record of scholasticism and pioneered the world's first anti-cancer cobalt bomb, although it only celebrated its 50th anniversary in 1959. Its next-door neighbour in Alberta, which has just opened up a new School of

Music, was founded one year earlier. Perhaps typical of interests on the Prairies today was the division of University of Alberta students among the various faculties that I found in 1958; Arts and Science, 1121; Engineering, 1074; Medicine, 212; and Agriculture only 101. In standards and aims, the University of British Columbia, the youngest, largest and perhaps most vital of the four, comes closest to resembling an American West Coast university. Its dynamic, tirelessly campaigning President, Dr. N. A. M. Mackenzie, told me that he considered the UBC's principal function was to provide a good education to the 'most', and to even out the uneven education possibilities provided by the BC schools. As a result entry qualifications are more 'liberal' at UBC than elsewhere.

Dr. Mackenzie himself (together with Dr. Bissell, who, President of University of Toronto at the age of 40, was described to me as a 'hard-headed egghead') is perhaps typical of modern Canadian heads of universities — a distinguished academician, but in his position as President rather more concerned in expansion and the material development of the university than in scholastic fields. And the 'physical plant' of most of these newer Canadian universities is really impressive; Alberta, for instance, has the most magnificent new library I have seen in any university of its size. Contrary to what I had heard, and seen, of the atmosphere of Canadian schools, at the universities it was impossible not to sense an immense enthusiasm and keenness. I suspect that more work gets done in Canadian universities than at Oxford and Cambridge; if this is so, it is probably because — in the North American scheme of things — the great majority of Canadians 'work their way' through university by taking summer jobs, and are therefore perhaps more determined to make their efforts worthwhile. It may be relevant that only an estimated 14 per cent of Canadian undergraduates receive some kind of financial aid, compared with 70 per cent in Great Britain.

Despite the high standard of university equipment, Canadians are disturbed that this may not be enough. Each year the universities receive some $16 million in Federal grants, and now they will receive another $50 million (spread over about ten years) from the Canada Council. But, in 1955, the Gordon Commission claimed that if universities were to meet the 'upsurge' [1] expected within the next ten years, they must receive at least $40 m. a year. Since SPUTNIK, Canada has become seriously worried at the quantity of scientists she is turning out (although, to an outsider, what Canada achieves in the scientific world is quite remarkable) — particularly when every year a steady flow of her best brains is drained away by the United States.[2] To meet the problem, a lot of valuable work is done by two bodies that — in scope, anyway — are more or less unique; the National Research Council and the Defence Research Board of the Armed Forces. The former has an annual budget of $17 million, of which about a seventh is channelled to the universities, and affiliated to it is Atomic Energy of Canada Ltd. The DRB receives some $52 million a year and, with a payroll of 2500 (including many British scientists), is Canada's biggest employer of scientific brains.

An essential feature of the Canadian university is its 'Extension' programme. This consists of lectures given to outside adult audiences, in courses ranging from Drama to Prospecting, from Choral Music of Bach and Handel to Child Psychology, Space Technology and the Art of the Interview (or how diplomatically to sack an employee). After seven or eight years of some of these night courses, it is possible to get a BA from a number of Canadian universities; including Toronto. Bizarre as some of their titles may sound, these Extension courses undoubtedly do much good. At Antigonish, the Catholic University of St. Francis Xavier has long been renowned for the success it has had both in improving the economic standing and developing the intellectual interests of the Nova Scotian fishing families through its extension programme. On the Prairies, these programmes

[1] According to the Dominion Bureau of Standards, university applicants may be doubled by 1965, and trebled by 1972.

[2] For this state of affairs, the Gordon Report blames largely the lack of research facilities for graduates at Canadian universities. '... In the academic year of 1953-4 more than 1200 Canadians entered United States graduate schools. We know well that scientists must have made up a considerable proportion of these two categories and also that relatively few Canadians trained in American graduate schools returned to Canada,' says Rollo Earl in *Culture in Canada, ibid.*

seem to be a particularly active function of each university, with lecturers spending their entire year in planes and trains journeying to give courses in remote areas; I was told of one such lecturer from a Western university who had had to wait while inhabitants of an outlying hamlet cleared grain from the village barn before he could use it as an *ad hoc* lecture hall. Courses are extremely well attended; the University of Alberta estimated that in 1956–7 it provided some 1700 talks to audiences totalling 100,000. This university also maintains its own radio station for the same purpose. In 1933, virtually as an extension of its Extension programme, it launched the Banff School of Fine Arts, which holds summer courses in music, painting, drama, ceramics, weaving and oral French, and, in the autumn, a school of Advanced Business Management.

A generation ago virtually all the textbooks and many of the professors at Canadian universities were imported. A good proportion of the books (including — a galling fact — works on Canadian history) still come from the United States, but Canada has now established a respectable cadre of professorship of her own. Yet, with her rapidly growing population, the problem of a dearth of competent teachers — especially in the schools — is always hovering there in the Canadian background. In 1955 one-third of Canada's teaching force had qualifications below a good leaving certificate from the XIth or XIIth grade. As a result, British teachers are still particularly welcome; just before I left for Canada 120 had been 'recruited' by British Columbia House alone. Unfortunately, as at home, the teaching profession is not handsomely rewarded, and there is no equivalent of the Burnham Scale in Canada. Some 3000 teachers or research workers are still said to leave Canada each year for the United States in search of better prospects.[1] According to the Gordon Report, the median salary for 3954 full-time academic staff at Canadian universities was only $5775 a year; or not much more than half what a hard-working truck driver in the Yukon can earn.[2] But, in terms of standard

[1] Miriam Chapin, *Contemporary Canada*.
[2] This was in 1955, but since then the earning power of teachers has not appreciably moved ahead in comparison to truck drivers or other members of the community.

of living, this still means that at both university and school level teachers can in fact do better for themselves in Canada than in Britain. Because of the country's rapid expansion, advancement is also quicker; several of the Principals of Canadian high schools I met were men in their thirties. One snag, however, of which Britons frequently seem unaware, is that before taking a permanent teaching job in most Canadian Provinces, immigrants have to pass an exam, and possibly a 'conversion course' to bring them to conformity with Canadian educational methods. This often irks experienced British teachers, but because of the need for standardisation that I have mentioned earlier, it is really hardly surprising that Canadian educational authorities should require it.

In conclusion, perhaps the most heartening factor common to the entire Canadian cultural scene is the awareness of deficiency and the urge for improvement. Most Canadians realise that their educational system is not perfect, and are determined to do something about it. (And what about ourselves? — or are we smug enough to think ours needs no perfecting?) As long as concern about her cultural status continues to goad Canada on, one cannot help feeling that, remarkable as her progress has been over the last ten years, it will be nothing to what she may achieve over the next ten. If the present rate of advance continues, by the end of the coming decade 'New Canadians' will have no justification whatsoever to grumble 'there's no culture in Canada', and the day may not be so very far distant when promising young Britons will actually go to Toronto to have their voices trained — just as today famous men from many lands make pilgrimages to Ottawa to be photographed by the great Karsh.

CHAPTER TEN

FROM LIQUOR TO LABOUR

Some people say that Canada has contributed no great thing to the world's culture. They have overlooked the Canadian summer shack. (BRUCE HUTCHISON, *Canada, Tomorrow's Giant*)

The wilderness remains a partner in the venture. (The Gordon Commission Report)

THE late Hermann Goering is supposed to have remarked that whenever he heard anyone speak of 'Culture' he reached for his revolver. One could sympathise with him, if for no other reason that there is no more hackneyed, overworked or unsatisfactory word in the English language, having to convey so much but in fact ending up by meaning so little. At Cambridge I pursued one of the undergraduates who had complained about the deficiencies of Canadian 'culture', to find out just what he understood by that word. 'Well,' he said, 'to begin with, there aren't any pubs.' I remember thinking at the time, a little scornfully, that this was a fair indication of the frivolity of the rest of his complaints against the Canadian cultural scene. But after travelling from coast to coast across Canada and meeting, in the process, many serious-minded British immigrants with the same complaint in the same context, I was no longer so sure. Culture, after all, does mean more than just books and pictures; when a French Canadian speaks about 'defending his culture', he means everything from St. Joseph's Oratory to Quebec's delicious traditional pea soup. At the Brussels Fair of 1958, one of the main exhibits in the United Kingdom pavilion was a typical British pub. And why not? For pubs are as integral a part of our heritage as Shakespeare or Hogarth. This is a serious matter. Let it be said at once, they do not exist at all in Canada, and this is a deficiency that genuinely causes more distress to more British immigrants

222

than the absence of Covent Garden, Hatchards, the Tate or the Old Vic.[1]

For many years the Canadian Liquor Laws (which vary from Province to Province) have provided an unfailing reservoir for music-hall jokes. Eighty years ago Corporal Donkin, an Englishman with an acid wit serving in the Northwest Mounted Police, remarked that 'in Canada there are no barmaids; society is not sufficiently educated for them.' In the days of American Prohibition, a gay little ditty used to be passed around in a Canadian border town:

> Four and twenty Yankees, feeling very dry,
>   Went across the border to get a drink of rye.
> When the rye was opened, the Yanks began to sing,
>   'God bless America, but God save the King!'

But when the United States gave up the unequal struggle, for long years Canada remained the drier of the two countries. Why it did so is hardly a matter for discussion here, except to note in passing that in most of the Canadian Provinces the anti-alcohol movement has had strongly religious undertones, led by such powerful lobbies as the Women's Christian Temperance Union, and forces within the Nonconformist Churches (sometimes known to their foes among the 'wets' as 'Iced Water Baptists'). Because of this moralist background, the approach to the Liquor Laws has been that 'all drinking is a sin, and if you have to sin you must do it in private'. The result has been that, until quite recently (outside of Quebec Province, which, as might be expected, has always shown the most broad-mindedness in its licensing laws) there were virtually no common drinking places throughout Canada; what there were were limited to dreary heavily-controlled, men-only 'Beer Parlours'. At the hub of the laws was (and still is) the Liquor Commission, in some cities (like Winnipeg) disguised under the more genteel title of 'Retail Stores', a state-owned commissary rationing out liquor to approved permit-holders. (Ironically enough, at least one of the most passionately dry Prairie Provinces has in the past been saved from bankruptcy largely by the

[1] A view backed up by a *Financial Post* Survey carried out in 1957 to ascertain what British immigrants missed most in Canada; 34·4 per cent, the largest single category, said pubs.

revenue gained from the sale of liquor through these com-
missaries.) On leaving the Commission store, your purchase
is discreetly wrapped so as not to injure the susceptibilities
of the public; if the paper should perchance fall off before
you reach your den, you may be as heavily fined as if you
had committed indecent exposure. In Ontario, men have
been fined for drinking a glass of beer on their own front
lawn — because it was in the public gaze. In Alberta,
dentists have been prosecuted for having a 'wee nip' themselves from a brandy bottle nominally kept on the premises
for 'relieving the pain of patients'. The finding of an opened
bottle of Scotch in a car (even if the driver had not had a
drink for a week) could bring more severe penalties than if
the bottle were empty and its contents inside the driver.

The various laws made life particularly harrowing for
barmen on transcontinental trains. As the tax on all drink
consumed in a Province while the train is in transit is earmarked for the government concerned, each bar-car had to
have eight or nine separate and identical lockers of drink, to
be sealed or opened up the moment an invisible frontier was
crossed. In the days when BC had gone 'wet' while
'Bible Bill's' Alberta was still dry, half-way through the
Rockies there would be shouts of 'Drink up, please' and
down came the bar shutters with a slam. Worse still, in
some Provinces individual towns were permitted their own
'local option', so that for the two minutes it took the CPR
express to rattle through the dry hamlet of Bowmanville,
Ont. (population 5407), the harassed barman would once
again have to close up shop.

The idiocies of the laws were legion, and it is hardly
surprising that they have had profound effects on Canadian
social life. Boot-legging has been widespread; the unhappy
'treaty' Indians, banned all alcohol, have rotted away their
systems with illicit brews made from vanilla extract, after-
shave lotion or simply liquid boot-polish with the dye filtered
out through loaves of bread; and impatient, sinful drinking
in sombre hotel rooms has undoubtedly done as much for
many a white Canadian. What in other societies might have
been merely a bonhomous tipler was turned into a patho-
logical drunk. Setting out for a party, the prevailing custom

at many levels of Canadian society has been to 'tank up' in hotel rooms, or at private homes, then pile into a car to steer a lethal course to a near-by restaurant, there to be sobered up by a meal gloomily washed down with iced water; for lunacy, and sheer discomfort, a *modus vivendi* only rivalled in the Commonwealth by Australia's 'six o'clock swill'. Things admittedly have changed a lot in Canada in recent years, but habits built up over so long a period die slowly. Currently, there are reported to be 10,000 new alcoholics each year in Canada, and the 'wets' and the 'dries' debate furiously as to whether this is the legacy of the licensing laws or the result of their relaxation. Despite these apparently high figures, the really remarkable thing — when one recalls what happened in the States as a consequence of Prohibition — is that the Canadians have managed to remain, by and large, such a sober and law-abiding race; a fact which must reflect great credit upon the national character.

One does not know what circumstances provoked the Duke of Edinburgh into his widely quoted attack on the Canadian Liquor Laws during the Royal Tour of 1959 — perhaps he had just been called upon to drink the Queen's health in iced water for the hundredth time — but did he realise on what deadly dangerous ground he was treading? Politically, the issue has been such dynamite that for years few public figures have dared touch it. A newspaper owner in the Maritimes told me that after he had printed an editorial condemning the Liquor Laws, he was nearly run out of the Province: 'I can't describe to you the abuse that came in. If I'd been a politician, I'd have been finished.' But in the last few years big progress has been made. When we were in Calgary during Stampede Week in 1956, I innocently asked the receptionist of a hotel where we could get a drink. She gave me a look of virtue outraged — as if we had asked for a room for the afternoon — and snorted 'there's a Men's Beer Parlour back of the hotel, and one for *her* at the other end of town'. But a plebiscite a year later voted overwhelmingly in favour of mixed cocktail bars, so sin has now triumphed in Alberta. Still, as a concession that rings somehow like a popular music-hall song from Victorian days, bars have to close between 6 and 7 o'clock to give the working man a sporting chance of returning safely to the family bosom. The laws have been similarly relaxed in BC and Manitoba; they needed no relaxing in Quebec, still the most liberal of the Provinces; in Toronto, formerly 'the Good', Liquor Laws in application are now little more oppressive than in London — except that, as almost everywhere else in Canada, you still have to buy your own booze through the Liquor Commission, with a permit. The Maritimes remain the most stubbornly 'dry', with New Brunswick still not permitting even male beer taverns, though even in these Provinces there have been some advances; Prince Edward Island, where a few years ago it required a doctor's prescription to get a bottle of Scotch, now generously allows you four bottles of spirits or four cases of beer a month.

Despite these recent changes in the laws, they still permit the emergence of nothing remotely resembling the cheerful, uninhibited atmosphere of a British pub — or anywhere you might want to relax with your friends over a pint of beer. The nearest approach, the 'Men Only' beer taverns of Canada are soul-destroying institutions, designed either to send a man to serious drink or the nearest Temperance Society, it matters not which. On my first evening in Canada I visited one in Halifax, Nova Scotia, and noted down my impressions before custom rendered me insensitive to the horrors of this institution. A gloomy bunker of a room, with clusters of metal tables containing either four quietly despondent drinkers, or one totally despondent solitary; each with two beers in front of him (the law allows only half-pint glasses, so if you want a pint you simply order two at a time). Surly waiters, anxious for a chance to bounce somebody, and a surlier 'beverage dispenser' glaring at his customers from behind a stainless-steel bar, through the inevitable bottles of blue-tinged hard-boiled eggs that look like some rather nasty laboratory exhibits (I never saw one of those eggs actually eaten). No windows to affront the innocent outside world with this scene of sin, no pictures or decorations on the bleak walls — save admonitory excerpts from Part III of the Regulations of the Nova Scotia Liquor Control Act, informing the sad topers what it takes to get bounced; *i.e.* standing up with a glass in hand — singing —

Repairing salmon nets,
Vancouver Island, BC

Ski school at Mont Tremblant, near Montreal

THE QUEEN IN CANADA

*Behind the scenes at
Stratford Festival
Theatre, 1959*

The Hudson's Bay Company pays its 'rent' to the Crown, 1959

causing a disturbance — loitering — being under 21 —
going from table to table without permission — having more
than four persons at one table. The only thing missing was
'No Talking'. Finally, just before I left, a policeman came
in, suggestively toying with a pair of handcuffs, and leaned
for a while against the bottled eggs — presumably checking
that there was no infringement of Part III in this model
estaminet; which was, I sadly discovered, a fair prototype
for many thousand other 'taverns' and 'beer parlours' across
Canada. The nearest I was to come to finding that British
pub atmosphere was in the Far North and in the officers'
messes of the Canadian Armed Forces. The 'No Culture'
faction among the British immigrants, with their pining for
a 'Bunch of Grapes' or a 'Baron of Beef', indisputably had
a case.

One day on our wanderings through the interior of
British Columbia we came across a strange-looking house set
on the edge of a lovely secluded lake. Shaped like a toy fort,
its outer walls appeared to be entirely of glass. It turned out
to be the handiwork of a prosperous local undertaker,
ordered by his doctor to find a hobby that would take his
mind off his work. So he had set to building himself a
country retreat — using as materials the square-ended em-
balming fluid bottles collected over the course of many years'
successful business. For all its bizarre design, the undertaker's fort in fact represented an unusual example of a most
important aspect of *Canadiana*. It was the log cabin of the
20th century, the hideout in the wilderness, the Canadian's
country manor; or more simply, the 'week-end shack',
which Bruce Hutchison sagely rates as Canada's great
contribution to world culture.

In the vast expanse of Canada, there are no major
centres more than an hour or two by car from the unspoilt
land of woods, lakes and rivers (even arid Regina has its attractive Qu'Appelle Valley). When summer days arrive, every
other car on the Canadian highways has either a canoe or a
dinghy lashed to its roof, or a small motor-boat bouncing
along behind on a trailer. You can be fairly sure that most
of them, crammed to the roof with children, fishing tackle,

Q

outboards, hot-dogs and a thousand-and-one pieces of domestic equipment, will be heading for the delectable paradise that is the week-end shack. In most parts of Canada, a paternal acre of Crown Land in the wilderness can still be bought for only a few dollars; an acre where there will be no neighbours to make you conform, no town-and-country planners to tell you what you may build and how, where for the price of a $10 licence some of the best fishing in the world is yours. Land at Lake Simcoe, the nearest to opulent Toronto, may now fetch astronomic prices of over a hundred dollars a square foot, but in the Muskoka district, less than 140 miles out, you can still find small, uninhabited lakebound islets for about $500. In 1958 2155 would-be shack-dwellers were registered as having bought Crown Land in Ontario alone.

'Shack' can be something of a misnomer; it may be a millionaire's fishing lodge up in the Laurentians; equally it could be a patched-up prefab on a mosquito-ridden muskeg that would shame even a Dogrib Indian. The typical week-end shack is generally a home-made affair; sometimes hewn, old-style, from the forest, but more often put together lovingly from 'Do-it-Yourself' blueprints in week-ends and odd evenings, starting the instant snow leaves the woods. The great thing is that it should never be quite finished; from summer to summer there is always some improvement to add, something that needs doing. What in older parts of the world would be a rich man's hobby is one that in Canada is shared alike by tycoon and taxi-driver; it is one that any immigrant, the moment he has a car (one of the first acquisitions under the North American scheme of things) and a few dollars in the bank, can share in. And he *should*, for the week-end shack is one of the real joys of life in Canada; it is a harking back to the fundamental way of life of the men who pioneered Canada; it is also perhaps Canada's way of compensating a man for her failure to create a pub.

But, the average British housewife may think suspiciously — looking forward to a leisurely Sunday after her busy week, to a quiet week-end in the country — it is hardly any compensation *for me*. She should, however, be prepared to face the facts; the Canadian week-end shack is just one not-to-be-mistaken warning that this is a man's country. While the man spends his Sundays on his back in a boat, idly fishing for succulent Small-mouthed Bass — or perhaps merely dreaming of what he will do to the shack next summer — she, consumed by black fly 'No-See-Ems' on the shore (he, of course, forgot to buy any insect repellent), has the job of washing up in a bucket of cold water and sand, of cooking with watering eyes over a wood fire, of seeing that the children don't fall into the lake, or get eaten by a bear. (Unhappily, this is not mere flippancy. There were at least two cases of children being savaged by bears while we were in Canada in 1958 alone. Even the friendliest black bear in a National Park should be treated with respect.) For her it would all seem about as miserable a way of spending a weekend as could be imagined. Yet, for generations, Canadian wives have been submitting to this kind of punishment, and — being North American women — they would presumably not continue to put up with it unless, secretly, they quite enjoyed it.

Each summer Canada becomes one of the world's greatest tourist grounds — a fact that is not always realised abroad. Americans flood over the unguarded frontier in their millions, and they are joined by more millions of Canadians who either do not take part in the week-end shack cult, or whose women have, for a season, staged a successful revolt. Some head — often year after year — for a hideout among the lakes and woods like Mr. Brown's establishment at English River, which we visited in Northwest Ontario. But many will be bound for one or other of the forty-odd 'National Parks' scattered across the country from Cape Breton Highlands to Tweedsmuir Park in BC. The word 'Park' hardly does justice to the size or scope of these huge reserves; the adjoining parks of Jasper and Banff in the Albertan Rockies alone exceed the total area of Northern Ireland and are only a little smaller than the whole of Wales. Their size saves them ever from becoming overcrowded — in the British sense. We spent the week-end of Labour Day (the Canadian and US equivalent of August Bank Holiday) at Jasper, the most popular of all the Canadian Parks; accommodation in the town was crowded, but a few miles away it was all too easy to lose sight of humanity, to find wonderful fishing in a lake shared only by an imperturbable cow moose. The parks are extremely well organised and strictly protected wild-life sanctuaries, carefully selected from some of the most beautiful country on the continent, where fishing is allowed, but no shooting, and where no building is permitted — except for discreetly sited holiday lodges sanctioned by the Park Authorities. These lodges, whether in or outside a National Park, form the core of Canadian summer holidays. They generally consist of a group of small cabins or 'chalets' on the motel system, one to a family, some with their own cooking facilities, otherwise centred around a main building with a communal dining-room, etcetera. Ranging from the ultra-luxurious to the primitive where the only running water is the near-by stream, they are pleasant, informal and friendly places, where everybody seems to know everybody else — and if they don't, the amiable proprietress soon makes sure that they do.

In a small town in British Columbia, a recent British immigrant who had just returned from a holiday in the Rockies with a car full of huge trout remarked to me: 'Where else in the world could you have a millionaire's holiday?' Later, in the same town, a metal-worker from Edinburgh summed up his approval of Canada by saying, simply, 'You live nearer to Nature here.' You have to be prepared to accept this fact and all that it implies, plus and minus; be prepared to drop tools at a moment's notice, to spend days fighting the forest fires that scourge Canada from time to time (if you refuse, it may cost you a heavy fine, whoever you are, and the censure of your neighbours). The wilderness remains a partner in the venture. On my way out from Kitimat to the airport, a 200-foot Douglas crashed just ahead of the bus, bringing with it another giant tree and completely blocking the only road out from the great aluminium city. At home, I suspect, things might have remained that way for hours while County Councils sought around for authority and removing tackle, but within half an hour a huge mobile crane with a gang of 'buckers' had arrived. Thirty-five minutes after the trees fell, they had been carted off in neatly sawn sections and the road opened, in that unostentatiously quiet and efficient manner with which Canadians have been trained to meet the emergencies Nature throws up. This 'closeness of Nature' is a fact in most parts of Canada, it is an integral part of Canadian 'culture'. Exploit the joys that its unlimited freedom, its 'millionaire holidays' and its cult of the week-end shack can bring, and you will have travelled a long way on the road to contentment in Canada. This is, one feels, what Canada is for.

Clarence Campbell, a former Rhodes scholar and — as President of the National Hockey League — one of the most important figures of the Canadian 'Establishment', once commented that ice hockey 'is a way of life in Canada'. It is indeed. The fastest and most thrilling game on earth, and — in my opinion — one of the most aesthetically satisfying, it too might be rated as one of Canada's leading contributions to world culture. Canada is still the home of hockey; without its steady infusion of Canadian players British ice hockey (though at best a poor replica of the real thing) would cease to exist. Each year, the Montreal Canadiens and the Boston Bruins, the Toronto Maple Leafs and New York Rangers, the Chicago Black Hawks and Detroit Red Wings, fight it out for supremacy, but even on the American teams most of the players are Canadians. It is both the top spectator and top participant sport in Canada; most of the seats at Toronto's Maple Leaf Gardens are sold out before the season begins, and a top player can earn about $25,000 a year — to say nothing of the perks that he can pick up through advertising and on TV. It is a game every Canadian boy plays at school, and some 100,000 between the ages of 8 and 21 play regularly in organised leagues. Nothing stimulates Canadian emotions quite like ice hockey; the last serious 'race riots' in Montreal were sparked off when Clarence Campbell barred the great French-Canadian hero, 'Rocket' Richard, from the ice for beating up a referee. For two days angry supporters broke windows up and down St. Catherine's Street. Two years later there was a strong move to get the 'Rocket' appointed to the Federal Senate. Now, one of the latest innovations in the rules of Canadian ice hockey has been the provision of a 'sanctuary' for the referee at one side of the ice; when an argument becomes too heated, he merely has to skate off over its protective red line, and any player following him is automatically hauled away to the penalty 'box'. It does not, of course, protect him from the spectators' beer bottles.

In the parts of Canada where there are hills (*i.e.* in the Rockies or the Laurentians), ski-ing is an ever-growing participant's sport in winter. But it is not always the kind of ski-ing a European might be accustomed to. In the Laurentians close to Montreal, Canada's principal ski-ing centre, runs are short and mostly through narrow trails cut in the woods. Ski-lifts tend to be two to three times as expensive as in Switzerland. And with temperatures often many degrees below zero, there are few days in the year when you can take off nonchalantly in a shirt or light sweater; most of the time you require to be dressed as for an Antarctic expedition, and you still count your fingers, toes and noses at the end of each descent. In recent years, curling has gained tremendous popularity throughout Canada, among both young and old, and has even drawn heavily from the ranks of the hockey players. A star Canadian team actually triumphed over Scotland, a historical occasion, in 1959.

During the unfrozen times of the year, Canada's favourite participant sports are those of water and woods. The leading, notably spectator sports are Canadian football and baseball. Canadian football is a very close relative of the American game, played with twelve men instead of eleven a side. In their ferociously flattering, but necessary carapaces, the teams surge back and forth across the field, like well-led Panzer armies, every once in a while pulling off a daring raid through a long pass over the heads of the enemy. At half-time, massed bands and gambolling majorettes in scanty skirts take over the pitch. Each season culminates in Grey Cup Day, which has been described as 'savouring of civil war', when East meets West for the all-Canada championship. It is all very North American, and great fun. I could do without the majorettes, but (heresy though it may be) I must admit to finding a good game of American or Canadian football considerably more exciting, and more skilled — though perhaps less fluid — than rugger. It is only unfortunate that the price of tickets is so high in Canada ; it is almost impossible to get a seat at a major game for less than $2·50 to $5·00. And this applies to hockey and baseball as well.

Rugger and cricket are still played in Canada, but confined largely to the playing-fields of private schools ; though cricket still maintains its stronghold on the West Coast. Rugger seems to be on the wane, while soccer is rapidly increasing in popularity. There is no greyhound racing in Canada, and only a few small, locally organised football pools. Horse-racing is limited, though at its Woodbine Track, Toronto claims to have one of the most modern and best-laid-out courses in the Commonwealth.

When Prince Philip launched a bombshell at his installation as President of the Canadian Medical Association, by declaring that Canadians were not as fit as they might be, he was on a much surer wicket than in his remarks about the Liquor Laws and, in fact, put his finger on a source of great national concern. On the strength of criticism that has come from Canada herself, it would seem that progressively since the end of the war, the rugged Canuck from the woods, the tanned and brawny farmer, the superbly fit fighting man of two World Wars, may have become a legend of the past. According to figures cited by the Duke, 34 per cent of Canada's male population were unfit for military service, and an investigation subsequently made by *Maclean's* revealed that 81 per cent of freshmen at one of the University of Manitoba's colleges were 'well below average' of physical fitness, that even the 26-year-old goalie of the Toronto Maple Leafs could only chin himself three times. A Toronto professor followed up with the discovery that the average Canadian woman was 10 lb. fatter than her mother; her overweight being the consequences of too many labour-saving gadgets in the kitchen.

The background to all this is largely the same as why young Canadians won't go North ; material prosperity, the comforts of city life, and — of course — that great atrophier of muscles, the automobile.[1] The impact on sports has been

[1] Relevant statistics in the Gordon Commission Report show that already two-thirds of Canada's population live in urban centres, and this will rise to 80 per cent by 1980; that there is now one car between every six Canadians, and in 1980 there will be one for every three.

that Canada threatens to become a nation of spectators, rather than participants, perhaps even more so than Britain. In international field athletics, recent Canadian showing has been extremely disappointing. One of the young English school teachers at Kitimat offered an explanation when he told me that he had tried to organise cross-country runs, but had only had four candidates out of 300—one of them an English boy — the attitude being 'why exert yourself when you can go by car?' (My wife and I came across the antipathy to walking, which in North America generally is fast becoming an inability, when we went to examine the fish ladders in the Fraser Canyon. At the top of the path leading down to the river was a large sign gravely warning visitors they had a strenuous walk ahead of them, to be attempted only by those in tip-top condition. Without being conspicuously fit, and without pushing ourselves, we made it in little more than half the time estimated by the sign.) At Quebec's Collège Militaire Royal near Montreal, I was somewhat surprised to be told that, although there were fourteen compulsory sports, they were giving up Canadian football because so many cadets had been getting hurt. (Imagine Sandhurst dropping rugger for that reason!) It seemed very un-Canadian. Yet a predominant number of the top professional players in Canadian football are today recruited from the United States — presumably because of the lack of participant interest at home — and even though Canada remains the principal exporter of ice-hockey players, it may be symptomatic that more and more young Canadians seem to be turning from hockey to the less exacting sport of curling.

At the heart of the Canadian way of life, and accountable for many of the differences with our own, is the Canadian home. With Canada's rapidly growing population, accommodation often presents a problem; one which varies greatly from region to region. It is generally particularly acute in Ontario, and especially in Ottawa, where hundreds of civil service employees and members of the armed services seem to spend months living in motels, waiting for somewhere permanent to live. Before descending on any area with his wife and family, any immigrant would be well advised to enquire first about the housing situation. Today, about three-quarters of all Canadians live in their own houses. They tend to buy rather than rent their accommodation, and — in both town and country — prefer to live in totally detached small houses rather than flats. Because of the pressure of population, the average immigrant will be faced with the prospect, sooner than later, of having to buy, or build, for himself. There is no such thing as a subsidised council house in Canada, but under the National Housing Act of 1954 substantial loans can be obtained on fairly generous terms. At many of the new 'company towns' the companies have their own parallel house-purchasing schemes.

In a fairly typical Ontario housing estate, a small three-bedroom house with living-room and combined kitchen-dining-room might cost (at the time of writing) $14,000 to build, including its plot of land. It could be financed with a down payment of $2000–$3000, the loan amortised over twenty-five years, with monthly payments, plus municipal taxes (or rates), totalling about $80. Rents are much higher in Canada, and before moving into his own house an immigrant should reckon on spending as much as one-quarter of his earnings on accommodation alone. Estate agents and building contractors both tend to have a rather less leisurely attitude towards business than their British counterparts, and Britons should be wary of being 'stampeded' by high-pressure salesmanship. They also should be wary of whom they select to do the work; in a booming, expansionist society such as Canada's the contractor who goes bankrupt on the job is by no means a freak — nor is the jerry-builder.[1]

The typical modern Canadian home is closely patterned on contemporary American design. A pleasant-looking bungalow, with perhaps two small bedrooms in the attic, of white-painted wood and cheerful, red, blue or green slatted roofs, it sits in its own small plot of lawn and garden, un-fenced from the road — or the neighbours — amid a neatly laid out housing estate, looking like a model lifted from an

[1] For a warning of the pitfalls of this kind that can swallow up the inexperienced, *Pardon my Parka*, an entertaining account of life in a Quebec mining community by an Englishwoman married to a Canadian, is well worth reading.

architect's office. Its cheerful colours have done much to brighten the predominant grey of Canadian cities in winter. One of the most important features is the basement 'play-room' that runs the length of the house, and is, of course, heated. In the compact living of the modern Canadian home, this represents the one chance (and a limited one) for parents to find isolation and peace from their offspring. As in the United States, 'help' is either non-existent or pro-hibitively expensive, so the Canadian home is designed for the 'home-maker' (as the housewife is often euphemistically called) to do everything for herself, supported by a battery of washing-machines, dish-washers and other gadgets (gener-ally bought on hire purchase). Consequently, rooms are small, inhabitants tend to live 'all of a heap' and — except in price — there is not all that much difference in size or shape between the house of the high-paid executive and his humblest employee. Yet, in some magic way, Canadian architects manage to impart a surprising individuality to houses on their new estates so notably lacking in British 'ribbon development'.

With their bright and summery, and perhaps slightly fragile appearances, the new Canadian homes seem hardly designed to withstand the savage winter. But, in fact, in-geniously insulated and centrally heated by (fairly cheap) automatic fuel oil furnaces, they are extremely snug; to anyone reared in the draughty deep-freeze of an English home, possibly too snug. A British visitor of the 1790s [1] remarked: 'One circumstance, however, renders the Cana-dian houses very disagreeable, and that is the inattention of the inhabitants to air them occasionally by opening the windows', and he might not find much change today. Walking muffled to the eyebrows along a Montreal street in freezing winter temperatures, it always seems curious to see through brightly lit office windows men at work in their shirt-sleeves. At home, as at work, Canadians — like all North Americans — generally like to have temperatures closer to eighty than sixty.

In all things, the emphasis of the Canadian home is decidedly on comfort — and on informality. Living arrange-

[1] Isaac Weld, from *Early Travellers in the Canadas*.

ments in the home undoubtedly contribute to the less-formalised relationships between parents and children in Canada, just as they have their impact on social habits as a whole. Little elaborate entertaining is done in Canada, most of it is highly informal; hamburgers on paper plates and coffee in paper cups more often than a sit-down dinner. Nobody seems to mind what you give them to eat or drink — just as long as you don't try too hard to separate the men from the men. In notable contrast to the United States, segregation of the sexes at Canadian (though not *Canadien*) gatherings seems to be the accepted norm — this is, after all, still a man's country. After I had observed this several times, I could not help wondering whether it did not to some extent reflect habits formed by Canada's segregational drinking laws. In either its pleasurable or social function, food itself is definitely not one of the most important factors in a Canadian's life. By and large, one eats well in Canada, but not ingeniously, and often with little variety. This may be part of the British heritage. A Scotswoman who had cooked on ranches in the Cariboo told me that any culinary variations she produced were seldom appreciated; 'they preferred pie, which all could recognise'. Eating out is not a favourite Canadian pastime, and a good restaurant — unless you pay the earth — is all too rare. French Canada is, of course, the great exception, with Montreal boasting some of the best restaurants on the continent.

Despite the 'Do-It-Yourself' role that is inescapably hers, the Canadian 'home-maker' manages to lead a remarkably emancipated, drudge-free existence. According to recent statistics, she devotes only 1 hour 36 minutes of each day to preparing meals for her family, compared with $5\frac{1}{2}$ hours a generation ago. Apart from the labour-saving devices in the house, the refrigerators and the deep-freezers which she considers necessities, not luxuries, 'baby-sitting' is a highly organised institution and — above all — there are the super-markets and the concentrated shopping centres which have rapidly become indispensable elements of Canadian life. Now to be found in most larger towns and city suburbs, these enable her to buy all her food under one roof in a matter of minutes, do all the rest of her shopping within a

few yards' walk. A new $30,000,000 shopping centre in the
heart of Montreal, all covered in by a huge (appropriately
enough, golden) dome, will have space within it equal to a
70-storey skyscraper, and will contain nearly 100 shops;
two supermarkets; a one-hour laundry and dry-cleaning
service; a hospital and huge supervised crèche; a 3000-seat
theatre, and a beauty parlour with 100 attendants. Special
conveyor-belts will take shoppers' parcels right out to the
vast car park. This is the pattern of the future in Canada —
and probably in Britain too, one day. In the remoter parts
of Canada today, the mail order house with its thick catalogue of an astonishing variety of goods still plays a most
important role. In the towns, newcomers would do well to
caveat emptor, particularly when the ubiquitous travelling
salesman calls. Anybody who has not encountered the
North American breed simply does not know what he is up
against, and I was constantly being astonished at the genuine
distress caused to newly arrived Britons by their persistence,
and often unscrupulousness.

Society is certainly better organised for the Canadian
housewife than for her British counterpart, and she is herself
perhaps better organised. Lunching with two young Canadian wives in Montreal, my wife remarked that several
British women she had met had complained sadly of loneliness — forced upon them because they were so tied to
household work that they never got out to meet anybody,
or make any friends. Both Canadians jumped on this
vigorously; it was nonsense and quite unnecessary, it was all
a matter of 'organisation', they said. The trouble with
English women was that they just would not change the ways
they were used to at home. For instance, was it not idiotic,
one of them asked, for a housewife to have to go marketing
every morning? She did hers just once a week, by car from
the supermarket, and that was that. The other remarked
that she washed and ironed on just one set day a week and
that every day she was through her household chores by
mid-morning, with the rest of the day to do as she pleased.

'What I don't like about Canada is the *conformism*,' complained the English wife in Toronto. 'Everything seems to

be so standardised; what you eat, what you buy from the supermarket, what you wear, how you entertain and what you read, and even what you talk about.' It was, in itself, a fairly 'standardised' European critique of life in North America. Conformism in the United States, about which so many millions of words have been written, has of course its simple causes; a new country with a multi-racial population that somehow has to be broken down into a single recognisable norm, and now the impact of the age of automation. Since the war, these causes have come to apply with increasing force to Canada, with her great influx of non-British immigrants. On my first day at home after four months in Canada, I remember feeling some surprise at seeing a man with long shaggy side-whiskers obliviously working on a music score in the Tube. None of his fellow passengers showed the least surprise, or interest, and I realised I had become acclimatised to Canadian norms where — I am quite sure — on the Toronto Metro the composer would have been an object of considerable curiosity. There is nowhere in the world — except perhaps France — where eccentricity and ultra-individualism flourishes, and is accepted, as happily as in England. The ground for the eccentric is not so fertile in Canada, and he tends to be looked on with some suspicion — as a famous British TV star discovered when he left his Toronto hotel in dressing-gown and bedroom slippers to visit a near-by drugstore.

But the impression one has is that the conformist urge in its strictest sense is less strong in Canada than in the United States; there is, for one thing, too much space between people. In its place there is a different phenomenon — for want of any other word, call it 'community-mindedness' — springing from a rather different set of circumstances. The days when pioneer settlements in Canada had to fight for their existence against hostile nature are not so very far away, and then the individual who would not pull his weight in the community, the 'maverick' in the herd who wandered by himself, could be a real danger to the rest. In countless isolated Canadian hamlets, neighbours are still the most important things in life, and the spirit of co-operation and mutual help is tremendous; if a man's house burns down, the neighbours will not only take in his family but the men of the town will often get together and help rebuild his house. In the medium-sized towns, and particularly the new towns that are thrown back so much on their own resources for providing a full life for their inhabitants, 'community-mindedness' may take other shapes. Gregarious clubs or orders, like the Rotary, the Kiwanis, the Knights of Columbus, Shriners, Elks or Lions are an integral part in Canadian life, and a British 'New Canadian' would probably do better to start off by joining one of these than the clannish, backward-looking club for local Scots or Englishmen. In Kitimat, after little more than five years' existence, there were already something like 150 active community organisations — ranging from the 'Broken Spokes Square Dance Club' to the Canadian Legion, from the 'Toastmistress Club' to the 'Cosmopolitan Theatre Society' and the Kitimat Garden Club.

Whatever form 'community-mindedness' takes, it is a factor of greatest importance, and the immigrant who stands aloof may lose, irretrievably, his best chance of being 'accepted'. One of the most contented of the hundreds of 'New Canadians' I met was a Londoner in his forties, who accompanied me around a mining centre in British Columbia. He had had a good job on the Gas Board, and had not really wanted to emigrate, but his wife's health, ruined by the war, had forced it upon him. In the job he had found I suspect he was materially not much better off than at home, but he had found himself in other ways. He was a Scout leader, an executive of the local Red Cross, on the Church Finance Committee as well as many others, and had recently been appointed Trustee to the new high school. 'At home,' he confided to me, 'I was not involved in any community activities, because I felt there were others who could do them better, and I was not needed. Here I feel I have something to contribute, and I am needed.' He emphasised that to participate in community existence was the best way of becoming 'identified' with Canadians, and that anybody who did not tended to be 'rather suspect'.

Finally, in passing, it is worth mentioning that at the hub of most community activities in Canada is the Church. Most of the Churches in Canada are vigorous, dynamic organisations with strong and active followings. The United Church (a union formed in 1925 of the leading nonconformist sects) numbers over three million, the Anglican Church two million, the Roman Catholic over six million and Jewish about two hundred thousand. They are also financially strong (in most Provinces contributions to the Church are exempt from tax) and in various ways — one of which was mentioned at the beginning of this chapter — wield a powerful influence on political affairs. Altogether they represent a far more important factor in the life of the nation than in modern Great Britain.

I once read — I forget where — the wise comment that it was foolish to expect Canadians and Britons to be similar when even the most fundamental words in their mutual language had to convey such very different things. To a Canadian, the word spring for instance connotes something far removed from our associations of a long-protracted, gentle and well-mannered period of rebirth. In Canada, spring comes, and goes, with a wild rush. One day it is hard winter, with temperatures several degrees below zero. The next day ice on the ponds and lakes goes soft, and school ice hockey comes to an abrupt end. A crackling noise like a forest fire sweeps through the firs as the melting snow cascades off the branches. Unpaved roads turn into quagmires, and the municipal road-graders appear everywhere like large yellow butterflies emerging out of hibernation. On the big rivers, the ice breaks up with the creaking and grinding of a wooden Armada driven upon the rocks. The syrup begins to flow from the maples, and leaves appear overnight. The roads harden up again, and summer is here — all within a matter of a week or two. There is nothing gentle or gradual about the Canadian spring. And, compared to ours, there is seldom anything very unpredictable about the Canadian summer (the temperate West Coast is of course an exception at most times of year, and the Rockies can lay on snow for you any day between Boxing Day and Christmas). You can rely on it to be short, intense and hot, glorious in the country, but often not so glorious in Toronto and Montreal, where the heat can be as stifling and humid as New York, or in Winnipeg where, when July temperatures pass 100° F., Manitobans are left wondering whether it really could have been 140 degrees colder only five months ago.

Throughout Canada, as in New England, the Queen of the seasons is the Fall. This is no sad time of falling leaves and rapidly shortening grey days heralding a soggy, smoggy winter. After the sharp shock of the first frosts has come, there follows a long period of pure, clear sunshine and gentle, fresh days — that fabulous 'Indian Summer', a sort of English springtime in reverse, when the frost-nipped maples turn to their dazzling gold and scarlet. A new fighting spirit enters into the great Tyee of the Pacific, the trout and Arctic Grayling of the Shield; and the first flights of Canada Geese head south in their tens of thousands over the heads of the expectant 'hunters'. A new feeling of well-being, a final promise of next year's summer, enters into the souls of Canadians, preparing them to face yet another long cold winter.

Of all the seasons, it is of course winter that has its most divergent meanings in the two vocabularies. Readers may think that I have deliberately glossed over the hard fact of the Canadian winter, by describing the various parts of Canada basking in summer sunshine. This is, I admit, how I like to remember them, and anyway it is hard to describe nuances of colour and variations in a country when the whole of it lies under a uniform blanket of white. But winter cannot be ignored. It is too closely tied up with everything that constitutes Canadian life. Between the end of Indian Summer and the onset of real winter, there is often a short period of indetermination, of grey days when the clouds are drawn like iron bars across the sky. Then suddenly the freeze-up begins; sometimes the ice spreads across the lakes so rapidly that diving birds have been known to get trapped. It is a hard bitter winter, with temperatures reaching as low as − 20° F. (or fifty-two degrees of frost) even in Toronto, and with Montreal's January temperatures averaging nearly seventeen degrees of frost over the past thirty years. But after its sombre beginning, it is a winter more often of crisp blue skies (especially on the

Prairies) than heavy cloud. On a really cold night, the stars seem to hang down on pendants in the extraordinary clearness, or else, in the higher latitudes, the sky flares up with the strange kaleidoscope of the Northern Lights. That dry, exhilarating Canadian cold penetrates less ferociously than temperatures well above zero in a damp English winter. Canadians claim that you hardly notice the difference between fifteen above and fifteen below zero; it is only when the mercury sinks to the minus twenties and thirties that the cold makes you gasp, literally. But Canadian society is geared (as of course it should be) to taking the sting out of winter. Houses are properly heated, no outside plumbing, clothing carefully designed, roads cleared promptly, so that — unless you indulge in such carelessness as taking off your gloves to open an outside door (you won't do it twice) — winter in Canada is now no more alarming, and often a lot less unpleasant, than at home. Worst of all, as Canadians themselves will freely admit, is its length; five months (seven, or even more, in the North) is a long time under snow and ice.

For all modern technology's success in mitigating Canada's winter, it has been so far unable to eradicate the gloomy spectre of 'seasonal unemployment', with its profound influence on Canadian life. The severe temperatures limit such activities as outdoor construction to an extent unknown in temperate Britain, and since earliest days, as regularly as the coming of the snows themselves, thousands of Canadians have grown accustomed to finding themselves jobless from December to March. Over the last five years they have totalled as high as 10 per cent of the whole working population, and seldom much lower than 6 per cent. Figures vary with the trade; most affected are those employed in the construction of bridges and highways, where an average of 40 per cent are seasonally unemployed; next, at 30 per cent, the building industry and water transportation, notably on the St. Lawrence Seaway which freezes up early in December. But cutbacks caused by the dislocation of winter spread like a chain reaction throughout the whole Canadian economy. Canadian labour is largely conditioned to it. Higher summer wages, plus overtime, in seasonal industries mean that

R

a bulldozer operator in Ontario, for instance, could earn £2000 or more, then freewheel over the winter, drawing unemployment insurance. It is, in fact, possible to draw such benefits for as long as five and a half months, on the basis of having worked merely fifteen weeks the previous summer. Nevertheless, the prospect of being unemployed for perhaps a quarter of every year is psychologically a grim one. It is especially grim for a Briton, brought up under full- and full-time employment, and probably starting in Canada with no money in the bank; which is one good reason why Canadian Immigration urges migrants to come early in the spring, so as to be established and prepared for the next winter.

Some serious efforts are being made to mitigate this problem. In Alberta, for instance, builders have successfully experimented with shielding-in open roofs and walls with polyethylene film, heating the unfinished interior with cheap natural gas, and continuing work throughout the winter. But a Briton in Winnipeg, who had prospered and seemed to be regarded locally as a man of sound sense,[1] suggested to me that the prevailing tendency in Canada was rather to accept winter unemployment as something inevitable, part of the national heritage. Much of it was unnecessary, he thought. It now took no more than an hour or two to clear the roads around Winnipeg after a snowfall, yet there was still little road haulage in winter — largely because of 'tradition'. Even he knew that in his completely 'unseasonal' trade he would have to lay off some of his workers that winter, because firms would suddenly become 'cautious' and cancel orders for signs, although they too were not directly affected by the freeze-up. 'It's very largely psychological,' he claimed. 'At the first sign of winter, you can literally feel the gloom setting in. People pull in their horns and become disinclined to take risks.' (Two months later, watching winter close in at Knob Lake in Labrador, I knew exactly what he meant, and I remembered experiencing the same sensations at the onset of a Canadian winter during the war. A drowsiness

[1] Emigrating in 1946, he had started up his own one-man sign-painting business, and now employed eighteen men in a very lucrative concern. The Provincial Government (who sent me to see him) obviously looked on him as something of a showpiece 'New Canadian'.

and a torpid lethargy comes over you, like a wasp in autumn, and you have no incentive to undertake anything drastic. It is the natural animal urge to hibernate.) 'It's a serious matter,' he concluded, 'and until Canadians can get over this winter recession mentality, it's likely to retard progress more than almost any other single factor.'

It is the impact of winter that, combined with the innate canniness of her two most dominant strains — the Norman and the Scot — is largely responsible for one of the most clearly delineated features of Canada's national character, cautiousness. A Canadian writing for *The Times* recently (in an article entitled 'Is Adventure in Abeyance?') went so far as to claim that his countrymen 'are not an adventurous people'. For all their apparent reluctance to go North or take violent physical exercise, this seems to be selling the Canadians a bit short; their achievements since the war certainly do not suggest that they are unadventurous. But cautiousness is a different thing, a positive thing. It means that the Canadian is seldom swept away by over-optimism, thinks matters over carefully before he leaps; and thus in the past has escaped many disasters that might otherwise have befallen him. It is a characteristic that strongly differentiates him from his southern cousins. Canadian caution manifests itself in a number of ways. One is that Canadians take out more insurance *per capita* than any other race in the world. Another is that they buy considerably less on hire-purchase than the Americans. Only about 3 per cent of the gross national product is channelled, on average, into buying on credit. The average Canadian is also cautious about his savings, favouring Government Bonds and savings banks. Whereas over the years the American big investor has tended to take a risk on the future of Canada and invest heavily in more speculative Canadian enterprises, the wealthy Canadian cautiously puts his money into Standard Oil of New Jersey. As a result, something like half of all Canadian commercial profits ends up in the pockets of foreigners.

Tangent to the amount of insurance bought by Canadians is the fact that there is — as many Britons have discovered — considerably less security in Canada than at home, though

perhaps more than in the United States.   Conditions of
employment, for both employer and employee, are less
secure; several times British immigrants remarked to me
how workers in some Canadian industries would be quite
apt to walk off without warning in the middle of a shift,
collect their wages, and move on elsewhere.   Equally, men
can be laid off with considerably less ceremony than in
Britain.   One reason for this is that, although some 70 per
cent of Canadian Trades Unions are affiliated to the mighty
US giants of labour (but not to any political party), they are
far less powerful in Canada — with the possible exception of
strike-ridden BC — and in fact only 35 per cent of Canadian
labour is 'organised'.   Even in BC, management tends to
be able to take a tougher line with labour than it dares in
Britain.   At the mining community of Kimberley, I was told
of a newly arrived British shop-steward who had organised a
stoppage in protest (shades of 'I'm All Right Jack') at a
time-and-motion experiment.   The company promptly sus-
pended him for a week; the whole mine did not go out in
sympathy.   Absenteeism is treated severely in Canada;
Alcan at Kitimat, publishing a list of disciplinary actions,
makes an inviolable rule that first offence brings a warning
— second offence, suspension — third offence, suspension or
discharge — fourth offence, discharge.

As with the Americans, Canadian workers are also more
prepared to accept mobility as a necessary factor of working
life.   Again in Kitimat, a Briton told me with some astonish-
ment of a Canadian friend who had unexpectedly come to
say goodbye one morning; the previous night it appeared,
the Canadian had been visited by people looking for a house
in Kitimat, and over dinner he and his wife decided to sell
theirs to them, plus all contents, and move East for 'a change
of scenery' and a new job.   After being settled in Kitimat for
three years, they were moving out that same day.   A distinctive feature of Canadian life is the highly skilled transient
miner or construction engineer, who moves from job to job
often carrying — like a snail — his house on his back, in the
shape of a monster caravan.   At Elliot Lake in Northern
Ontario there was still a small city of 1500 'trailers'.   In one
such trailer I visited — 45 feet long, complete with bath,

running water and (of course) central heating, and about as roomy and comfortable as a two-bedroom city flat — I found an engineer who had been living in trailers for seventeen years. It was a good way to save money, he said ('your wife can't spend all your pay on furniture and stuff — there's just no room for it'), he was putting his son through Harvard on the savings, and he had a smaller, 'vacation', trailer in which he took off for Florida each winter.

Far more than in Britain, Canadian labour is geared to 'following the jobs'. Canadian employers frequently complain of the relative immobility of Britons, and the Canadian Immigration authorities make sense when they urge new arrivals not to become tied to any permanent dwelling too soon; recommending the purchase of a car as incomparably more immediate.

The average Canadian works shorter hours than the British worker, a 40-hour week now being almost universal in Canada, with 37½ hours or less for most office employees. Many Britons, representing both labour and management, however, commented to me that, when he was not moving to another job, the Canadian seemed a steadier worker; not constantly in need of a tea break, more responsible, and generally identifying himself more closely with his work — which in turn probably means more to him. Management, they nearly all agreed, also gave the impression of working harder. Those hearty business-expense luncheons that de-vitalise so much of British management over so large a part of its working day play no part in the Canadian scheme of things; as in the United States, multi-million dollar deals are done over iced water, not port. In the event of a mechanical breakdown in a factory, the 'boss' is quite likely to take off his coat and join the manual workers in putting it right. Because of its hard-working, down-to-earth approach, Canadian management expects — and probably gets — more out of its employees.

One of the happiest features of Canadian life is the almost complete absence of the bitter rift along class lines between labour and management, that eternally bedevils industrial relations in Britain. Because Canada is so genuinely a land of opportunity where anyone can rise to the top, where many

of the greatest and richest men have in fact had the humblest
beginnings, there is little envy of wealth.   In a big factory
near Toronto, a machinist who had been a staunch union
man and Labour Party supporter in Glasgow, remarked to
me on how much better labour relations were in Canada:
'There's no line running down the centre here.   I can go
into the boss's office any time I like, and feel that we're both
on the same side.'   Time and again I heard similar comments
from British workers across Canada.   Canadian management
tends to take a more patriarchal interest in those it employs
than in Britain (at times I was strongly reminded of German
industry with its vast fringe benefit schemes, works' enter-
tainments, and vacation hostels), and naturally this is particularly so in the remoter centres where 'the Company' has
to be responsible for so much more than just the running of
an industry; the Canadian employer is also apt to be more
ruthless with the loafer or the disaffected than his British
counterpart.   Conversely, the Canadian workers themselves
impressed me as showing a far greater interest in their Company, and in really finding out about the wider aspects of
its affairs.   At Trail BC, a former Scottish amateur wrestler
in his late forties, now working as a paid hand in the scrap
division of Consolidated Mining, told me that he and many
of his co-workers — in the absence of football pools — dabbled
regularly on the stock markets.   'When Inland Natural Gas
was at $5, we were all buying it, because we realised how
much gas was going to be used at this plant.   Now the shares
are up to $7, and that's very nice for us.   We also invest
in our own Company, so we're really anxious to know
everything about its business, and when the market prices
drop we want to know why.   Of course, I just speculate
— seldom hold anything.   It's like the pools, only more
certain.'

One of the strange contradictions of Canada is that
although it has never had anything resembling a Socialist
Government in Ottawa, the list of its 'nationalised' industries is almost as imposing as Britain's;   more than half the
railways;   the principal airline;   most of radio and television;
the Atomic Energy Corporation and one of the largest

uranium producers; a big plastics industry; many of the power utilities; and the entire liquor retailing business. Like many things in Canadian life, the system represents an intelligent compromise based on necessity that works rather well; as noted earlier, state-financed broadcasting competes against commercial programmes, Canadian Pacific Airlines gives battle to TCA (with the result that Trans-Canada is probably one of the best-run airlines anywhere — also one of the few nationalised airlines to make a fairly regular profit), CPR competes with CNR (with perhaps rather less success), and BC Electric Company provides some challenge to the British Columbia Power Commission. In fact, the system bears very little relation to what we understand by Nationalisation in Britain. It is more a form of 'State Capitalism', based on the principle as once stated by Mr. C. D. Howe, Minister of Trade and Commerce under the Liberals, that in a country of limited financial resources 'you can't go without something just because private enterprise won't build it'. Canadians as a nation are strongly opposed to any socialistic experiments. For this same reason, Canada is also very definitely not a Welfare State, either in practice or in outlook; although in the last few years several provisions comparable to those that constitute Britain's welfare services have made their appearance on the Canadian scene. A people who until relatively recently still had to struggle against nature for survival, are perhaps less likely to vote for the 'pampering' of the less fortunate members of their civilisation. Canada is still a country of challenge; a doctrinaire Socialist might claim that the Law of the Wild still thrived there, but he would of course be exaggerating. The fact is that Canadians, like Americans, approve of the philosophy of every man for himself; they do not admire the man prepared to stand patiently and endlessly in a queue, but they do admire — and will usually go to great lengths to help — anybody who will help himself.

A good proportion of the British immigrants I interviewed in Canada claimed to have left Britain to get away from the 'Welfare State Mentality', which they felt had deadened incentive at home. But I found many — especially among the younger ones who had spent most of their adult life within the security of the Welfare State — to whom some nasty shocks had been administered during their first months in Canada. The difficulty of finding immediate employment, the high cost of unpegged rents, but worst — and commonest of all — the realisation of what it means to have to pay a doctor's bill, had taken them by surprise. Until 1959 most Provinces in Canada had no National Health Service of any kind, and Canadian medical bills can be astronomic. An elderly Canadian in Montreal told me of a friend of his who regularly put away a sum each year against the eventuality of a serious illness, and by the time he was sixty it amounted to some $7500; but one major operation took the lot. I heard all too frequent, heartbreaking stories of Britons who had arrived with young families, totally unaware that there was no National Health in Canada, to find their life savings rapidly eaten away by minor children's ailments; or even just dentists' bills. Prior to 1959 it was estimated that an average Canadian family of four spent $100 a year on medical care, without any special illnesses.[1] Wisely enough, Canadian Immigration officers have in the past advised newcomers as a priority to buy first a private Health Insurance Policy (widely subscribed to in Canada, which partly accounts for the Canadians' high extent of insurance), then buy a car, and lastly a home.

By 1959 all Provinces except Quebec had established Hospitalisation Insurance Plans, which although not co-ordinated on a national basis are fairly similar. In some provinces this requires payment of a premium of between $2 and $4 a month, in others financing of the plan is carried out by means of 'sales taxes'. Only royalty-rich Alberta is paying for it out of existing revenues. In Quebec, many employers have their own private hospital schemes to cover employees, but usually with rather less generous benefits. The standard of hospitals — and doctors — is extremely high in most parts of Canada; the new Montreal General Hospital which I visited is reputedly one of the two or three most modern and best-equipped hospitals in the world, and appears to offer a degree of comfort and cheerfulness more like a luxury hotel than a place of healing. From all accounts,

[1] T. W. Beak, *We Came to Canada*.

Canadian mental hospitals are the exception, and are even behind British standards. Otherwise, under the new Hospitalisation scheme, free patients in a Canadian hospital can probably look forward to better treatment — and certainly less waiting — than in Britain. In none of the provinces, with the sole exception of Newfoundland, do government-run plans provide medical service for out-patients. Most Canadian firms have their own Medical Insurance Plans, to which employees contribute $3 to $4 a month and which cover outside doctors' bills, but there are no facilities — private or otherwise — covering free medicines or dentistry; although expenses are to some extent deductable from income tax. With both major political parties strongly opposed to anything that smacks of 'socialised medicine' it seems unlikely that Canadian health services will go as far as Britain's NHS in the foreseeable future. In Canada there is no real equivalent to the British 'family GP'. It is a country of specialists, and when anyone is not sure whom to consult he simply rings up the Out-Patient's Department of the nearest hospital. This system provides more specialised care; but it does also result in an additional snowballing of medical costs. As the Principal of the Montreal General (himself a refugee from Britain's NHS) remarked to me: 'This is definitely not the country for the not-well-off neurotic'.

What other social security benefits can an immigrant expect in Canada? *Unemployment Insurance* is handled by the Federal and not the Provincial Government, but the major part of the cost is split between the employee and employer. Under the most recent legislation the employee pays a weekly deduction from his wages of up to 94 cents (maximum), and in return can receive an increasing scale of benefits of up to $36 a week if he is married ($27 if single), with an additional allowable earnings of $18 a week, for a period of unemployment of up to thirty-six weeks. An *Old Age Pension* of $55 a month is payable to every Canadian on reaching 70 (or 65 if need can be proved). But it is only valid for those who have lived in Canada for at least ten years prior to application. Some provinces pay additional pension supplements of up to $20 a month, on a means test basis. *Family Allowances* of $6 a month for every child under 10, and

$8 for each between the ages of 10 to 15, are paid to every Canadian mother regardless of means. Children of immigrants qualify after one year of residence. There are no state-subsidised *Sickness Benefits* in Canada, but most employers have private schemes which carry employees on half-pay while away because of sickness.

Things change so rapidly in Canada that, in a book of this kind, it is obviously impossible to provide specific details of employment conditions that would remain valid for more than a few days. The best places to obtain up-to-date information on employment prospects in various fields and in the different Provinces, as well as prevailing wage rates, are the Canadian Immigration Offices abroad; such as the one that has its headquarters at Green Street in London. But, even with information provided by these offices, there is always the danger that has to be accepted of the time-lag between the date it was gathered in Canada and the date the potential immigrant arrives on the spot. At least one recently arrived immigrant made the complaint to me that immigration officials in London had told him there was no unemployment problem in Toronto, but when he had arrived he had found some 30,000 out of work there. The most closely in touch with local current conditions and prospects are the branches of Canadian Immigration located in each of the Provincial capitals. Most of the officials I met at these branches gave me the impression of being extremely alert, helpful and sympathetic. A further valuable source of information of Canadian wage rates and the current cost of living — as well as a lot besides — is an excellent booklet called *We Came to Canada* by a British immigrant, T. W. Beak, which is circulated by the Canadian Immigration Service, and regularly revised. Also worth reading, and kept well up to date, is another entitled *Working and Living Conditions in Canada*, published by the Economics and Research Branch of the Canadian Department of Labour, and, for more general information, the very handsomely produced *Canada Handbook*, brought out each year by the Dominion Bureau of Statistics, price $1.00.

For several years, immigrants have been drawn to Canada

by the fact that she has the second highest standard of living
in the world, surpassed only by the United States. Despite
her recent recession and the subsequent boom in Britain,
this is still true; but there are qualifications. Wages are
certainly higher, and — although they change so rapidly,
and also vary widely from province to province — for pur-
poses of comparison it might be worth mentioning some of
the typical earnings I came across in touring Canada. An
electrician was getting paid $1.94 an hour in Halifax and
$2.00 in Montreal; but $2.40 in Hamilton Ont., and $2.81
in Vancouver. On the other hand; a senior female clerk
earning $66 a week in Montreal would have been reduced to
just under $57 in Vancouver. At International Nickel in
Sudbury Ont., skilled tradesmen were earning $100 a week,
and the minimum wage was $1.84 an hour. At Orenda
Engines near Toronto, a huge new plant making jet engines,
basic wages were between $1.63 and $2.49 an hour. In
Alberta, union rates for carpenters were $2.00 an hour, while
plumbers were earning $2.35. At Macmillan and Bloedel
on Vancouver Island, $1.72 was the basic wage in the saw-
mills. At B.C. Packers outside Vancouver, it varied between
$1.75 to $2.00 for men, and $1.50 for women. At an aircraft
plant at Malton, Ontario, I met a British technical illustrator
who had been earning £16 a week in England, and was now
getting $115. In the same plant I calculated that the average
employee at all levels was earning at least twice as much as he
would at home. Earnings were often swelled appreciably by
the wife working as well; a young English mathematician,
who had been working for the aircraft company for just two
years, told me that he and his wife — working as a typist —
between them brought in $680 a month. At another factory
in Ontario, a Glasgow gear-box assembler and his wife, doing
a clerical job in the same plant, were jointly earning $580;
though $110 of that went on the rent of their apartment
alone. The inspector of his assembly line, also a Scot, was
earning $360 a month. In Montreal, another Scot who had
been only 5 months in Canada, told me he was earning $400
a month as a draughtsman with a firm of construction
engineers; his wife was making a further $260 as a short-
hand-typist; they had already paid for all the furniture in

their three-and-a-half room apartment, and were about to buy a car.[1]

The proportion of women at work in Canada is rather smaller than in England; perhaps because more women are tied to their domestic-less homes, and partly because the national average is lowered by Quebec where relatively few women go out to work. But those women that have jobs in Canada do considerably better for themselves than the British. In all Provinces except Quebec and one or two of the Atlantic Bloc, there are equal pay laws for women. Today something like three-quarters of all Canadian teachers are women; a third of all Canadian laboratory technicians, 15 per cent of the professors, 15 per cent of the statisticians, and 5 per cent of the doctors.[2] In an industry outside Toronto, a 24-year-old girl from Belfast operating a computer told me that she was making $280 a month, compared with £8 a week at home. Everywhere I had impressed upon me the need for high-grade British stenographers and typists. In the major cities, a secretary can earn $250 a month (at least one executive I met was willing to pay as much as $450), and a married woman simply taking on casual work by the day as a typist in Toronto can bring in $10 a day. At a place like Schefferville, typists of the Iron Ore Company were being paid $300 a month — not bad, even if you have to live in Labrador to earn it.

One paradoxical result of high Canadian wage and cost levels was brought home to us several times in Winnipeg, where, on the menus of restaurants we found 'Danish brook trout' listed. It was apparently cheaper to fly trout all the way from Denmark than to have them caught and shipped from the inexhaustible lakes of the Shield, a few hundred miles away. High as Canadian wages are, they are, however, still between 15 and 25 per cent below American levels, a fact that — as the Gordon Report noted a few years ago — reflects a 'roughly equivalent difference in *per capita* productivity of the two countries'. At the lower end of the wage scale the gap is much less pronounced and now very

[1] A survey carried out by the *Financial Post* in 1957 discovered that two-thirds of British immigrants possessed their own cars in Canada, while only one-third of them had had one in Britain.

[2] *Opportunity in Canada*, by John Dauphinee, Rockliff.

small, nevertheless it is probably not exaggerating to say that the overall Canadian standard of living is as much as 30 per cent below that of the United States. The reason for this is that wages also buy less in Canada. Basic foodstuffs cost marginally less, but processed foods more in Canada and clothing is very much more expensive there than in the United States. On top of this, the exigencies of the Canadian winter mean that rather more clothing has to be bought, and similarly heating bills are markedly higher. There are tariffs on many manufactured necessities imported from the United States; notably cars, which may cost between 10 and 25 per cent more, and depreciate quicker — due in part to the corrosive chemicals sprayed on Canadian roads in winter. Compared with Britain, the Canadian cost of living is very considerably higher;[1] though such items as cars, petrol, long distance transportation and mechanical devices (notably for the home) are cheaper and of course not subject to heavy purchase tax. The high cost of living is to some extent offset by less severe taxation. Despite the fact that when Britain cut her income tax rate in 1959, Canada increased hers, taxation is still perhaps a third lower in Canada and it does not 'progress' upwards nearly so rapidly. Though Canadian tax laws encourage incentive, and favour the 'top men' more than in Britain, death duties, however, are very high and less open to evasion.

All in all, high costs do deflate sharply those alluringly fat Canadian pay packets. A British businessman in Toronto told me that, when trying to relate the two countries' wage levels, 'we divide the pound by 5.50 instead of 2.70'; and in my own haphazard calculations, I came to the conclusion that a Briton in Canada in order to improve his standard of

[1] Appended for the purpose of comparison are excerpts from a rough guide, 'The Cost of Living Round the World', published by the London *Financial Times* of October 14th, 1959. Out of 26 capitals listed, New York came second highest to Caracas, with Montreal a close third; London was only fourteenth.

	Dinner-Bed-Breakfast at a 4-Star Hotel	20 Cigarettes	Gallon of Petrol	Food Basket	Wardrobe	Rent (p.a.)
	£ s.	s. d.	s. d.	s.	£	£
New York	9 0	2 0	2 1	46	28	1100
Montreal	8 10	3 0	3 0	40	41	950
London	4 10	3 11	4 3½	27	22	700

living by 50 per cent would in fact have to earn about two and a half times as much as he did in England. But this in fact is what a great many Canadians do earn. That the average Canadian's material standard of living is still well above our own is shown by a survey made in the autumn of 1959 by a Canadian journalist, who found that : 'Two out of three Canadian families own automobiles ; in Britain, one out of four. In Canada eighty per cent of households have telephones, ninety per cent have washing-machines, ninety-five per cent have refrigerators, in Britain the corresponding fractions are only eighteen per cent, twenty-seven per cent and twelve per cent respectively. . . .'[1]

Perhaps one of the most noticeable contrasts in the Canadian wage and salary structure when compared with both Britain and the United States is the lack of differentials. I have remarked on this where it affected the Press, and it is a factor to be found in most fields of Canadian enterprise. No executive in Canada receives more than a fraction of the £199,000 paid out annually to the President of General Motors ; at the same time, few earn as much as the £10,000-plus which is the average director's emolument of a firm like British Electric Traction (by no means in the First Eleven of British industry), although the lowest basic wage paid by the company might be less than half as much as its equivalent in Canada. Similarly, a truck driver working overtime in the Yukon can earn $10,000 a year ; which is little less than many a highly-qualified engineer might expect to receive ten or fifteen years after graduating from college. It is clear that there is a fundamental distortion of values here. The reasons for it are that, despite her wealth, Canada is still a small country — yet, through the affiliations of most of her unions, the minimum wage rates of her labour force are pegged to those of the biggest and richest power in the Free World ; in itself a dangerous economic maladjustment. This reduction of differentials may mean that, in some respects, Canada is a more truly egalitarian society than either Britain or the United States. It has been well said that Canada is an emphatically middle-class country, and, with no very poor

[1] 'Are the British Better Off than We Are ?', by Blair Fraser, *Maclean's Magazine*, September 12th, 1959.

and few very rich, from the standpoint of incomes today this is certainly true. On the other hand, even though Canada's tax structure may favour the man at the top, it also means that the 'investing class', which should normally be putting its savings into the development of the country, has very little risk capital left over once enough has been set aside to put the children through college; a contributory cause of why Canadian expansion is so dependent upon outside capital.

As in the past, it is still the skilled craftsman, the technician, and certain classifications of professional man, who — in general — can do best in Canada today. But even the most highly qualified Briton should not assume that he can automatically step into a position equivalent to the one he had at home. This is an easy way to disillusion. Standards and requirements can be very different in Canada, and in professions ranging from plumber to Harley Street specialist the Canadians impose 'qualification exams' before an immigrant can fully practice his calling. Tradesmen may find themselves drawing lower than the regular rates until they have passed the necessary exams, and this is often a source of disgruntlement. But the Canadians have good reasons for demanding this standardisation; similar to those mentioned earlier that prevail in the teaching profession. It hardly needs to be said that any plumber who cheerfully ran pipes, à l'anglais, up the outside walls of Canadian houses would probably be strung up to the nearest tree before he had completed very many contracts! The process of qualification can, however, be an expensive one; especially for immigrant doctors. All doctors setting up in Canada, regardless of past experience, must pass a Licensing Examination. This is roughly equivalent to a final exam in Britain, but it obviously poses considerable hardship to a doctor who has been ten years or more out of school. Also the stipends paid to interns awaiting full qualification are quite incredibly low in Canada. A young English doctor, who had been a contemporary of mine at Cambridge and was now in his third year of post-graduate work at Montreal General, told me that he was only earning $60 a month, plus $40 marriage allowance (or about two-thirds of what a junior female clerk might earn). In Canada it is in fact virtually impossible for a young married doctor with no capital to keep his head above water while waiting for his licence to practice. Many doctors, I was told, enter their life in practice up to forty or fifty thousand dollars in debt; which no doubt explains the high fees charged by Canadian doctors upon qualification. Once over the hurdle of the Licence, however, the prospects for an able, and energetic, young doctor are unrivalled in Canada.

Against all the disadvantages of seasonal unemployment, the lack of security, the need to pass qualifying examinations, there is the fact that in most spheres of activity in Canada's expanding society there is far more opportunity for advancement. This is something that was emphasised to me by countless British and other European immigrants who had made a success in Canada. In 1958 approximately one in eight Presidents of Canadian companies were not born in Canada. Despite the setback Canada has received as a result of more than two years of recession and her worst spell of unemployment since the war, and despite the recent boom in Britain, in general the prospects of life for a good man — and particularly a skilled one — are still relatively better in Canada. And it is almost a certainty that they will grow better still, in the future.

CHAPTER ELEVEN

THE WIND THAT WANTS A FLAG

What are you ? . . . they ask, in wonder.
And she replies in the worst silence of her woods:
. . . I am the wind that wants a flag.
I am the mirror of your picture
until you make me the marvel of your life.
(From *Poem of Canada*, by PATRICK ANDERSON)

I am a Canadian, first, last and all the time. I am a British subject by birth, by tradition, by conviction — by the conviction that under British institutions my native land has found a measure of security and freedom which it could not have found under any other regime. (SIR WILFRID LAURIER, 1910)

Our nightmare is Anglo-American rupture. Canada loves and cherishes the Commonwealth connection, but she could not survive a break with the United States. If the terrible choice ever had to be made, geography would dictate it. (MATTHEW HALTON, on BBC in 1952)

IN a speech he made in Quebec soon after the war, Field-Marshal Montgomery coined the image of Canada as a 'hinge of purest gold' coupling the Old and New Worlds. It was a pleasing conception that struck the fancy of many a Canadian, and at least one distinguished author drew on it for the title of a book.[1] Yet, when analysed more closely, it somehow falls short. You might as well try to fix a mechanism as rigid and brittle as a hinge between the Cyanean Rocks as between two highly mobile mammoths like Britain and the United States. When the two veer away from each other, one can visualise the fragile link simply rent asunder. It is altogether too big a job to expect of even a hinge of Canada's substance. Tethered at each end as she is to one of the two Great Powers in her life, Canada does indeed provide a linkage of a kind; one that transmits pulls in both directions, and is in turn even more strongly influenced itself by these forces. But it is a linkage that is far more

---

[1] Leslie Roberts, *Canada: The Golden Hinge.*

flexible and ductile — sometimes an elastic sinew, sometimes a shock absorber — than can be conveyed by the image of a hinge, and far more loosely connected at its terminals.

Over the past centuries since the Capitulation of New France, Canada's initially tight-bound connections with Britain have been steadily loosened, until it is hard to find today any mooring point at all. Educated by the nasty shock of 1775, Britain's rulers ensured that the process of casting off in Canada has been a generally amicable one of 'evolution, not revolution'. Politically, Britain's relationship with Canada has probably received rather less than the credit it deserves on both sides of the Atlantic. With one or two exceptions, Britain sent the best administrators she has ever produced to govern Canada, and the administration they provided is greatly responsible for the stability and highly efficient government that Canada enjoys today. Economically, the record has been rather less magnificent, and could in part be held responsible for at least one of the weakest features of Canada today — her dependence on the United States — as well as for the flabbiness of her surviving ties with Britain. Following the American Revolution, in shame and embarrassment and lack of confidence, British merchants averted their gaze from the remaining North American colonies. Well into the mid-19th century 'Little Englandism' thrived at home. By the 1840s, an associate of the great coloniser, Gibbon Wakefield, was protesting that although Britain had already sunk £40 million in the United States 'hardly a shilling of English capital' had been invested in the Canadas.[1] The Repeal of the Corn Laws and the advent of free trade in Britain was a severe blow to Canada, and brought her closer to annexation to the United States than at any other time in her history. Then came Disraeli and a new era of imperial awareness, spurred on by the rise of German nationalism — though still a cloud no larger than Bismarck's fist. In the late 19th century most of the capital for Canadian development was provided by Britain (although little enough interest could be aroused among British investors for Canadian Pacific's olympian project).

It was late in the day for a revival of the Imperialist

[1] John Robert Godley, *Letters from America*, 1844.

ideal in Canada. In 1891 the great Conservative leader, Sir
John A. Macdonald, could still win an election with his
dying gasp on the slogan, 'A British subject I was born, a
British subject I will die.' But a few years previously, for all
his staunch devotion to Britain, he had declined to commit
Canada to an Imperial customs union and had briskly
refused to help Gladstone in his embroilment in Egypt,
declaring — shape of things to come — 'the Suez Canal is
nothing to us.' At this time there were irritants to Canada's
growing national pride when Britain, still responsible for the
Dominion's foreign affairs, acted in an apparently high-
handed fashion over her head; a notable example being the
surrender to the United States of the Alaska 'panhandle',
which still rankles in British Columbia. With the coming to
power of Macdonald's French-Canadian, Liberal successor,
Wilfrid Laurier, Canada strode out along the road to full
sovereignty. In 1905 she rejected British proposals for
setting up a permanent secretariat in London to prepare
the agenda of the intermittent Colonial Conferences. Five
years later Laurier upset the British Admiralty by founding
a separate, Canadian Navy. The Kaiser gleefully took this
as one more sign of the disruption of the British Empire,
ignoring Laurier's eloquent warning that : 'If England were
on trial with one or two or more of the great Powers of
Europe . . . we will put at the disposal of England all the
resources of Canada.'

The Canadian Prime Minister was as good as his word.
The same day Britain declared war in 1914, the splendid
Canadian volunteer army took to the field. Its sacrifices
were superb and terrible; out of the 600,000 men it raised
(in a population of only 7½ million) 48,121 were killed or
wounded, equal to all the war casualties of the thirteen times
more populous United States. The tragic losses left a legacy
of bitterness; there was a feeling that the Canadian soldiers
had been used as 'storm-troops', their lives thrown away by
inept British generals. It strengthened the urge for independence. Canada, backed by the other Dominions, declared
that the Imperial War Cabinet should not speak for them as
a whole at the Peace Conference, and demanded representa-
tion. In 1926 she was the initiating power behind the

Imperial Conference which gave the Dominions full sovereignty over their affairs, and at a blow converted the Empire into the Commonwealth. Meanwhile, as if to prove her new independence, in 1922 Canada had refused to support Britain in the Dardanelles crisis with Ataturk, mishandled as it had been by Lloyd George's government. During the inter-war years, Canada went her own way; disillusioned with Europe and frankly isolationist. But once again, when the call came in September 1939, Canada responded as before, this time entirely of her own free will. Again her contribution was magnificent; 12 million people raised armed forces totalling over a million, and by 1944 one-quarter of the air crews bombing Germany under British command were Canadian. Again the losses were severe; 41,700 killed and missing. Finally in November 1956, a fully sovereign Canada, with a heavy heart and a badly divided population, took to the floor at the United Nations against her two mother countries. As an 'equal' member of the Commonwealth, there was no doubt that Canada was treated shoddily by the Eden Government during the Suez episode. In her indignation, she had never made her voice in the world councils more effectively heard; and this voice was one of the leading factors that made Britain — faced with a possible dissolution of the Commonwealth — pause at Suez.

Five main strands now tenuously link Canada with Britain; race, commerce, tradition, the Crown, and the Commonwealth. One of the reasons that Canada in the 'twenties sued for nationhood harder than Australia and New Zealand was her large minority of non-British stock. Since then the British element in Canada has become even more diluted. During the inter-war period, an American writer noted: 'The old British impulse to go out and settle in remote parts of the world seems to have died out. Most people of the type that would formerly have emigrated seem to prefer the dole.' [1] After the war Canada still received the bulk of the British immigrants, but large inroads were made into the quota available by the competing attractions of New Zealand and Australia who, unlike Canada, offered

[1] W. H. Chamberlin, *Canada, Today and Tomorrow*, 1942.

to pay part of the transportation costs of selected immigrants. Between 1946 and 1954, years when one might have thought the attraction to leave Britain had never been stronger, Britons in fact comprised less than a third of the 'New Canadians'. In the post-Suez year of 1957, of the record total of 280,000 immigrants, the large majority of 41 per cent were British. But it was a freak; the following year, for the first time since the war, Britain was displaced from the top of the list — by Italy. This was more typical of the trend of events. Of the 356,000 who immigrated to Canada in the three years after 1945, nearly half were European DPs. In the 1901 census there were by origin 5682 Ukrainians, 10,834 Italians and 16,131 Jews registered in Canada. Fifty years later the figures had risen to 395,043, 152,245 and 181,670 respectively. Meanwhile over the same period, the French-speaking population had nearly trebled, while those of British origin did little more than double. The result is that whereas in 1901, 57 per cent of all Canadians boasted British origins, today the proportion is rather less than 48 per cent. Perhaps a sign of the times is that of the 265 present MPs in Canada's House of Commons, there are several Ukrainians, a Dutchman, an Italian, an Icelander, a Chinaman, a German from the Crimea, a man with a Lebanese father and a Swedish mother, and another of Swedish and Norwegian parentage, and the Prime Minister himself is of course partly German. More and more Canada is coming to resemble the 'melting pot' that America became in the 1870s, less and less a British domain.

Commercial trends have followed in the same direction. During the last war Canada was forced to turn for obvious reasons to the United States for her trade, and patterns were established that Britain has not yet managed to alter — and maybe never will. Pre-1940 17–18 per cent of Canada's imports came from Britain (from United States, 66 per cent), and 35–40 per cent of her exports were bought by Britain (United States also 35–40 per cent). In 1958 Britain supplied only 11 per cent of Canada's imports, while the United States' share was 69 per cent. This showed a trade switch in Britain's favour of 5·5 per cent over 1956, but the change in the export picture was far less spectacular; in contrast to pre-war days, by 1958 Britain was still buying only 16 per cent of Canadian exports, the Americans 59 per cent, a swing against Britain of 1 per cent over 1956 and an improvement of only 1 per cent over 1954. In 1956 British goods sold to Canada, the largest market in the Commonwealth, represented only 5·5 per cent of our total exports. Canada's grain trade, which above all others has traditionally looked to Britain as her principal customer, sold only 36 per cent of its wheat to Britain and 28 per cent to continental Europe in the five years from 1950 to 1954, compared with 61 and 16 per cent respectively over the previous five-year period. Thus the picture of Canadian trade swinging away from Britain, and strongly tied to the United States, is one that has remained fairly constant in the post-war years. With an alarming trade deficit of as much as a billion dollars with the United States, thirteen times as high as in 1950, Canada would dearly love to make a big increase in her trade with Britain. The Gordon Report, however, was pessimistic about any trade swing on a really large scale, and it may well be that Mr. Diefenbaker with his election postulate of bringing about a 15 per cent swing to Britain was being too optimistic.

Irritations over trade disappointments between the two countries operate both ways. In wheat-buying agreements of 1948, Britain's Socialist Government bought wheat from Canada for the first two years of a four-year period at a price substantially below the world level, promising to take this into consideration when fixing the price for the remaining two years. When the time came, however, she refused to pay more than world prices, with the result that Ottawa had to step in with a subsidy for Prairie farmers. Ten years later Britain was equally incensed when one of the first acts of the new Diefenbaker Government, a matter of weeks after it had declared its intention of increasing trade with Britain, was to raise tariffs on wool cloth imports from Britain; thereby hitting a British industry that was already down.

Today a new question mark hangs over Anglo-Canadian trade in the form of Britain's own relations with the European Common Market. Some Canadians fear that any deepening British involvement in the economies of the Six, and the death of the probably outmoded system of Imperial Preferences that must ensue, would only throw Canada further into dependence upon the United States. Other, perhaps more far-sighted Canadians, see Britain's entry into Europe as opening to them, eventually, a way for their own products to benefit from the greatly expanded markets that they believe the increased prosperity promoted by the Common Market will bring to Europe as a whole.

Meanwhile, any expansion of trade with Canada still depends to a very large extent on the enterprise of British business, and it is impossible to make a prolonged visit to Canada without getting the impression that British exporters could be a great deal more energetic. Each year teams of British industrial heavyweights flit across Canada, but the results when they return all too seldom seem to justify the self-congratulatory pomposity of those after-dinner speeches. While I was in Canada, many Canadians — and Britons — complained bitterly to me of the apparent inability of British firms to appreciate the vital importance of advertising and public relations in North America. The Dollar Exports Council, headed by Lord Rootes, which had toured Canada a few months earlier duly noted this tendency in its report; but it seemed rather late in the day to make such discovery thirteen years after the war, thirteen years during which more aggressive and publicity-minded American — and German — concerns have been grabbing potential British markets.

In Canada one is also constantly running into those two other bogies that seem to have plagued British exporters everywhere in the post-war years; loss of orders due to failure to meet delivery dates and an apparent inability to adapt to the peculiar needs of the country. At a logging camp in Vancouver Island I met a harassed mechanic sent over by a big British firm to cope with a workshop full of 'crocked' heavy earth-moving machinery. Most of them had repeatedly stripped their gears, and it was obvious that these were simply not designed for the heavy work met with in the forests of Canada. The lumber company was now turning instead to the United States for its requirements. In Edmonton, a senior official of the Alberta Government told me of a British firm that had placed a large order of 2″ by 4″ timber for a building contract. 'They were informed that the standard Canadian size for the same purpose was $1\frac{3}{4}''$ by $3\frac{3}{4}''$, but they still insisted on having the materials they were accustomed to in Britain. They got them, but it cost them just about twice as much.' These were but two, unfortunately all too typical, examples.

In the field of direct investment in Canada since the war, Britain has also lagged behind. By the end of 1957 Britain had $1150 million thus invested in Canada, the United States $8200 million. Over the previous four years, American long-term investments in Canada had increased by 61 per cent, those of other overseas countries (notably Germany) by 156 per cent, Britain's by only 55 per cent. From 1945 to 1953 the US stake had shot up by 78 per cent, Britain's by a mere 13 per cent. In 1958 the Dollar Exports Council reported that of 1200 new plants established in Ontario between 1953 and 1957, 37 per cent had been started by Canadians, 46 per cent by Americans, but only 11 per cent by British companies. Though every bit as needful of new sources of iron ore as the United States and Germany, Britain has apathetically stood by while Herr Krupp and the Ohio steel-makers moved into the Commonwealth, staking out claims to what is probably the richest deposit in the Western World.

In the past there has been altogether too much sheltering behind the difficulties, sometimes exaggerated, imposed by the Dollar Curtain. As the Canadian High Commissioner to Britain, Mr. George Drew, remarked pointedly a short time ago: 'There are still far too many exporters, in both our countries, who are busy looking for excuses instead of markets.' The time had come, he suggested, to replace the words 'buy British' with 'sell British'.[1] Now that Britain at last seems in sight of convertibility, things may — they certainly should — improve.

The Grosvenor Estate's imaginative project at Annacis Island near Vancouver is one example of how British enter-prise can play a part in the development of Canada. Here, at an initial cost of $25 million, a 1200-acre island in the estuary of the Fraser has been raised several feet and is being opened up as a highly modern industrial estate. The

[1] Speech on the retirement of the Agent-General for British Columbia, March 5th, 1959.

hundred-odd factories eventually to be built on this site will provide an important source of dollar earnings for Britain, as well as giving a great impetus to the further growth of B.C. (though it may be a further indication of British lethargy that of the first thirty-six plants constructed — despite the emphasis placed by Grosvenor Estates on proposals from home — only four were for British firms). Perhaps the best recent example of what Britain can do in the way of revitalising economic bonds with Canada was given during the Commonwealth Trade and Economic Conference at Montreal in September 1958. That summer the BC salmon fisheries, basis of the province's second biggest industry, had had their all-time record catch and were then anxiously wondering what they could do with it. Before the war Britain had been the leading customer for BC canned salmon, but for twenty years she had been importing only a dribble on a strict quota, and the British Columbians expected to have to spend several million dollars in advertising over a period of two years before they could market their huge catch. Then at Montreal Sir David Eccles suddenly announced that Britain would remove all quota restrictions on canned salmon. Within two days the whole of British Columbia's exportable surplus had been sold. I was in British Columbia at the time, and the delight at the British action — especially coming at a time when the province was still suffering from a recession — was almost unbelievable. Papers spoke of a 'miracle' and a 'heaven-sent *deus ex machina*'; probably no other event since the war had made that distant corner of the Commonwealth feel more gladly aware of its remaining links with the Mother Country. The official in the Board of Trade behind the timing of the Eccles announcement deserved a decoration. Nothing emphasised more clearly the true purpose and potential of the Commonwealth.

Canada has inherited, and proudly maintains, many British traditions, and with them go invisible — sometimes intangible — links with the Mother Country. Her justice is British justice; which may partly explain the noteworthy absence of graft and scandal in Canadian public life outside Quebec. Her civil service is closely based on Whitehall;

as incorruptible as it is slow-moving. Her parliamentary system is that of Westminster, not Washington. Her Prime Minister is not elected like the President, but chosen by the party which the electorate has given a majority in the House of Commons, and there is no division of authority between the executive, legislative and judicial branches which so often hamstrings government in the United States. The Canadian Senate, or Upper House, is more like a House of Lords composed of life peers than its American counterpart, in that its members are appointed for life on a generally non-political basis representing the elite of the country's elder talent, and that it has delaying but no veto powers. The progressives and youth of Canada frequently call for its abolition; though from time to time it provides an invaluable platform for non-party criticism of official policy. Each province has its own unicameral legislature (except Quebec, which — always different — also has a Senate) that is a miniature of the Commons in Ottawa, in turn a miniature of Westminster. Government and Opposition glower at each other across a rectangular floor, instead of all jumbled up in a semi-circle around the Speaker's rostrum as in American or European practice. The only concession to the men of 1775 is in having a written Constitution (the British North America Act), though it is seldom brandished as a sacred tablet, and a Supreme Court to interpret it and — if necessary — disallow legislation passed by either Federal or Provincial Governments; though it is an oracle that in comparison with its overworked counterpart in Washington is seldom invoked.

These traditions still provide some kind of invisible bond between Canadians and Britons. But it is usually intangible, as well as invisible, and the average Canadian while enjoying the benefits of British justice naturally enough does not feel that he owes the Mother Country tribute for these benefits. (After all, we do not respect the modern Italians for what their ancestors did for us.)

At the summit of the Canadian pyramid is the Governor-General, the Queen's personal representative and the last remaining political link between Britain and Canada. Up to 1951 the Governor-General had always been a Briton appointed by the Crown. All illustrious men, some were

brilliant successes, others less so; the last of the line, Field-
Marshal Lord Alexander, was probably one of the most
popular of the lot.   But the tide of Canadian nationalism
demanded that his successor be a Canadian.   Canada's
choice, Mr. Vincent Massey — scholar, industrialist, diplomat, patron of the arts and man of infinite wisdom and tact
— turned out to be unique and almost irreplaceable.   His
five-year term of office was twice extended before Canada
could find a successor approaching his stature.   It seems
almost a certainty, though, that the clock will never now be
put back and — barring an outstanding Royal candidate
like the Queen Mother — Canada will not again come to
Britain to find a new Governor-General.

During the Royal Tour of Canada in 1959 the *Montreal
Gazette* printed a cartoon eloquently depicting the Commonwealth as a chain held together by the Crown, entitled 'The
Vital Link'.   The Crown is indeed the vital link between
Britain and Canada today, and the attitudes of Canadians
towards it often contain a microcosm of their wider feelings
about Britain and the British.   Attitudes are highly complex.
After reading the floods of criticism and thinking-out-loud
that appear in the Canadian Press when a Royal visit is
in the offing, Americans sometimes rashly recommend to
Canadians that they become good Republicans like themselves.   They are usually astonished at the vehemence of the
Canadian response.   At its lowest common denominator,
to the average Canadian — whether of British, French or
Ukrainian extraction — the Crown is the one thing he has
that the rich and mighty Americans have not got.   It makes
him feel a little superior; in the fantastic greeting accorded
the Queen — *his* Queen, the Queen of Canada — at Chicago
in 1959, he detects a note of envy (as *Time* had a Canadian
business man scathingly remark, 'After all, you can't rally
round the country's most prominent golfer.'), and he feels
confirmed in his superiority.   But at the same time he may
be a great deal more critical and outspoken when discussing
the Royal connection with a Briton (and this in itself provides
one of those strange personal links which he cannot share
with any American).

Attitudes to the Crown vary greatly across Canada; they

vary with race and according to age group. By and large the
Crown means more in Newfoundland than perhaps elsewhere
in Canada, with the Maritimes and the surviving pockets of
Loyalist Ontario vying for second place. French Canada has
its own peculiar emotions. The welcome the Queen received
there in 1959 was hardly exceeded in other parts of the
country, and far excelled the warmth of her reception as a
Princess by French Canadians less than a decade ago. The
enthusiasm might in part have been explained, as a faintly
cynical French Canadian suggested to me the previous year
when the *Montreal Matin* ecstatically declared '*Les yeux bleus
de Margaret ont conquis Montréal*', by Gallic susceptibility to
beauty and charm. But there is little doubt that, as the
Crown as the instrument of British imperialism has receded
in French-Canadian eyes, many today reach out towards it
in a way they never did yesterday as a further shield against
American cultural encroachment. Out West and in the back
streets of once true-blue Toronto, it is hardly to be expected
that New Canadians born in Brest-Litovsk, Leipzig or Naples
should share the mysticism that an English Canadian from
London, Ontario, feels about the Crown. Curiosity, more
than fealty, may be what brings them out on to the streets
during a Royal Tour.

Today the strength of the Crown depends so much on its
mystic symbolism. Yet to a highly rational, down-to-earth
people like the Canadians living cheek by jowl with the
world's greatest Republic, founded on pure rationalism, this
very mysticism often provides a source of awkward conflict;
a conflict that may partly explain the controversy provoked
by the Royal Tour of 1959. Few Canadians are entirely
resolved as to the precise role the Monarchy should fulfil in
Canada. The Dean of a Canadian university declared to
me: 'I'm strongly monarchist, but anti-nobility.' Canadians,
who abolished titles soon after the first war,[1] do not really
approve of the Court, and in 1958 many were frankly disturbed that a young Princess should tour Canada with a

---

[1] An unknown Canadian poet gleefully wrote at the time:

'Away with honours, knighthoods, swords;
In proof of high endeavour
We'll wear where Adam wore the fig
The Maple Leaf forever.'

large retinue on what was supposed to be an essentially 'informal' holiday tour (though Ottawa was probably as much to blame for this as Clarence House). Yet, for the minority who felt the following year that the Queen's tour should have been more informal and who raised their eyebrows at the cost, the majority obviously favoured that full pomp and circumstance and panoply should accompany the Crown itself. I met several Canadians who genuinely felt that the inherent contradictions were too powerful, and that Canada was predestined sooner or later to become a Republic. More than one spoke to me of an 'absentee Monarchy', commenting that it should stay that way, 'because all Royal Tours do is show up the cracks in the structure'. But most Canadians, aware of the fate of absentee landlords in Canada in the past, seemed to feel that the Queen should come still more often to Canada and stay longer, though not necessarily on a set-piece attack like a Royal Tour. Great interest had been aroused by Nevil Shute's futuristic fiction *In the Wet*, in which the Sovereign, unappreciated by a Socialist Britain, divides her time equally between a permanent residence in Canada and the other Dominions. Probably the only ideal solution that would satisfy the greatest number of Canadians in their present dilemma would be to have the Queen all to themselves, shared with no one else!

The Royal Tour of 1959 crystallised conflicting Canadian emotions about the Crown, and in this the frequently heated arguments thus brought to the surface probably did a lot of good. Several points emerged; one was that the Canadian Press as a whole treated the Queen with considerably more respect and affection than did our own. There was no mistaking the genuineness of emotion in the often simply stated editorials from all over the country. The *Montreal Star* wrote: 'In the streets today the Queen is being accorded the warmest of welcomes by a people conscious of her demanding role and of how much it ennobles us to share it.' The Southam Press remarked of the Duke of Edinburgh: 'This is quite a guy.' The Toronto *Telegram* (admittedly more Royal than the Royals) described the Queen as 'a symbol of the best in national life'; in Winnipeg the less susceptible and usually eloquent *Free Press* admitted: 'Words cannot convey to Her Majesty and His Royal Highness the feelings that move Manitobans today.' A Gallup Poll found that 69 per cent of Canadians approved of the Royal Tour, that only 10 per cent thought it 'not good' for Canada, and that a typical response was, 'There is little enough holding the Free World together.' It was unfortunate that some of the British correspondents covering the tour appeared to be more concerned with the comfort of their own arrangements than with the job in hand, and so in their often petulant reports they failed to see the spontaneity of Canadian reactions. Summing up, the Toronto *Globe and Mail* acidly remarked what was probably little short of the truth that 'these persons almost squandered all the goodwill won by the Queen and Prince Philip'.

The criticism was there too. Letters flooded into the Toronto *Star*, backing Joyce Davidson, the Canadian TV personality who had declared she was 'indifferent' to the Royal Tour. Some were extremely outspoken, demanding, as one correspondent did: 'Let's leave the Royalty in Britain and keep Canada for the Canadians.' The revealing thing about the attacks on the tour was the common denominator that ran through nearly all of them. Many of the more fiery letters to the *Star* claimed to see a 'Colonial' taint in the Royal Tour: 'Can't we stand on our own feet?' asked one. In an article published in America's *Look* under the caption 'Queen Elizabeth — Why the Canadians resent her', a Canadian woman journalist explained: 'Americans, who won their independence from Britain so many years ago, can afford to yell themselves hoarse over the Queen without any second thoughts about what she symbolises,' which were, she added, 'the apron strings that Canadians long discarded.' Joyce Davidson put forward what she thought were the emotions of 'most Canadians' by saying, 'We're a little annoyed at still being dependent.' As anyone who has read this far will have realised, Canada is no longer in any way dependent on Britain, but this cannot alter the fact that many Canadians today still become upset on recalling that they once were; nor should the Davidson-Callwood outcry be dismissed simply as the views of two vinegary female journalists. It is rather more symptomatic than that.

The *Star*, which had been more critical of the Royal Tour than any other major Canadian newspaper, itself noted, however, that of the deluge of letters it had received, 'very few people opposed the institution of the Monarchy'. (And not one of the critics attacked the Queen herself.) The bulk of dissension was directed against the elaboracy of the tour, the longest ever made by a reigning sovereign, and coming so soon after similar visits. By the end of the tour it became plain that there probably would never again be anything on a similar scale in Canada. In its place will be visits of a shorter duration, for a specific purpose; such as the opening of a new dam or a centenary celebration and, many Canadians hope, more *genuinely* informal, holiday visits where they could catch glimpses of the Royal Family in rather more natural surroundings than those ineluctably associated with a Royal Tour. This form of Royal patronage in Canada was pioneered by the Duke of Edinburgh in 1958 when he flew to Ottawa just to preside at a meeting of the English Speaking Union. Homeward bound, apparently acting on his own initiative, he made a detour to Springhill in Nova Scotia, to visit bereaved families of miners killed in the recent colliery disaster. This spontaneous act made a tremendous impression in Canada, and possibly did more good than a whole set-piece Royal Tour. But how often will such opportunities recur?

There is, alas, little doubt that — in line with the bonds that link Canada and Britain — the Royal connection has grown weaker since the war. In the emotions of a rising younger generation, steeped in American traditions as never before, it may grow still weaker. Just before the Royal Tour of 1959 a well-known British writer living in Canada wrote to me expressing concern at these trends. The only hope for the tour to be a success and capture Canadian imaginations, he said, would be for the Queen's own character to break through. Young Canadians, he thought, 'might be receptive to acquiring a personal devotion to the Queen.' Perhaps this did indeed happen — though in an unexpected fashion — and after the Queen had already left Canada. Canadians are a conscientious, dutiful people, and the realisation that the Queen had insisted on completing

this most arduous of tours despite her pregnancy, which
brought her to collapse in the Yukon, did more than anything
could to make them aware of her unique personal devotion
to duty, and her own loyalty. But can the Monarchy be kept
alive in Canada solely on the almost superhuman qualities
of the present Queen? Will fleeting visits from an 'absentee
monarch' suffice to replenish the flame over the years?
Added to this there is the tremendous strain that the rapid
travel demanded by these visits — remembering the equal
claims of the other Dominions — places upon the Sovereign.
It is hard enough for a young and healthy Queen, but what
about in twenty years' time, when her regular appearance
may be demanded even more urgently in far-flung parts of
the Commonwealth?

In the long run, the fate of the Monarchy in Canada
depends of course upon the Canadians themselves. It is up
to them alone to decide what they want, but this may not be
easy until they have resolved the wider problems of their
relationship with Britain and the British. And that, fundamentally, means finding a formula to exorcise that bogy of
the 'Colonial taint' which lurks at the back of so many
Canadian minds; that persistent image of Britain as a
superior, slightly condescending and sometimes still faintly
bossy mother figure.

These are also factors that profoundly affect the role that
Canada plays within the Commonwealth, the last of her
links with Britain. Off the public platform, the average
Canadian is not greatly inspired by the concept of Commonwealth (is, indeed, the average Briton?). To him it is a fine
idea, provided it has no great demands to make. His dealings
with Australia and New Zealand are virtually nil. Comfortably secure in having no colour problem at home, he dis-
approves of South Africa (though both Liberal and Conservative Governments have discreetly refused to take part in
public discussion of the Union's internal policies) and has
frequent reservations about British colonial policy in the rest
of Africa; with which again his contacts are few. Over the
last decade, Canada has felt a growing of sympathy for India,
which is apparently reciprocated; as *The Times* Delhi correspondent recently put it: 'Indians have a fraternal feeling

for Canada that often is quite lacking in their relations with other Commonwealth countries.' The reasons behind this harmony are partly that Canadians, by their nature, strongly approve of the sincerity of Indian efforts to find a peaceful and moral solution to the world's problems. But also there undoubtedly enters into it a certain subjective envy for the position as an influential, entirely independent 'third force' that India has attained among the Great Powers. As a whole, the Canadian tends to see the Commonwealth as a company operated exclusively out of London, and overshadowed by Britain — despite the 'equal status' bestowed on all full members by the Imperial Conference of 1926. He is instinctively suspicious of talk about 'strengthening Commonwealth ties', because this to him has a smack of colonialism about it and implies a regression into the orbit of Britain.

None of this is to suggest that Canada does not pull her weight within the Commonwealth. She does. Liberal or Conservative, her Government takes a vigorous part at the various Commonwealth conferences; she has subscribed more than $200 million towards the Colombo Plan and is largely responsible for its administration. In terms of national income, Canada has provided twice as much aid to India, Pakistan and Ceylon as has the United States. But could she not do more? Canada's position within the Commonwealth is unique. Because of her spotless record for unaggressive peacefulness, no country in the world is more universally trusted. To the African and Asian she is a nation virtually free of racial prejudice (if you can ignore the immigration quotas on Asians), and completely free of any background of colonialism. There are occasions when her voice — already powerful — may be heard when a deaf ear is turned to Britain's, and in geographical terms alone she forms a bridge between East and West. Some indication of what Canada's role could be was conveyed by the importance Mr. Diefenbaker attached to his visit to the Asian countries of the Commonwealth following his re-election in 1958. (Yet when I asked Mr. Diefenbaker whether he favoured the creation of some kind of standing secretariat to co-ordinate Commonwealth relations a little more closely, his answer was a firm *no*, and — dedicated as he appears to be to the idea of

T

a strong Commonwealth — I felt that his 'no' might also have been qualified by those Canadian fears of British domination.)

Nevertheless, if a permanent consultative body is ever set up (and to prevent the Commonwealth just gradually drifting apart from lack of cohesion, something of the sort may eventually be necessary), why should it not be based in Ottawa, rather than in London? The decentralisation of the Commonwealth away from Britain, and the strengthening of multi-lateral links within it are essential if it is to thrive, and certainly if it is to gain the full support of Canadians. With its 'middle position', Canada would be the ideal centre for a Commonwealth Secretariat; as she grows in power she is indeed likely to inherit more and more of Britain's apparel as guardian of the whole system. One way of stimulating the multi-lateral links might be for Canada to select say a distinguished Australian as a future Governor-General, New Zealand a Canadian and so on (though one prominent member of McGill University assured me that he and most Canadians would feel 'insulted' if any but a Canadian was ever appointed Governor-General); at least there might be more exchanges at lower administrative levels. There are one or two promising signs in the air; a Canadian, Professor Donald Creighton (one of Canada's most distinguished historians), and an Australian were included on the Monckton Commission for Rhodesia; a Commonwealth Institute of Social Research is to be set up in Ottawa with the Speaker of the Senate (a French Canadian) at its helm; the Second Commonwealth Study Conference will be held in Canada in 1962, with Mr. Massey in the chair (the Duke of Edinburgh was Chairman at the First Conference). Finally, the new Canadian Minister of External Affairs is regarded as one of Canada's staunchest exponents of the Commonwealth (even to the extent of preferring that archaic title, 'the British Empire').

From a reading of Canadian history, noting its progress by 'evolution not revolution', a Briton might think that Canadians are over-sensitive about the 'colonial taint'; especially now that more than a generation has passed since they received full independence of the Mother Country.

(And does more than one Briton in a million really still think of the Canadians as 'Colonials'?) Nevertheless, this is a factor that exists and Britons intending to live in Canada would be much better advised to try to understand, or at least take cognisance of, this sensitivity than let irritation bring them to criticise it. Because of the very closeness of past ties, like blood cousins, the Canadians feel a special, not always easy, relationship to Britons on the personal level. They are apt to interpret British diffidence as arrogance, restrained enthusiasm as disguised disparagement, and sometimes to sense a snub where none is intended. One of the most cultivated, intelligent men I have met anywhere, head of a great Canadian publishing empire, admitted to me: 'I so often feel frankly uncomfortable in the presence of the British, an unaccountable sense of inferiority.' There it is, the deadly word is out. For much of Canadian sensitivity towards the British amounts to little less than a devastating inferiority complex (excluding from this generalisation, of course, the French Canadians who — like their European cousins — feel inferior to nobody). When one considers the miracles Canada has achieved at home, and the honour and admiration she has gained abroad in the few short years since the Statute of Westminster, it is certainly hard to account for this feeling of inferiority. Canadians themselves cannot always explain it. A young lawyer in Toronto gave me a remarkably honest, and rather revealing, analysis of his own feelings. At a cocktail party he had overheard a British friend of long standing go up and introduce himself to a newly arrived Briton, lightly excusing his forwardness with the words, 'I hope you don't mind, it's an old Canadian custom.' The Torontonian told me: 'I suddenly felt really upset, upset to find someone I looked on as a close friend apologising to a fellow Briton for Canadian customs. But the next day I was ashamed at myself. Why should I have allowed myself to get upset at all? That upset me even more.'

Canadians have good excuses for being sensitive, and the Britons in Canada have a certain amount to answer for. Every native-born Canadian since the war must have met at least one Englishman (more likely, a hundred) who has impressed upon him how much better things are done 'at home'. All too many are long on criticism and short on praise. The curious thing with the British in Canada is that many an immigrant, having severed his security-giving roots at home, seems to clad himself in his own protective armour — which also displays itself as a kind of inferiority complex. When complex works upon complex, the result is mutual uneasiness. The insecure Briton adopts positions he would never adopt at home, criticises things that he would mutely accept; and the less successful he is in life in Canada, the more critical he becomes. This frequently comes out in letters to the Canadian Press. Some of those published while I was in Canada were quite incredible; nobody outside a padded cell could have written them in England. One appearing in the Vancouver *Province* declared indignantly that although the writer was a British subject with ancestors he could trace back to A.D. 1120, and could boast a 'substantial bank balance', at the Canadian Immigration Office in London he had been made to sit 'among a motley crowd of Hungarians, Poles and other nationalities in a stuffy and overheated building, with screaming children and unwashed immigrants. . . .' This lack of consideration convinced him (by the end of a column-long diatribe) 'that it is evident that British people are no longer welcome in Canada.' For the next few days, my thoughtful Canadian hostess removed all the papers before breakfast to save me the distress of reading the outraged rejoinders.

In Toronto, there is a hotel where the proprietors, concerned about the walls in the men's lavatory, have installed a large blackboard above the principal piece of equipment — to canalise their patrons' literary and artistic urges. With unfailing regularity, in large letters across the top is chalked a strongly worded comparison between the contents of British and Canadian beer; below the equally inevitable response: 'IF YOU DON'T LIKE IT HERE, WHY DON'T YOU . . . ING WELL GO HOME.' It was symptomatic of Anglo-Canadian relations at their lowest level.

British immigrants may sometimes be irritated by this Canadian hypersensitivity towards themselves, but they should learn to live with it, examining their consciences as to how many times they have proclaimed British Bitter

superior to Canadian Ale. Canada is in a state of psychological flux at the moment, trying to establish a character for
herself that is neither entirely British nor entirely American.
When she succeeds her people will be more sure of themselves
and altogether less sensitive to what others think of Canada.
Already the rising generation in Canada shows a sureness
that its elders lack.   Between the three generations of
Canadians (and I mean principally those of British descent)
living today, there is a considerable disparity in attitudes
towards Britain and the British. The eldest generation, with
a cherished portrait of the Royal Family — possibly also one
of the Athlones or the Alexanders — on the piano, still looks
back with some nostalgia to the great days of Empire, to the
days when the life they led was the British way of life. They
wish that the image Britain projects today was a more potent
one, and sometimes feel that Canada, on casting off from
Britain may have gone a little adrift in a turbulent stream.
The men of that generation know how durable are bonds
forged by sharing the same trench for four years ; time has
softened down the more bitter memories of huge casualties
in attacks mounted by an apparently callous British High
Command.

To their sons, today in their forties, the Second World
War is closer ; they remember its seamier sides still, they
remember Dieppe and the sacking of General McNaughton.
They have seen post-1945 Britain's impact on the world
grow feebler ; they have been to London, seen the tarts
thronging Park Lane, seen the Cairene degeneracy of Piccadilly Circus and the apathetic squalor of British Railways,
and finally seen themselves universally mistaken for Americans
by Britons ignorant as to whether Montreal is east or west of
Toronto, and caring less. Was this really the nation their
parents reverently called 'the Old Country'? But then they
are also concerned at the way the United States seems to have
slipped into Britain's chair at the head of the Canadian
table. Unlike their parent's generation which largely supported Britain, they were bitterly divided over Suez. Too
many changes have taken place in their lifetime, so they are
a little confused, a little unsure.

Things are much simpler for their sons, now just leaving

school or university. They cannot really remember a time
when British influence in Canada was all-powerful. The
only Britons they have met on their home ground have been
travelling salesmen, complaining immigrants and an occasional itinerant travelling on a handful of illegal dollars and
a suitcase full of introductions, of whom they may hear their
fathers complaining that he left without paying his laundry
bill, their grandfathers muttering that Englishmen they used
to know were different. Unlike their parents who stumble
after its opening bar, they know all the words of 'O Canada',
but may not be so good on 'God Save the Queen'. For years
Canadians have been unable to agree upon a national flag,
but (if one can rely on a poll taken of the high schools in
1958) Canadian youth is much more certain of what it wants
than their elders; what the majority of boys and girls voted
for was an entirely new flag, and rather less than 13 per cent
wanted to retain the Union Jack. America is their guiding
star; from her originate the comics they read, the television
they watch, the clothes they wear, most of the games they
play and much of the education they receive. A typical
Provincial high-school syllabus sets out: 'The English programme should contribute to an understanding, apprecia-
tion, and faith in the basic values of democracy.' Nothing
about an understanding of Canada's British heritage. The
young Canadian resembles a young American far more
closely than either of the preceding generations, and to many
of them the United States is the country they would like to
model Canada upon. They tend unconsciously to be more
republican-minded; they are not prepared to accept emotionally the Crown and the Commonwealth; they have to
be persuaded that both are good things. Today their discus-
sions may not be entirely flattering to Britain, but, out of the
surer, more confident Canada that their own self-confidence
will one day breed, a much happier, less self-conscious, relationship with Britain seems bound to emerge. If the ideal
of Commonwealth can be sold to them (a big if), their
Canada may feel its way to a far closer collaboration with
Britain, unembarrassed by the stigma of 'colonial' associations. As Dr. James, the Principal of McGill University
remarked at a dinner of the Royal Commonwealth Society

celebrating Empire Day in 1958: 'Today does not remember with affection the debt of yesterday; it dreams of the promise of tomorrow.'

During his television appearance with Mr. Macmillan in 1959, President Eisenhower referred eloquently to the US-Canadian frontier as 'defended by nothing but friendship'. No after-dinner speech on relations between the two neighbours is ever complete without some mention of the 'longest unguarded frontier in the world'. The amity with which Canada and the United States have lived together for nearly a century and a half is indeed a remarkable thing, deserving of rather more worthy tribute than those plushy, post-prandial platitudes. But relations have not always been idyllic, and even today they are far from being a honeymoon without strife. From time to time, Canadians still find themselves in tacit agreement with Trollope's acid verdict of nearly a century ago: 'The star-spangled banner is in fact a fine flag, and has waved to some purpose; but those who live near it, and not under it, fancy they hear too much of it.' [1] On several occasions in Canadian history, the United States would have liked to gobble up part or all of Canada, and missed their chance — generally through lack of tact. When the Americans under General Montgomery 'liberated' Montreal in 1775, they failed to ignite the spark of revolution among the French *habitants* because of their intolerance towards the Church and their payment for services in valueless 'Continentals'. In the War of 1812 Jefferson boasted that the conquest of Canada was not likely to be more than a matter of marching; but most of the few spectacular victories on land during that dismal conflict were won by Canadian troops. Strongly pro-American tendencies in Lower Canada were rapidly reversed by the harsh threats of the invading General Hull. Post 1812 the ebullience (some contemporary writers call it arrogance) of the rapidly expanding United States made Canadians glad, whatever their difference with the Mother Country, to have British troops on their soil, where they remained until 1871.

In 1854 the signature of a Reciprocity Treaty dropping

[1] Anthony Trollope, *North America*.

tariff barriers on trade between Canada and the United States brought Canada unprecedented prosperity, and brought her closer than at any other time to annexation. But a decade later good feelings came to an abrupt end when the victorious Unionists, enraged by Britain's support of the South in the Civil War, abrogated the Treaty and turned a blind eye on raids over the border by the Fenians, wild Irish precursors of the IRA. In the opinion of at least one Canadian writer, if Washington had cracked down on the Fenians, 'the birth of Canada might have been indefinitely postponed, and conceivably would never have happened.'[1] Instead, Confederation was hastened along. When, in 1911, Canada was once more on the brink of resuming Reciprocity with the United States, her rejection of it was clinched by a statement of the Speaker of the United States' House of Representatives, 'Champ' Clark; 'I am for it,' he said, 'because I hope to see the day when the American flag will float over every square foot of the British North American possessions clear to the North Pole.'

In 1940 the war and Canada's virtual economic isolation from Britain forced her into a new intimacy with the United States that continues to this day. First came the Ogdensburg Agreement between Roosevelt and Mackenzie King and the establishment of a Permanent Joint Board on Defence, then the Hyde Park declaration a year later providing for close economic co-operation between the two countries. The one paved the way to the complete integration of North American defence structure that exists today, NORAD and the DEW-Line; the other to American exploitation of Canadian resources. Thousands of Americans poured into Canada to rush through the Alaska Highway. During the first post-war decade, US-Canadian relations had seldom been better, but Canadian fears that they may have merely exchanged dependence upon Britain for an even tighter dependence on the United States have brought about a cooling down recently. The Diefenbaker landslide in 1958 was largely won on a platform promising to combat American influence; though, paradoxically enough, probably no politician in Canadian history ever conducted a more American-style electoral cam-

[1] Leslie Roberts, *Canada: the Golden Hinge.*

paign than Mr. Diefenbaker, perhaps in itself a proof of the extent of US influence in Canada.

Canada has a number of sources of grievance with the United States today, some small, some big. On the personal level, some of the irritants are very similar to those with which Britons manage to bring Canadians out in prickly heat rash. Ignorance is one. When Toronto (then York) was captured and burnt in 1813, outraged Americans regarded the Speaker's wig they found hanging on his chair in the legislative buildings as conclusive evidence of Canadian scalpings. (In the same war, Britain showed just as profound an ignorance when the Admiralty laboriously shipped kegs of fresh water to Kingston, apparently on the assumption that the Great Lakes were salt!) Today many Americans seem to believe that Canada still pays some kind of tribute to Britain. A Canadian veteran of Korea told me how infuriated his men became when GIs amiably asked: 'Why doesn't Canada shake off the British yoke, instead of paying taxes to keep the Royal Family going?' or 'Why doesn't Britain trade Vancouver Island to the USA in payment of her war debts?' The reaction to this kind of remark usually leaves the American baffled that Canadians could still be so 'pro-British'. In 1958 American members of the Kiwanis businessmen's club boldly suggested that henceforth the Red Ensign of Canada should replace the Union Jack at Kiwanis meetings, declaring that they were 'not interested in the spreading of a former empire by showing the Union Jack.' Whatever individual Canadian members of the Kiwanis may have really thought about the ever-burning flag issue, their replies were vitriolic, with the Toronto Branch retorting that they were proud to be members of the British Commonwealth and that the Union Jack was regarded as a symbol of common unity and allegiance.

Canadians complain, with some justification, that — despite her proximity — Canada gets even less coverage in the American Press than in the British. As somebody once remarked, 'While the American is benevolently ill-informed about Canada, the Canadian is malevolently well-informed about America.' Out of ignorance arises a big-brotherly indifference which, in a penetrating article for an American

magazine in 1958,[1] Bruce Hutchison isolated as one of the
principal causes of anti-Americanism in Canada. It infuriated
Canadians, he said, to be 'taken for granted as good, steady
neighbours. . . . What the American people must understand
. . . is that tomorrow they will be dealing not with a small,
weak people but with one of the earth's major powers.'

Beneath the mask of this indifference, Canadians sometimes see a high-handedness, a kind of arrogance they used
to associate with Britons.   At a country-club in Calgary
(which is the home of the biggest American 'colony' outside
the United States), a Canadian ex-colonel told me how
furious he and his co-members had been when the rich
American contingent had railroaded them into tearing down
their beloved clubhouse; because, at 25 years of age, the
Americans considered it antiquated. At another club, also in
Calgary, Canadian tempers had been raised still higher when
American members declared they would blackball a local
editor who had published anti-American editorials during
the Suez crisis. Travelling in the States, Canadians are irritated to find shops will not accept their dollars, or if they
do, disregard the premium on it, although the US dollar is
universal currency in Canada. They are even more irritated
to find Americans taking credit for the lion's share of the St.
Lawrence Seaway, despite the fact that it was obstructionism
in the US Senate which nearly forced Canada to 'go it alone'
and that, in any case, more than two-thirds of the bill for
the navigational part of the Seaway was footed by Canada.
Like Europeans, Canadians occasionally note their sensibili-
ties bristling at the floods of those shrill-voiced Midwesterners
pouring in each summer, treating the country as a 'cute'
kind of vacation colony (while they remain perhaps oblivious
to the millions these self-same American tourists are investing in 'English Bone China', curios and fishing licences).
Canadians were deeply resentful at US interference in their
affairs as revealed by the Norman suicide in Cairo. They
are outraged by remarks such as the following, made by one
of the United States' more provocatively nationalist writers:
'Were we not generous, good-natured and sentimental, we
might find means to send Canada's economy whirling into a

[1] 'Why Canadians are turning Anti-American', *Harper's Magazine*, 1958.

nice little vortex by evading purchases there, when Canadians complain about our investments in that country.' [1] They were not much reassured when President Eisenhower, during his visit to Ottawa in 1958 and in answer to Canadian concern at severe US restrictions on raw-material imports, merely told them that their troubles were a result of the times we live in.

Where the principal object of Canadian resentment used to be the sophisticated, 'elders-and-betters' attitude of the Mother Country, it has now become the thick-skinned might of the rich uncle. The mantle has been transferred in many ways. During the Korean war, Canadian feelings about the US High Command, under whom their force served, had a strong resemblance to what was felt about the British General Staff after 1914 and 1939. Today many Canadians are worried to find the RCAF in Canada tactically under the command of an American general at NORAD. Remembering the words of 'Champ' Clarke, they are sometimes concerned by the implications of the American flags that now float over DEW-Line bases in Canada's untenanted North, especially when they read in their press of senior Canadian officials having to receive security clearance from Washington to visit these bases.

Some of the most serious matters casting an occasional cloud over the love relationship between the two neighbours stem simply from the proximity to a small country like Canada of such a huge power, unconsciously exerting such potent gravitational forces. Often the United States can hardly be blamed; as for instance in the problem of emigration *from* Canada, whereby — generation after generation — much of her best talent is regularly siphoned off southwards, drawn by the promise of greater opportunities. Between 1851 and 1941 the number of *emigrants* (nearly all to the United States) virtually balanced out the total immigration into Canada. Figures improved during Canada's great post-war boom, but still between 1955 and 1957 alone 2472 engineers, 3643 nurses, 535 doctors and 1073 teachers left Canada for the United States, a heavy loss for a nation of 17 millions. The moment there is a breath of a recession in

[1] George Sokolsky, in the New York *Journal American*, October 24th, 1957.

Canada, up goes emigration. In 1958 roughly as many Canadians are estimated to have emigrated to the United States as Britons entered Canada. In 1959 as soon as AVRO announced that it would have to dismiss 14,000 workers, because of cancellation of the Arrow fighter contract, Toronto newspapers were filled with 'wanted' ads. put in by the American aircraft industry. And it hardly escaped Canadian attention that pressure from the United States had quite a bit to do with the dropping of the Arrow project. At least 25 of the sacked personnel — about half of them highly skilled immigrants from Britain, the type Canada most needs — are already reported to be at work on the United States 'Project Mercury' to put a man in space.

It is in economic relations that Canada is most vulnerable to the whims of the American giant, and here Canadians frequently feel that she falls short of being everything a good neighbour should be. Mention has already been made of the curious relationship between the US and Canadian Trades Unions; in no other country in the Western World can strikes be ordained from a Union HQ outside its own borders. Today the United States also dominates Canadian trade, as well as her capital structure. She is by far Canada's biggest customer, with nearly 85 per cent of her newsprint alone originating from Canadian forests, and Canada is also the biggest buyer of American exports. But where foreign trade occupies about only a twentieth of the US economy, it represents at least *one-quarter* of Canada's. Thus the United States can afford to ignore the fluctuations of international trade, but Canada cannot; especially when some 80 per cent of her products are still exported as raw, or semi-raw, materials, which are the first to feel the draught when markets recede. On imports of these raw materials — now essential to her own economy — the United States places a low tariff, but she places progressively higher tariffs on Canadian manufactured goods. The result has been the inhibition of the more profitable secondary industries that Canada badly needs to transform herself into a major industrial power; the piling up of her alarming trade deficit with the United States; and imposition on Canada of what some of her more nationalist economists call a 'colonial economy', with the United States simply exploiting her for the benefit of the treasure lying under the Laurentian Shield.

Canadians felt they had particular cause to be piqued when, during the recent recession, the US Government slapped drastic import restrictions on Canadian oil and raised tariffs on lead and zinc, thus closing markets to the very resource industries that the United States had been encouraging Canada to build up. And while Canada, in the grip of the recession, was anxiously searching for markets for her manufactured goods, Fords in Detroit stepped in to forbid the sale of 1000 trucks to Red China by their Canadian subsidiary. Canadians exploded at this latest interference in their affairs, and the incident undoubtedly added many thousand votes to Mr. Diefenbaker's majority a few weeks later. It also underlined a factor that today worries Canadians more than any other; American control, direct or indirect, of her key industries.

When Canada strode off into her tremendous post-war boom, with Britain virtually out of the running she had to depend on American capital to develop her new industries. American investment dollars pouring in also counterbalanced Canada's large trade deficit, thereby saving her from the kind of trouble that has consistently plagued Britain since the war. Thinking Canadians appreciate that without this American investment they would not be enjoying the prosperity they have today, but they also wonder whether things have not gone a bit too far, and are fearful lest they may have sold their birthright for a mess of US capital. The figures are genuinely alarming. *The Canadian Journal of Economics and Political Science* of November 1956 was not exaggerating when it said that 'No other nation as highly industrialised as Canada has such a large proportion of industry controlled by non-resident concerns'. Two years later, the *Financial Post* listed 102 Canadian companies, representing $2,000,000,000, that had passed into foreign hands since the war.

Despite the efforts of the Diefenbaker Government, things are still worse today. According to figures produced by the Dominion Bureau of Statistics at the end of 1959, in the three years 1956 to 1958, 44 per cent of all new capital investment in Canada was directly financed from abroad. Of all the

long-term foreign investment, $14,600 million was American,
and only $3100 m. British. This meant that (by the end of
1957) some 52 per cent of all the capital employed in the
Canadian mining, petroleum and manufacturing industries
was controlled in the United States,[1] 10 per cent in Britain,
and only 38 per cent in Canada herself. Control of more
than half the chemical industry, and over 95 per cent of
automobile production is today in American hands. Although
AVRO, one of the two biggest aircraft firms in Canada, is
still British controlled, the replacement of the cancelled
Arrow project by a contract to build a 'flying saucer' for the
US Government means that this industry is also now overwhelmingly dependent, indirectly, if not directly, on the
United States. So is the uranium industry, bound as it is
by the United States' buying contracts. In 1955 the Gordon
Report warned that the United States controlled 68 per cent
of the Canadian petroleum industry, but this has now risen
to 71 per cent, while Canada's own portion has sunk from
31 per cent to a depressing 24 per cent. When I was last
in Alberta, no less than fourteen members of the Board of
Governors of the powerful Canadian Petroleum Association
were American, only six Canadian. US tax laws have strongly
favoured American investment in Abertan oil, to the disadvantage of Canadian operators ; Canadian laws, having
no Capital Gains Tax, have also encouraged more and more
American investment. Finally, as the Bureau of Statistics
noted in its 1959 report — pointing a faintly accusing finger
at Canadians themselves — home savings which might have
paid for another 9 per cent of Canadian investment during
the 1956–8 period were actually invested abroad. Thus
Crown Zellerbach of San Francisco was busy buying up
Canadian lumber companies, while Garfield Weston was
purchasing Fortnum and Mason, and Roy Thomson *The
Scotsman* and the Kemsley empire.

Aside from the crude symbolism of financial power, what
does this preponderant American control over Canadian
capital really mean to Canada ? For one thing, it means that
bright young Canadians often find the top reaches of industry

---

[1] A further interesting point was that for this 52 per cent control, the United
States in fact actually *owned* no more than 45 per cent of the capital.

barred to them by American executives. Of some 4000 US
subsidiaries in Canada, not more than about eighty have
Canadian directors on their boards. Thus there is the added
enticement for administrative talent to slip off over the
border. Secondly, when for instance there is a world oil
surplus, as there has been since 1956, the natural inclination
of the US controlled oil companies is to cut production in
Canada rather than at home. The same applies to the other
producers of Canadian raw materials, in time of recession.
But, in the long term, probably the most damaging effect on
Canadian development may be that, in return for the extraordinarily rapid development of the first stage of Canada's
post-war expansion, the second stage — that of building up
the processing and manufacturing industries she must have
in order to fulfil her promise of true greatness — may be
seriously set back. The impact of the American-controlled
Iron Ore Company of Canada provides one example of this,
although many Canadians I spoke to hardly seemed to see
it themselves. Every year the IOC digs up millions of tons
of an exhaustible Canadian capital asset in Labrador and
ships it off to the States. The recovery and transhipment of
the iron ore does provide jobs and prosperity for perhaps
10,000 Canadians, but that is all. Meanwhile, in the States
the far more profitable business of turning this Canadian raw
material into steel ingots and thence into automobiles may
give work to ten, twenty or thirty times as many Americans.
And it is obviously in the IOC's interest to keep things that
way, so that it is most unlikely to do anything that would
encourage the establishment of any competitive Canadian
enterprise for processing that iron ore at home.

Canada is in a quandary. She must have outside capital
for her future development. She would badly like more from
Britain, for that would at least dilute the proportion of her
investments held by one set of outsiders alone (therefore it
is a little sad to see British enterprise, the moment dollars
become less tight, spending $25 million to erect a skyscraper
in New York with all its vast sources of capital, rather than
investing money in Canada). She cannot take any action
against the United States that might smack of expropriation,
as Mexico once did — to her lasting ruin. Yet the present

evaporation of capital assets to the United States cannot go unchecked. It may be that there should be some kind of legislation, demanding that foreign subsidiaries should appoint a majority of Canadians to their boards in Canada; should earmark substantial minority holdings of their shares for the Canadian market; and — perhaps most important of all — demanding that some reasonable percentage of the raw materials produced in Canada be processed *in Canada*. Meanwhile, if things continue as they are, for as long as Canadians sniff economic imperialism in America's approach to them, there will be a major source of anti-Americanism in Canada.

It is a mistake, however, to be misled by the fierce voices occasionally raised in Canada into underestimating the bonds that do exist now between Canadians and Americans. In 1958, when Mr. Diefenbaker won his election on a distinct anti-American bias, and then announced his plans of a big trade switch to Britain, this was heralded by certain sections of the British Press as a sure sign that Canada was coming closer into the fold of the Commonwealth once again. Yet one could not help feeling at the time that at its roots this might be a negative reaction rather than a positive trend; perhaps a little reminiscent of the 'annexationist' flirtations with the United States, that manifested themselves in mid-19th century Canada, on occasions when Britain had driven Canadians to despair by indulging in one of her more disgraceful bouts of Little Englandism or Imperial indifference. Today, continental consanguinity may be more potent that the purer ties of race and tradition, attenuated as they are by 3000 miles of Atlantic, and these North American orientations seem to be growing stronger and deeper all the time. When Stephen Leacock was invited to England on his retirement from McGill, he refused, giving as one reason: 'I'd hate to be so far away from the United States. You see, with us it's second nature, part of our lives to be near them.' Every year, some fourteen million Americans pass in and out of Ontario alone, and a proportionate number of Canadians trek over the unguarded frontier, equipped with no papers but a driving licence (to do the same, a Briton needs a passport and a US visa). When we stayed in Regina, the city was overflowing with a convention of 'Shriners', a

flamboyant Masonic order who justify their hideous good
cheer and annual prank-playing by great works of charity.
With lodges in most cities in the United States and Canada
and some twelve thousand Canadian members, they are but
one of the many organisations and clubs (like the Kiwanis)
that unite Canadians and Americans socially.   Most Britons
would, I suspect, be a little embarrassed by the 'Shriners'
ritual, by the spectacle of paunchy middle-aged business men
clowning in fezzes and Turkish pantaloons, but a Canadian
accepts it all quite naturally as part of the North American
heritage.   In much the same way, a Torontonian can laugh
at the same jokes as a San Franciscan, feel quite at home and
comfortable in New York or Chicago, whereas he might not
in London.   After her first couple of weeks in England, a
thirty-year-old Canadian girl admitted to me: 'Before I
came here, I never realised just how North American I was'.
Pondering about this North American 'solidarity', I remembered the loggers hidden away in the wilds of Vancouver
Island, raptly listening to the baseball scores of the US World
Series at the other end of the continent.

With the great material power she has gained since the
war, Canada today quite naturally wants to be something
more than just a hinge, however golden, between the two
great powers.   She wants to be a force in her own right.   She
is 'the wind that wants a flag'.   In the world of foreign
relations she has already succeeded to a remarkable degree.
In 1914 the total staff of her foreign service numbered fourteen, including two messengers.   Today it is closer to two
thousand, and includes many diplomats of the very highest
ability.   Her contributions to world affairs have far exceeded
what would normally be expected from a nation of seventeen
million, and so has the respect she has earned.   The great
concept of NATO first originated in the mind of a Canadian,
a French Canadian, and ever since Canada has played a
leading role there.   It was also from Canada that the suggestion of a United Nations Emergency Force came, at one of
the earliest UNO sessions, and it is in UNO and its affiliated
organs that Canada has won particular acclaim.   Few representatives have been more active than Mr. Lester Pearson,

U

who was President of the General Assembly in 1952. It was through the inspired handling of the Canadian delegate that the East-West deadlock was partially broken in 1955, and a 'package deal' admitting sixteen new nations accepted. The first Director of the World Health Organisation, and a strong influence on its inception, was a Canadian, Mr. Brock Chisholm. As well as her participation in the Suez UN Force, Canada made significant contributions to the settling of the Korean war, working closely with the Indians in their mediatory function, and a hundred and fifty Canadians joined with India and Poland in the Indo-China Truce Commission of 1954; more recently she sent troops to join the UN Force in the Congo. In all these commitments, Canada found herself assuming responsibilities on behalf of the West, where other Western Powers would have been unacceptable; indication in itself of the hugely important role Canada may continue to play in the work of breaking down barricades of distrust and relaxing international tensions.

When Canadian foreign policy deviates a degree or two from the American or British, from time to time it gives the impression of having been slightly conditioned by this great urge of Canada's to be truly independent, to be something in her own right. But this is only a small part of the truth. In addition to her loyalty to the Commonwealth, her commitments to NATO and her ineluctable ties in North America, Canada often senses she has another vital responsibility as a leader among the Third Powers, in the cause of peace. Canada is one of the very few countries where that rather sickly, overworked epithet 'peace-loving' has any meaning at all. The fact that Canadians at the end of the First World War erected a Peace, not a 'Victory', Tower in Ottawa, is in itself symbolic. The many pacificist groups like the Mennonites, Hutterites and Doukhubors, who sought refuge in Canada from the bellicose insanity of Europe, may well have had their influence, but above all and embracing all there is the sheer passive remoteness of the Canadian environment.

At the extreme tip of Cape Breton Island, a place as peaceful and far-removed from the rest of the world as any that one could imagine on earth, we stayed overnight at a guest-house run by an elderly Canadian Scot. He had lost a

leg and an arm in the First World War. As he moved painfully upstairs to show us our room, I could not help wondering what possible claim far-off Flanders could have had upon
him; or indeed what Cassino had to do with the men from
Saskatchewan who died before it a generation later. The
farther one travels across Canada the more one marvels at
the qualities, higher than mere loyalty, that brought her into
both World Wars. She does not share the anxiety, the greed,
the passions, of Europe, nor the stresses world leadership
imposes on the United States. Why should she? It is perhaps
all the more remarkable that today, casting aside her isola-
tionism of the 'thirties, she has accepted any responsibility
for Europe at all. Yet her approach to world affairs can
never quite be the same as that of the 'Supermen of Europe',
as Mr. St. Laurent dubbed Britain and France at Suez. Split
by Suez (and many Canadians were deeply shocked by the
moral issues), Canadians were also disturbed by the US
landing in the Lebanon of 1958. They see a peaceful solution
to world affairs lying perhaps somewhere between the United
States and Russia — with special importance attached to the
emerging desires of the underdeveloped, uncommitted countries of Asia and Africa.

For all her remoteness from the world's trouble spots,
Canada reinforces her position among the powers by maintaining a highly efficient defence force, numbering about
120,000 men, and devotes some 7–8 per cent of her Gross
National Product to defence expenditure, or only slightly
less than Great Britain. After Britain, she makes the highest
per capita contribution to NATO. Today all three Canadian
services are tightly integrated, more so than the British,
under one Joint Staff responsible to one Government department; the Ministry of National Defence. Officer cadets
receive identical courses at one of Canada's three military
colleges, and wear the same uniforms while there, regardless
of whether they are destined for navy, army or air force.
There is one medical service for all three, and the research
functions in Britain formerly scattered between the three
service departments, the Ministry of Supply and Ministry of
Defence, are united in Canada within the Defence Research

Board, also responsible to the Defence Minister. All services are composed of volunteers; there is no National Service in Canada.

The Royal Canadian Navy, which during the war grew to nearly twenty times its pre-war size to become the fourth largest naval force in the world, today numbers about 20,000 men. Consisting principally of destroyers and destroyer-escorts (most of the newer vessels designed and built in Canada), it is cast for an almost exclusively anti-submarine role under NATO command. The Canadian army of 50,000 mounts a force of four infantry brigade groups, of which one (totalling, with its ancillaries, 12–13,000 men, and costing Canada $30 million a year) is permanently stationed under NATO, at present at Soest in Germany. Army units are also serving with the UN Emergency Force in Sinai, until recently commanded by a Canadian, Major-General Burns. As in the British Army, Canadian regiments have strong regional affiliations. The RCAF, which has nearly trebled in size since 1952, now numbers about the same as the army. Symbolic of Canada's role among the powers, the RCAF is a purely *defensive* force, possessing no bombers.[1] Its interceptor squadrons are equipped with CF-100s (designed in Canada) and F-86 Sabres, both built in Canada, though now obsolescent. In 1959 the RCAF had no less than forty squadrons in service. Twelve of these (representing 6000 men) form the Canadian NATO air division in France and Germany. Most of the remainder come under NORAD, with a USAF C.-in-C. and a RCAF deputy. As noted earlier, the RCAF is also responsible for operation of the Mid-Canada and Pinetree radar lines. With the shadow of the ballistic missile hanging over it, its future is neither more nor less uncertain than air forces of other nations.

Integrated as they are, the Canadian armed forces give the impression of outstanding efficiency. Fifty per cent of the army's manpower is now in actual fighting units, which shows a reduction of nearly half the numbers it took to keep a Canadian division in the field during the war; a feat of

[1] Canada is also probably the only power with the potential of making an atomic bomb that has steadfastly devoted itself to peaceful uses of nuclear fission only.

streamlining that makes the Canadians believe that —
despite their high standard of living — their forces today
have a proportionately smaller administrative tail than
either the American or the British. The RCAF (admittedly,
I saw more of it than the other services) is particularly
impressive, its administration run on lines more resembling
that of a brisk North American business corporation. Its
division in Germany currently has the highest efficiency
rating of all the Air Forces (including the British and American), in having the highest proportion of planes operational
and in being the quickest into the air in an emergency. The
RCAF's spirit is remarkable and after a few minutes with
one of its units you feel that nothing is too difficult for it.

Conditions are extraordinarily good in all three services
(with the RCAF having a slight edge on the others), and as
a result they have in the past been able to pick and choose
among men wanting to join up. In the RCAF alone, the
re-engagement rate after the first term of five years has been
as high as 75 per cent. Wages are high ; a recruit in any of
the forces receives a basic pay of $104 a month. A Squadron
Leader with nine years' service receives (at the time of
writing) $545 a month, plus generous family allowances.
The Canadian services also have attractive schemes whereby
if a young man signs on for five years they will finance his
university education prior to joining.

Any British subject may join the Canadian services, and
many officers with the RCAF today have in fact transferred
direct from the RAF. Two of the RCAF stations I visited
had C.O.s who had been in the RAF, and at least one
member of the crew in each of the three RCAF planes I
travelled in was British. With their traditions closely related
to those of the British armed forces, there are few environ-
ments in Canada where the atmosphere is so much that of
Britain. (There was actually once a Royal Commission to
investigate whether the Canadian navy needed de-anglicis-
ing !) Britons are made welcome in the Canadian services,
and for a young man wishing to immigrate it is hard to think
of any better way of collecting both a little capital and a lot
of experience about Canada, than by signing on for a stint
of five years.

CHAPTER TWELVE

THE NEW CANADIANS

The principal cause of failure in immigration is the wrong people coming for the wrong reason. (T. W. Beak, *We Came to Canada*)

There is a freedom, an independence, and a joyousness, connected with the country, which dazzle those who have visited it into a forgetfulness of its defects. . . . (JOHN HOWISON, *Sketches of Upper Canada*, 1821)

The greatest single land under the sun,
The planet's greatest hope, her friends believe.
(JOHN MASEFIELD, 'Lines on the Occasion of Her Majesty's Visit to Canada, 1959')

How are the British 'New Canadians', the post-war generation of immigrants, settling down? Are they making a success in Canada? What makes them emigrate in the first place?

All the way across Canada, officials of the Department of Citizenship and Immigration filled my ears with depressing tales of Britons who were too arrogant, too choosy or too lazy, who told the 'natives' how much better things were done at home or who expected a Welfare State to bail them out when things went wrong. There was, I knew from my own observation, a solid background of truth to their remarks; but if one had taken all they said at face value, one would have returned with a hopelessly gloomy and rather distorted picture.

Contrary to the complaints of the Briton in Vancouver who could trace his ancestry back to the year 1120, British subjects still enjoy certain privileges and a certain priority when they emigrate to Canada. They can vote, stand for Parliament, join the Canadian forces or the RCMP without having to wait, like foreign immigrants, for five years to take out Canadian citizenship papers (Canadians also have reciprocal rights in Britain). Because of the Commonwealth ties, the common language and the closer proximation

of both living and professional standards, Canadian policy
places a preference on immigrants from Britain; and will in
all probability continue to do so. For the same reasons, the
doors to many walks of life in Canada may open more easily
to a Briton. Thus, from the moment he arrives in Canada,
he is really in a special category. Add to this the slightly
'special' relationship between Britons and Canadians that I
have tried to analyse in the previous chapter, and Britons in
Canada do have a case for believing that they are under a
more intense spotlight than other nationalities. Because of
his advantages, more is expected of a British 'New Canadian';
when he succeeds his success attracts less attention than if
he had been an impoverished Pole struggling with broken
English. On the other hand, when he fails his failure sticks
in the minds of Immigration officials and employers more
glaringly. On top of this, since the war there have, of course,
been far more Britons than any other single nationality of
immigrants into Canada, making them just that much more
conspicuous.

In Toronto, the successful British immigrant who had
complained so bitterly about the British journalist wanting
to go by 'overnight' train to Vancouver, and who had such a
poor opinion of his fellow countrymen in Canada, remarked
to me: 'The pity is that none of the British come here for a
specific purpose — they're all coming *away* from something.'
By the end of my trip I realised there was truth in what he
said, but was not sure how far it actually affected the quality
of the immigrant. I had met machinists who had left home
because of the housing shortage; doctors, professional men
and executives who had pulled out in disgust at Welfare
State apathy; *entrepreneurs* who had just come out to make
money quickly so that they could retire in comfort, back in
England; a great many in all walks of life who had migrated
simply to improve their material standard of living; many
who (in '57) had been scared stiff by Suez; some who had
relations in Canada and had come largely out of curiosity;
and a few who really didn't quite know why they were there
at all. With a large proportion of these one felt that the
positive appeal of Canada had little to do with their decision;
if they had been told that there were plenty of houses on

Mars, no free wigs provided by the taxpayer and no Mr. Frank Haxell, but much higher wages, they might just as happily have stepped aboard an interplanetary rocket as an immigrant ship. Several grades above them, but in the minority, were the men of forward vision; the over-35s immigrating to Canada for the sake of ensuring a better future for their children; skilled men coming with a definite purpose, confident that Canada offered them better chances of advancement, but also that they in their turn could bring Canada something; and above all, those few who had bothered to learn something about Canada before cutting loose from Britain, and had a positive conviction of its fundamental goodness as a country.

But a negative philosophy for emigrating is not just limited to today's Britons; and does it in any case necessarily preclude an immigrant from making an excellent Canadian one day? Many of the 19th-century Scots came solely because they were driven off their crofts by sheep-farming lairds, and they became some of Canada's greatest pioneers. Dutch and Italians have come since the war because of land-hunger and unemployment at home; Germans and East Europeans, because of political repression.

Who can say categorically that any one nationality of post-war immigrants has proved itself more satisfactory than another? In almost every Canadian Province I was told that the Dutch were wonderful immigrants, the best of the lot; but on probing a little farther I found that although they had indeed established a tremendous reputation for farming, in industry there were always cases of Dutchmen who had not done quite so well. All in all, I decided that the Britons were probably not much better or worse than the others. On the other hand, the British who had failed or were unhappy in Canada generally seemed to form a fairly consistent pattern. You could be fairly sure that one of two or three factors was involved.

It was not until I reached the farthest point north of my tour that I came across a real failure, a really unhappy and embittered man, and I had already met scores of Britons before him. His name was Fred and he was working in the mill of the Keno Hill silver mines. A boiler-maker in Sunderland, he had come to Vancouver fifteen months previously. He had almost immediately found a job with a shipbuilding firm, earning $2.60 an hour. But recession had hit the firm, and inside a year he had found himself jobless. He had evidently not tried to find work that might have been available in other categories. His wife disliked Vancouver, had become fed up and gone home. With most of his savings spent, he had headed towards the high wages of the Yukon, just to earn enough to return home himself. He was bitter about his experiences. The 'lying bastards' in London's Canadian Immigration offices had, he said, deliberately deceived him with rosy propaganda of life in Canada. He complained that the Canadian Trades Unions did not do enough to look after the workers.

Working in the same section of the mill as Fred at Keno was an older Briton, a Somerset man, who had been thirty-two years in Canada, eleven of them at Keno. He was a fitter by trade, and told me that he had left Britain in the twenties after 'literally starving' in Birmingham on a wage of £2 a week. He had started off as a farm labourer in Saskatchewan during the depression (he could hardly have chosen a worse place) : 'It was four years before I could even buy a suit of clothes.' He then moved to a mining job at Timmins in Northern Ontario, where all his four children promptly caught typhoid and barely survived. 'In the early days,' he said, 'it was only my pride that stopped me going home again.' Now he was earning $600 a month, and spending his holidays in the Caribbean. Shaking his head, he added : 'I'm afraid Fred's the type who should never have come to Canada. He was too pampered; things were far too easy for him in post-war Britain. I doubt if he'd be happy wherever he went.'

I felt genuinely sorry for Fred, but thought he probably deserved rather less sympathy than Woods,[1] a highly-paid technician and supervisor I met a month or so later in a big aircraft factory in Eastern Canada. He had held a responsible post in one of the leading British firms in the industry, but had wanted to emigrate to Canada ever since 1951. An intelligent man in his late thirties, he had thought it all

[1] All names here are fictitious.

out most carefully, but his wife was reluctant; largely because of her family ties and social roots at home. Finally, in 1957, Suez persuaded her, and Woods moved straight into his present job, with a salary of $7200 a year; rather more than twice what he had been earning at home. For the first six months they were 'extremely unhappy' in Canada. They were swindled by an Estate Agent, driven nearly frantic by travelling salesmen, and found the neighbours unfriendly. His wife burst into tears when she first entered the tiny apartment they were to live in. She had been a teacher for seven years in England, had graduated from teacher's college, and so wisely decided to take a similar job in Canada as an antidote to her loneliness. But when she was told that she would first have to take a qualifying exam, she refused; 'as a matter of pride'.

They had since moved into a larger house, were generally happier, and had at last made a number of friends. But, Woods admitted to me, 'They're mostly all English.' They both still wanted to return home at the first opportunity; although, unfortunately, their teenage son now adored Canada.

In the same firm (which probably had a higher proportion of British immigrants than most industries in Canada), I met two other Britons whose stories are perhaps worth telling. There was Jack, now foreman of the engine-testing section. His parents had come to Canada eleven years ago, and he followed two years later, fresh from the RAF where he had been an engine fitter. Living at first in Windsor, Ontario, it had taken him two months to find his first job, with a paint and decorating firm far enough away to require a 40-mile hitchhike in and out each day. Meanwhile his father had been taken to hospital with TB. Jack's first job lasted exactly two days, and, with $15 in his packet representing the family capital, he trekked into Toronto in answer to an advertisement for an aircraft engine fitter at the plant where he was still employed. He had started at $140 a month, the lowest wage in the factory, and now — aged only 30 — his salary was $700. He had since married a Scots girl, and neither had any nostalgia for home, nor had any complaints against Canada.

The chief Public Relations Officer of this aircraft company — also not much over thirty — told me he had been sub-editor on a leading London newspaper. It was a well-paid job, but he disliked the hours and saw no future. Together with his brother, but leaving his family behind, he had set off for Canada. The brother, also a journalist, had found a job with a Toronto newspaper; but he had been less fortunate. However, taking the Immigration Officer's advice, he had accepted the first job that came along — as a slaughterman in a meat canning factory. Now his wife and child had joined him. They were comfortably established, and she too had taken a job as a typist, which more than paid for somebody to look after the child.

Fred, the boilermaker, and Woods, the aircraft technician, were not the only dissatisfied Britons I met in Canada, but I mention their cases because they contain so many elements of the faults that Immigration officials in various Canadian centres claimed Britons were particularly prone to. First, there was this problem of choosiness in employment. More strongly almost than anything else, Canadian Immigration impresses upon new arrivals that in a dynamic, fluid economy like Canada's — rather than hang about the labour exchange waiting for exactly the right job for their calling — they should leap at the first opportunity offered; then gradually look around for a more suitable opening. Fred had obviously erred against this precept of flexibility, and I felt (perhaps unjustly) that if Woods lost his job, he would go home a failure sooner than go to work as a slaughterer in a canning factory. But then I suspect that neither would have got the job of PRO in the aircraft company, when that had fallen vacant. With very little knowledge of an immigrant's background to go on, Canadian employers are likely to be just as impressed by what an applicant has been *prepared* to do in Canada as by what he knows how to do.

Canadian Immigration Officers, I found, were on the whole an intelligent and understanding race of men, with perhaps more sympathy and a deeper knowledge of psychology than some immigrants would give them credit for. They understood the reasons why the British tended to be choosy; the indoctrination of full-employment, the long columns daily of 'Wanted' ads. in the papers at home. They understood why, with the knowledge of what it is to be insecure, other Europeans sometimes succeed in Canada where Britons fail. Perhaps a good example of this is the story of a German I looked up in Vancouver who had been my assistant while I was a foreign correspondent in Bonn. He had been a refugee, what is known as a '*Volksdeutscher*' from Rumania, with no roots in Western Germany. A reasonably able journalist, he had emigrated to Vancouver five years previously, but — speaking very little English — he had not even attempted to find work as a journalist. Instead, he had started as a manual labourer, ditch-digging for only (I could hardly believe it) $45 a month, with the Forestry Commission. He was then moved to chopping cedar roof slats out of huge logs; 'we had to do so many thousand a day by hand — I can tell you that at the end of eight months my muscles were so huge I could not get my coat on'. His first promotion came when it was discovered he had learnt surveying in the *Wehrmacht*, so he was given a job laying down a line for sewer piping.

After a while, however, the job folded up, and he then took work 'cutting up rolls of lavatory paper in a pulp mill'. Three years had gone by, and he had not progressed very far; his standard of living was still well below what he had known in Bonn. His wife divorced him to return to Germany, and his second job collapsed. Then, by chance, he met another German who got him placed — again as a labourer — in a large new cement factory. At last fortune smiled on him; within a year he was managing the factory with a hundred men under him. He had remarried, had bought an $11,000 house in a pleasant suburb of Vancouver, owned a Volkswagen and a dog, and was blissfully happy hunting bears in the mountains each week-end. He had brought his mother and brother out from Germany, and the brother — who had been a singer in the Gelsenkirchen Opera — had set to work happily cutting glass for $1.60 an hour.

There are two similar expressions, with rather different connotations, that have a peculiarly deadly effect on all Canadians, when dropped from the mouth of a Briton in Canada. One is 'home'; the other 'at home', or 'back home'. An *Afrikaner* once assured me that the real division between his people and the British South Africans was that the latter still referred to Britain as 'home', with the inference that they could always return there if things got really out of hand in the Union. But to the *Afrikaner*, home was South Africa and nowhere else. To a lesser extent, this is also true in Canada today. Fred and Woods could both face the prospects of failure in Canada with the knowledge of being able to return 'home' and the fair certainty of being able to pick up ends again in a world of full employment. A Hungarian refugee could not return to Budapest; my *Volksdeutscher* could obviously not go back to Rumania, and West Germany was not his 'home'. In 1959 an article in *Maclean's* (written in fact by a British immigrant)[1] noted that between 1946 and 1957, 531,852 Britons had entered Canada; but between 1951 and 1957 (when two-fifths of them would have been eligible for Canadian citizenship), only 23,230 (or about 10 per cent) had — with their special privileges — actually bothered to take out papers. The feeling that British immigrants, more so than the others, may not be wholly committed to Canada, and may be keeping open an escape route, is a genuine source of irritation to Canadians; it may also be partly what prompts their Immigration Officers to say that some of the Europeans 'settle down' better than the British.

The moment a Canadian hears the words 'back home' uttered by a Briton, a powerful reaction takes hold of him; his face assumes a look of the defensive, or maybe just bored resignation. He has heard this preamble altogether too many times not to know what follows: 'At home we do things this way . . . at home the beer is stronger . . . at home this, at home that'. The retort discourteous bubbles up within him. At Keno I had noted the well-known expression come over the faces of Canadian mill-hands listening while Fred held forth on how much better unions 'back home' looked after the interests of their members. I could imagine the reactions of Mrs. Woods' Canadian neighbours when she announced she didn't see why she should take a Canadian conversion exam, having had a perfectly good teacher's

[1] Issue of October 24th, 1959.

certificate 'at home'; perhaps it was no wonder that they had found so renownedly hospitable people as the Canadians a little 'unfriendly'. Summing up the British 'back home' attitude, a Canadian Immigration Official in Alberta remarked to me: 'When Scandinavians, Dutch and Germans come here, they expect Canada to be *different*. Britons seem to expect it to be *the same*. If you can impress on them that Canada is *not* an extension of Britain, that they must adapt themselves to a completely different set of circumstances, you will be doing both them and us a real service.'

As Woods admitted to me, when he and his wife began to make friends these were nearly all fellow countrymen. When one arrives in a strange land knowing no one, the natural instinct is to seek the protection of one's own herd. In Canada, the British are certainly not the only nationality to do this, but through innate cliquishness and club-mindedness they are probably the worst offenders. A prominent Canadian businessman in Toronto complained to me how the large community of British executives in the city seemed to 'rotate on their own axes'. Many lived next door to each other in the same housing estates, regularly lunched together at Toronto's 'Piccadilly Club' (an extension of 'home' if ever there was one). 'Some of them have been here for years without ever getting to know any Canadians', he said, 'and they really don't know anything about this country at all.' Another Immigration Officer told me that he tried, as tactfully as he could, to recommend incoming Britons *not* to join the local 'St. Andrews Association' or 'Anglo-Canadian Club' until they had found their feet in the country, 'otherwise they will never become proper Canadians.'

This just about finishes the dissection of poor Fred and Woods. Two other related idiosyncrasies of the British in Canada — faults they may be — are immobility and the tendency to concentrate in urban areas. The first has been mentioned before, but it is so important that it may be worth reiterating the list of priorities for new immigrants: 'First, get health insurance. Second, find a job. Third, buy a car. Fourth, find somewhere to live.' Immigrants arriving in Canada have in fact a great advantage of mobility, which they should exploit, over Canadians rooted down by family ties and homes. For this reason, if it is humanly possible, they are well-advised to come alone — like the PRO of the aircraft company — ahead of their own family, until they are settled in.

Everybody knows about the tendency of Britons to throng into Toronto, in the vague assumption that it is the hub of Canada, and the place where the best jobs are concentrated. In the Immigration Department in Winnipeg, I was shown a map of the city and a large surrounding area, with different coloured pins in it, each representing the location of various nationalities of immigrants. Dutch and Germans, Scandinavians and Hungarians were dotted all over the countryside; in suburban developments of the capital, in small towns or on farms. The British were all clustered together in the centre of Winnipeg. I suspect that many of them who had had difficulty finding the right kind of work in the city would have done better if they had looked a little farther beyond the ends of their noses; and I know this to be true of Toronto. There I was told of several cases of Britons who had turned down good jobs, simply because they happened to be a hundred miles or more from Toronto.

Can one point to any set of factors of social background, education, or experience, as making for success or failure in a British 'New Canadian'? In Toronto, the organiser of a British ex-servicemen's association, which seemed to keep astonishingly close contact with most of its members in Canada, gave me some quite interesting facts. The association was in touch with well over a hundred former 'other ranks' in Ontario alone, and he knew of only two of these who were dissatisfied and wanted to go home, with another two who were changing their jobs. But out of perhaps a quarter as many ex-officers, during the last year no less than *seven* had actually returned home. The only generalisation that could be derived from this is almost too obvious to state; namely, that the Briton most likely to be contented in Canada is the one to whom life there represents a social as well as a material up-grading, the man who could afford to run a car which he could not in England; whereas those who may (even initially) face a down-grading in their way of life are likely to be less satisfied.

But so often a generàlisation collapses on the particular.
In the Province of Quebec, we met two English women of
about the same age who had both graduated from leading
British universities. They had both married Canadians with
Oxford or Cambridge degrees. One had been brought up
in a very conventional, upper-class environment in England
with every comfort; the other had probably been accustomed to rather less luxury. The first had married a Roman
Catholic French-Canadian, and was living in a typically
Canadian home, pleasant but confined, with no one to do the
work around it but herself. More than merely being faced
with the necessity to adapt herself to English-Canadian ways,
living in an almost completely French-Canadian community,
she had been plunged into a totally different culture and a
foreign language. Even her children spoke only *Québeçois*,
often barely intelligible to a European ear. Yet she was one
of the most contented English wives we met in Canada, and
in turn seemed to have achieved the remarkable feat of being
assimilated into the exclusive little world of French Canada.
By comparison, the second university woman — married to
an English Canadian and living in a predominantly English-
speaking quarter — had been faced with a considerably less
drastic psychological adjustment. But she had found it far
 harder to cope with. After more than five years in Canada,
she had still not been able to come to terms with Canadian
life at all; she genuinely missed the live theatre and the arts,
and found it hard to hold back her criticism. If it had not
been for her Canadian husband, she would almost certainly
have returned to England long ago. Eventually, I felt, she
would settle down to life in Canada, but meanwhile her path
would be infinitely the harder of the two women. There was
a certain amount of truth in the tailpiece of a pamphlet for
immigrants I came across in Alberta, quoting an old proverb:
'Even after the longest journey, one finds only oneself.'

The secretary of the regimental association in Toronto
told me that of the seven ex-officers who had returned home,
nearly all of them were persuaded to do so *by their wives*.
This brings into focus what is without doubt the single most
important factor in success and happiness in Canada;
whether the wives can take it or not. No Englishman should

underestimate the difficulties of adjustment for a woman in Canada; they are ten times as great as for himself. To begin with, as stressed elsewhere, Canada is a country where the pleasures of life are principally organised for men. Above all there is the problem of loneliness; a man at work automatically makes friends quickly, whereas his wife, tied to the kitchen, may meet nobody for the first few months but tiresome travelling salesmen. She has nothing to talk about except her life 'at home', which bores and probably irritates her Canadian neighbours. She misses her family more than she would have believed possible; during the summer holidays, or even an occasional week-end, there are no doting grandparents to whom she can send the children for a badly needed relief, so she has them clinging to her skirts 365 days in the year. On Sundays she cannot hop onto a tram to pour out her woes into the sympathetic ear of Mum. So little irritations pile up and are magnified within her, until she bursts forth her discontent upon her neighbours. A vicious circle starts; her flood of criticism makes her neighbours less sympathetic and her loneliness multiplies. She becomes desperately homesick and makes her husband miserable too.

There are really only two basic solutions to this problem. The first is for the woman to take a job herself, even — like the PRO's wife — at the expense of paying someone to look after the children. This seems to work wonders; throughout Canada I was repeatedly noticing that the British women who had jobs were seldom among the discontented ones. Secondly, there is the magic potion known as the '$1000 cure'. This is to send your wife home at the end of the first three years, neither sooner nor later. She will see Britain (so they assure me) through quite different coloured glasses, experience the sudden deflation of romantic pictures she had cherished over the past three years, bore her family to death with 'things are done so much more efficiently *back in Canada*', and return across the ocean a new woman, no longer looking over her shoulder. This sounds almost too good to be true, but I am told it happens with amazing frequency; if so, the price of permanent contentment is well worth $1000 (which is roughly what the 'cure' costs).

x

Britons miss a lot of little things when they come to Canada. They miss the real or abstract things that constitute 'culture' and they miss the pubs. They miss the food, soccer, football pools, and — surprisingly enough — the proximity of country walks to Canadian urban centres. They miss Mum, and at least one steelworker from Lancashire told me he badly missed 'the kind of fun you can have on a bus outing'. They miss fish-and-chips, the *News of the World* and the BBC. All these items can add up to quite a formidable list, and the longer you have been accustomed to them, obviously the more difficult it is to do without them. With every year over 30, the risk of not being able to adjust to these sacrifices grows logarithmically. Parents who go to Canada 'for the sake of the children' may be making a huge self-sacrifice. On the way to Sudbury, we gave a lift to a Dutch boy of about 16. He had been six years in Canada, was thoroughly Canadianised, and loved the country. But his parents, he said, were still very unhappy; his father, a school teacher, yearned to be back in Haarlem. There were too many things he missed. Not so long ago, we heard of a middle-aged British couple who had returned from Canada — unable to acclimatise themselves there — while all their grown-up children had remained. (Sometimes, though more infrequently, this tragic kind of family split happens the other way round.) One only hopes that in the rosy future ahead of them, young 'New Canadians' will appreciate the sacrifice their parents once made on their behalf.

One of the most intrinsic difficulties that seems to confront British immigrants particularly is the problem of what *to be* in Canada. As noted, Canadians do not take kindly to the 'back home' Briton who steadfastly retains all his old attitudes and ways of doing things. On the other hand, they do not much admire the Briton who in a few months slavishly apes everything Canadian, even to the accent (though admittedly it is difficult not to fall into quite automatically), and who may go as far as denouncing everything British. One frequently wished that Britons in Canada could be more themselves, strike a happy mean and remain proud of the good things of Britain, without ramming them down Canadian throats; that way they could undoubtedly contribute much more. But it is not easy to keep one's personality intact within a melting-pot.

So far this chapter has dwelt almost exclusively on the difficulties facing immigrants, and the shortcomings among the British. It is time to redress the balance by some reference to the successes. My German former colleague in Vancouver had a fairly remarkable 'success story' to tell, but in the East, the North and the West I met Britons with stories every bit as impressive. For every one that was discontented, I must have met ten or twelve who were on the top of the wave; despite the fact that 1958 was one of the most difficult years Canada had had since the war. On the whole it is estimated that about three per cent of each year's British arrivals decide to return eventually; a figure which has never exceeded five per cent even during recent years, possibly the glummest Canada has experienced since the 1930s.

It is practically impossible to describe the ozone of exhilaration and enthusiasm that literally emanates from the Briton who has really made good in Canada; an infectiously exciting thing, though selfishly it sometimes makes one wish that this quantity of enthusiasm had not been lost to Britain — where it is so badly needed. Talking to these happy men, again and again one felt that here was more than a trace of the great qualities of the ancient British race; qualities that had lain dormant under the stifling conditions of modern Britain. It wasn't just the fact of material well-being, of earning more and living better that awoke these qualities. It was the re-discovered sense of creation, of building up something utterly new and immensely worth-while, in a country where you were judged simply on what you personally could contribute, where the future counted for more than your antecedents, and where ability had more and quicker chances of proving itself.

At Schefferville I met a middle-aged West-countryman who had tried many trades at home, and apparently succeeded in none, ending up in bankruptcy as an unsuccessful farmer. Now he was a construction engineer (goodness only knows where he had gained the qualifications!), responsible for all the planning and building at Schefferville, as well as the new iron ore community starting up nearby at Wabush Lake. He was a contemplative, pipe-smoking kind of man, who made me walk around his house in socks so as to keep the ore dust out of the carpets. He had his criticisms of Canada and swore that he intended returning home, eventually — though I was by no means convinced that he would. But when he remarked, 'It's not bad to think you've built two new cities in your life', a look of quiet elation spread over his face. There was the London gas-board official in the heart of BC, delighted with finding himself a 'needed man' in the organisation of community life. There was the middle-aged Londoner in Calgary who in no more than three or four years as a 'New Canadian' had established a successful law practice, published a book about Canada, become elected as one of three Conservatives to the Alberta Legislature, and only missed nomination for chairmanship of the party in his Province by a very small margin. Also in Alberta, there were the two young Britons each helping manage one of the new Jubilee auditoria, fascinated by the exciting possibilities of creating, virtually from scratch, a new theatre from completely virgin raw material. There were, all over Canada, the British teachers and professors faced with the challenge — sometimes so vast as to be almost frightening — of building up new educational standards in a country young enough still to welcome experimentation and new ideas.

Finally, there was the ex-Corporal-Major of the Life Guards, a man in his mid-forties, who had been working for just over a year in the aluminium plant at Kitimat when I met him. After serving twenty-six years in the army, he told me, 'I felt I had had a good life, and now it was time to do something for my two boys, so I decided to emigrate to Canada.' Like many Britons, he had arrived with his family in Montreal possessing only a vague idea of what the country was really like, and a still vaguer idea of what he was going to do. 'It was rather interesting, having been looked after all my life by the army, suddenly to discover that there was no pay coming in on Monday, with a family to support.' They travelled out to the West Coast, and on reaching Vancouver he was rudely made aware of what the absence

of a National Health Service meant, when doctors' and
dentists' bills for his two children almost wiped out his
savings.

Undaunted, he continued up to Kitimat, where he took
a job as an hourly paid worker. A few months later, the
aluminium company was particularly hard hit by the recession, and as a rule the newest arrivals were the first to be
dismissed. Somehow he managed to hang on to his job by
the skin of his teeth, and was selected to help organise a
Time-and-Motion study in the plant. A year later he had
become foreman of a large machine-shop in the works,
earning $400 a month, and with a very comfortable flat of
his own. Like the Gas Board official I had met earlier in the
month, he was already prominent in community affairs and
was Sergeant-at-Arms of the Kitimat branch of the Canadian
Legion. That year he and his sons had killed fourteen hefty
salmon in the nearby river, and he was talking of building a
log-cabin retreat in the Peace River District one of these
days. He had little but praise for Canada, and obviously
it would have been hard for him and his family to have found
a better or happier life anywhere else. I hope his dream
continues.

So much is talked about how the immigrants adapt
themselves to Canada that one tends to overlook the other
side of the problem. By the time this book appears in print,
the two-millionth immigrant to enter since the war will have
landed on Canadian shores. This means that slightly more
than one in every nine of the population of Canada is a
'New Canadian'. Of the Hungarian refugees from 1956,
Canada took by far the biggest chunk of any nation —
42,000 — of which only 500 are said to have left dissatisfied.
History may well record the way in which Canada has
assimilated, and adjusted herself to, this huge influx as one of
the outstanding manifestations of the intrinsic greatness of
her people. There have been the occasional bad cases (some
of them read like a chapter out of *Martin Chuzzlewit*) where
an ignorant foreign worker, speaking little English, has been
disgracefully exploited; cases of swindling employment
agencies that take deposits of $100 or more (immigrants
should still beware of these), and then do nothing whatever

to find applicants a job; and there are always accounts of confidence men riding the immigrant trains — or, almost as bad, the HP salesmen who load down the newcomers with instalment purchase debts the moment they step off the ship, still hypnotised by the thought of Canada's high wages. But these cases represent a tiny fraction of the experience of the post-war immigrants. By and large the Canadians have taken them among themselves with a quite astonishing lack of discrimination, even though at times they have realised that a job given to a 'New Canadian' almost certainly meant a native son out of work. No nation, not even the United States, with its famed hospitality and vastly greater powers of assimilation, has ever welcomed immigrants with such open arms as Canada in the post-war era. In 1821 a British visitor to Upper Canada commented: 'The most extra-ordinary thing of all is the liberality which they exercise towards immigrants, in immediately admitting them to live on an equality with themselves . . . .'[1] The same could have been said with almost as much truth more than a hundred and thirty years later.

By 1958, however, Canadian newspapers were beginning to note for the first time an increase of ill-feeling, and also the creeping in of discrimination, towards the newly arrived immigrants. It was not really very surprising. The previous year, the alarms of Suez and Hungary had brought the greatest wave of immigrants — over 280,000 — since 1913; it had also brought the sharpest recession and bout of unemployment that Canada had experienced since the war. By 1959 sensational stories of soup lines reminiscent of the Great Depression, accompanied by pictures of British immigrants foraging in garbage cans or dossing down in Canadian Missions, began to appear in the London Sunday press. For 1958 immigration figures were reduced to 124,851, and the British contingent was down to less than a quarter of the previous year.

It was probably a good thing that there has been a let-up on the flow of 'New Canadians'; this has given Canada a badly needed respite in which to assimilate the hordes she had already taken in and to rediscover her original enthusiasm

[1] John Howison, *Sketches of Upper Canada.*

for a policy of steady immigration. There are in fact few Canadians who do not fully appreciate the benefits the immigrants bear for Canada over the long term. In capital alone, since 1945 they have brought with them over $1,000,000,000 into the country. Every Canadian knows in his heart that for the country to fulfil its promises of the future it must have more and more people; which means immigrants, as Stephen Leacock once put it, 'not thousands, millions — not gradually, but in a mass'.[1] The Gordon Report concluded soberly that it was in Canada's interests to encourage immigration over the whole twenty-five years, up to 1980, covered by its survey; while strongly advising the Government to resist 'the temptation to turn the administrative tap off and on with every temporary change in business conditions'. Thus it seems certain that Canada — once she has breasted the wave of her present acute unemployment problem — will resume and continue her open-armed attitude to immigrants; if anything, confronted with the competition of increasing prosperity in Europe, she may try to encourage them to come even more strongly than heretofore.

As the ex-Corporal-Major at Kitimat saw me off on the bus, his last words were: 'You know, there may be lots of things wrong in Canada, but you can find a good reason for all of them. That wasn't always so at home.' It was, I thought, one of the wisest comments I had heard from a 'New Canadian'. Education in Canada may leave a great deal to be desired at present; unemployment may be higher than it should be; trade may be seriously unbalanced, and the whole Canadian economy far too dependent on the United States. There are good reasons for all these things, as this book has tried to show. And the Canadians are aware of these things that are wrong, and overwhelming as the reasons for them may sometimes appear, they are vigorously determined not to let matters rest. Complacency is not a Canadian characteristic.

Much has been said in earlier pages about Canada's economic problems — about the lack of markets for her

[1] Stephen Leacock, *Canada, the Foundations of its Future*, 1941.

produce, about the headaches that face her railways, her coal and oil and aircraft industries — because it is felt that the 'booster' books have done harm to Canada abroad, and particularly in the eyes of potential immigrants. But none of this should conceal the basic economic strength of Canada. When I arrived in Canada, the recession and unemployment figures had already reached a high level, and, from accounts I had previously read in the British Press I expected to find a thoroughly depressed country. On the contrary, here was an atmosphere of boundless, assured confidence, and an overall level of prosperity that was still considerably in advance of Britain. The same remains true today. As Canada emerged in 1959 from the first bout of the worst recession she had had since the war, she displayed a far more robust economic health than might be gathered from the gloomy accounts that continued to flow out of Fleet Street. By June 1959 workers' income was up 8·6 per cent on the previous June; personal bank accounts were up 4 per cent, and unemployment down from 4·8 to 3·5 per cent of the labour force, compared with 1958. The first year of the Seaway already showed a 67 per cent increase in trade along the St. Lawrence. By autumn 1959 total production in both Canada and the United States had reached 5 per cent above pre-recession figures. Most important of all, an analysis of the impact of the recession showed that the economic contraction in Canada had actually been smaller than that suffered by the United States. (Among the worst hit Canadian industries were US-controlled car manufacturers and aluminium producers.) Ten years ago, the position would almost certainly have been reversed; the fact that in 1957–8 Canada was not harder hit by the recession in the United States was greatly due to the expansion of her own domestic market. This in itself was proof of how much stronger Canada's economic foundations had become since a Royal Commission [1] described her in 1940 as 'one of the least self-sufficient countries in the world'.

As this book goes to press, Canada is emerging from the worst winter of seasonal unemployment since the war; production figures have taken a bad fall; wheat exports are

[1] The Royal Commission on Dominion-Provincial Relations.

down; the automobile industry is suffering; the Stock
Exchanges of Toronto and Montreal have been stagnant
for some time. Poor publicity, the boom in Britain and the
simultaneous allure of the European Common Market have
diverted American and British capital that three or four
years ago would have found its way into Canada. All this,
coupled to prosperity in Europe, is keeping would-be
immigrants at home — for the time being. But in the New
World — and particularly in Canada — material advances
have seldom progressed in a straight line. Instead they take
the form of surges. Canada's great post-war surge came to
an end in 1957. Today one gets the impression of a young
giant that may temporarily have outgrown his strength,
pausing till his muscles grow firmer and consolidating his
foothold on the earth in readiness for the next mighty
effort. The great projects of the past decade — Kitimat,
the St. Lawrence Seaway, the Trans-Canada Highway and
Schefferville — are all now completed; work has yet to
begin on those of the next decade — the Peace River Hydro-
electric scheme, Pine Point and the railway to Great Slave
Lake, Labrador's Ungava Bay and Hamilton Falls projects.
But it will begin, and when it does Canada will make yet
another surge forward to even greater heights.

Canada's material growth is a tangible thing; so almost
is the exhilarating sense of creation that accompanies it. Her
economic future is a predictable thing. But many of the
attributes that make the country worth inhabiting and
raising children in are quite intangible, and her future in
other ways is quite unpredictable. One of the hardest things
about writing of Canada today is that the country is in a
state of flux, everything is changing all the time. One has
only to read a few issues of Canadian newspapers and magazines to realise with what vigour the Canadians are constantly arguing, trying to assess the nature of their own
country. Out of the argument may arise a totally different
Canada, which will negate all the predictions of today's
observers. If one dares predict anything, it is that Canada
will become both more North American and more herself.
She will *not* (as one competent American observer [1] recently

[1] Miriam Chapin, *Contemporary Canada*.

suggested might be to her advantage) solve her problems with
her gargantuan neighbour by entering the Union as a powerful lobby of one or more States; it will not even require a
'Champ' Clark to frighten her away from such a solution.
Whether she will come closer to Britain and the Commonwealth will depend very greatly on British initiative; on
whether Britain can devise new, dynamic relationships for
developing the Commonwealth that would give Canada a
greater interest in it; can provide her with the trade and
capital she needs to assure both her independence of the
United States and her future growth; and, perhaps above
all, on whether Britain can send her enough of the right kind
of immigrants. It is to be hoped that Britain will do all these
things, for Canada has become the keystone of the whole
Commonwealth and upon her rests the weight of its future
strength. She should be Britain's great hope in years to
come, and Britain hers.

One of the intangibles of Canada that becomes very
tangible after five minutes spent anywhere in the country is
the tremendous sense of excitement that it radiates. There
is not time to be bored in Canada. Canadians may sometimes complain that life is dull, but it should seldom seem
so to 'New Canadians'. There is always something new,
something exciting happening — or just about to happen —
just around the corner. This is perhaps why Canadians
occasionally comment on the triviality of conversation in
Britain; in an essentially static society, there are few really
new issues to discuss. Then, too, what is 'new' in Britain
does not necessarily equal what is 'good', or signify an
advance. Therefore the changes that life brings may not
always be agreeable to discuss. More people in Britain
simply means more congestion on the roads, more housing
problems, less countryside for everyone to enjoy, eventually
a lower standard of living, and — finally — less *freedom* for
all. But in Canada, more people means the opposite of
nearly all these things; and there is enough countryside to
absorb a hundred million people without any one of them
seeing the next-door-neighbour's washing. This is really
what is meant when people glibly say 'Canada has a better
future than Britain'.

Freedom is an intangible quality of Canada — one of its most important — that cannot really be measured until one has spent some time in the country and among the Canadians. In its simplest forms it is freedom from the wastefulness of petty snobberies and antique prejudices; freedom to stand and rise on one's own merit; and (still to a larger extent than in Britain) freedom from the tyranny of State and the Trades Union caucus. At its highest level, there is the sublime freedom that a country of the vastness of Canada alone can offer: the freedom that can only be gauged when one has heard the 'Canada Bird' piping his patriotic little song in the tranquil dusk by the St. Croix River; or canoed on an unnamed lake in Northwest Ontario; stood amid the rustling emptiness of a Saskatchewan wheatfield; watched the elk and mule deer grazing unconcernedly in a deserted valley of the Rockies; or experienced the wonderful rich silence of the North on a hill in Labrador. This freedom is Canada.

To end this book not so very far from where it began, Canada's principal asset — as with most countries — lies in the qualities of its people. For kindness and hospitality the Canadians can hardly be excelled by their American cousins. But beyond all this, there is a fundamental goodness and good sense that belong particularly to Canada. These people will never produce a Hitler or a Stalin; nor, very probably, will they produce even a McCarthy or an Alger Hiss, or a Huey Long. These Canadians, one feels, know both where they are going and what is right. If it is to Canada that the future belongs, a neurotic and uncertain world should indeed have cause to rejoice that the Canadians are the people they are.

SUGGESTED READINGS

Beak, T. W. *We Came to Canada.*

Bourinot, J. G. *The Story of Canada.*

Brebner, J. B. *The Explorers of North America.*

Burpee, L. J. *The Discovery of Canada.*

Calder, Ritchie. *Men Against the Frozen North.*

Campbell, Marjorie. *The Northwest Company.*

Careless, J. M. S. *Canada—A Story of Challenge.*

Chamberlin, W. H. *Canada, Today and Tomorrow.*

Chapin, Miriam. *Contemporary Canada.*

Craig, Gerald (ed.). *Early Travellers in the Canadas.*

Creighton, Donald. *Dominion of the North.*

Dalzell, Peter. *The Settlers.*

Dauphinee, John. *Opportunity in Canada.*

Dufferin and Ava, Lady. *My Canadian Journal, 1872–8.*

Easterbrook and Aitken. *Canadian Economic History.*

Glazebrook, G. P. *A History of Canadian External Relations.*

Gustafson, Ralph (ed.). *The Penguin Book of Canadian Verse.*

Hutchison, Bruce. *The Unknown Country.*
  Canada—Tomorrow's Giant.

Laugharne, Grace. *Canada Looks Ahead.*

Leacock, Stephen. *Canada, the Foundations of Its Future.*
  My Discovery of the West.
  Sunshine Sketches of a Small Town.

Levine, Norman. *Canada Made Me.*

Lodge, Tom. *Beyond the Great Slave Lake.*

Lower, A. R. M. *From Colony to Nation.*

Mackay, Douglas. *The Honourable Company.*

Massey, Vincent. *On Being Canadian.*

Moon, Robert. *This is Saskatchewan.*

Park, Julian. *The Culture of Contemporary Canada.*

Parkman, Francis. *Pioneers of France in the New World.*

Peck, Ann. *The Pageant of Canadian History.*

Roberts, Leslie. *Canada: The Golden Hinge.*

Ross, Malcolm (ed.). *The Arts in Canada.*

Royal Commission Reports. *Canada's Economic Prospects* (Ottawa, 1957).

Report on Dominion-Provincial Relations (Ottawa, 1940).

Report on National Development of the Arts, Letters and Sciences (Ottawa, 1951).

Stowe, Leland. *Crusoe of Lonesome Lake.*

Wade, Mason. *The French Canadians.*

Walker, Joan. *Pardon My Parka.*

Watkins, E. *Prospect of Canada.*

Watters, R. E. (ed.). *British Columbia, A Centennial Anthology.*

INDEX

THE END

PRINTED BY R. & R. CLARK, LTD., EDINBURGH

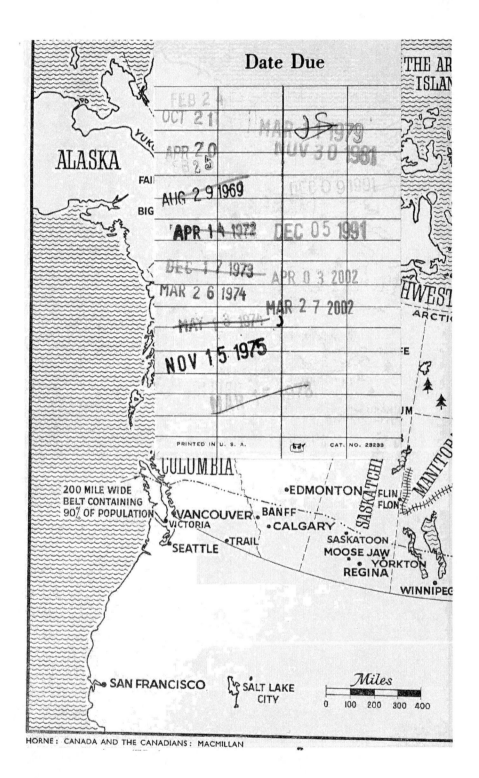

Date Due

ALASKA

THE ARCTIC
ISLANDS

200 MILE WIDE
BELT CONTAINING
90% OF POPULATION

COLUMBIA

VANCOUVER
VICTORIA
SEATTLE
TRAIL

EDMONTON
BANFF
CALGARY
SASKATOON
MOOSE JAW
REGINA
YORKTON
WINNIPEG

FLIN
FLON

SAN FRANCISCO

SALT LAKE
CITY

Miles
0 100 200 300 400

HORNE : CANADA AND THE CANADIANS : MACMILLAN